THE WEIGHT OF SILENCE:

EMERGING FROM THE SHADOWS OF FAMILY ADDICTION

Memoir by Melinda Velasquez

DEDICATIONS

For my niece. It is my greatest hope that by finally speaking my truth in an effort to heal, I can help break the cycle of addiction in our family and support you on your own journey toward healing.

For my family. I love you, and I always will.

For anyone with a loved one struggling with addiction, whether in the light or in the shadows, may this book help you feel seen, validated, and less alone on your own healing journey.

The Weight of Silence
by Melinda Velasquez

Copyright © 2025 by Melinda Velasquez
All rights reserved.

No part of this book may be reproduced, distributed, or transmitted in any form or by any means, including photocopying, recording, or other electronic or mechanical methods, without the prior written permission of the publisher, except in the case of brief quotations embodied in critical reviews and certain other noncommercial uses permitted by copyright law.

For permissions requests, please contact:
MelindaVelasquez.com

ISBN: 979-8-9923931-2-5
Cover Design by Laura Duffy of Laura Duffy Designs
Edited with the help of Jillian Navarro, whose insight and support were invaluable.

This is a work of creative nonfiction. Some names, locations, and identifying details have been changed to protect privacy.

Printed in the United States of America.

Trigger Warning: *This book discusses chemical dependency, suicide, trauma, bullying, emotional abuse, and neglect. I have included a list of resources I have found to be helpful at the end of the book. Although what I experienced is mild in comparison to some, it has been my experience that seeing ourselves or someone we love in another person's experience can be difficult. Please take care of yourselves if you feel triggered in any way while reading this book.*

Parental Warning: *Some of the content and language in this book may be intense and could be challenging for younger readers. Parents are encouraged to review the content before sharing it with their children.*

Disclaimer: *The stories in this book reflect the author's recollection of events. Some names, locations, and identifying characteristics have been changed to protect the privacy of those depicted. Dialogue has been recreated from memory.*

INTRODUCTION

"Forgive yourself for not knowing better at the time. Forgive yourself for giving away your power. Forgive yourself for past behaviors. Forgive yourself for the survival patterns and traits you picked up while enduring trauma. Forgive yourself for being who you needed to be."
~Audrey Kitching

Initially, this book began as an extension of my graduate research paper on female relational bullying, rooted in a profoundly difficult experience during eighth grade. I even presented my paper at the National Bullying Conference shortly after graduating with my master's degree in 2009, receiving rave reviews. However, after years of fits and starts, I struggled to bring that initial manuscript to conclusion.

I dedicated years to raising awareness about the dangers of bullying, sharing my experiences at conferences for youth and educators. However, I eventually grew tired of it being my main focus. While I still valued the work, I sensed that my story encompassed more than just my eighth-grade bullying experience.

I set the manuscript aside and focused on other work until 2017, when I felt compelled to revisit it. By then, I was ready to seek guidance. I found a writing coach who provided valuable feedback and encouraged me to continue, yet I still felt stuck. Deep down, I knew

I had something meaningful to share, but once again, I walked away from the manuscript and immersed myself in work.

In 2021, after working from home during the COVID-19 pandemic, I stepped away from the virtual world to partner with a colleague on an in-person training she had developed around Diversity, Equity, and Inclusion. Having delivered trainings for over ten years, I felt confident in my abilities. However, when the day came for me to present, I completely froze.

I experienced what I call a crisis of confidence. This colleague was not only a dear friend whom I admired, but also someone I didn't want to disappoint. The reality was that developing my own material and delivering someone else's were two very different challenges. I lacked the courage to tell her that I needed more time to feel comfortable with the material. Though it wasn't an unreasonable request, I feared she would lose faith in my abilities if I asked for more time.

The crushing fear of inadequacy had plagued me since early adolescence. Throughout my life, I struggled with this deeply ingrained insecurity that shaped how I presented myself to the world. By appearing capable, responsible, and helpful, I believed I could mask the pain I endured—from others and from myself.

As a member of Generation X, I learned that regardless of how difficult things became, the only option was to keep pushing forward and not dwell on the pain. Others valued my ability to take care of myself, to avoid complaining because someone always had it worse, and to see asking for help as a sign of weakness—though I didn't view it that way for anyone but myself.

So, in the limited time I had to prepare for the training, I stayed silent. I did what I always did: I pushed through without seeking help. The result? My crisis of confidence. Instead of speaking up and collaborating with my colleague on a different plan, I choked. This had never happened to me before, and as a consequence, I took a lesser role for the remainder of the training, spiraling into silent shame.

By the time I got home, I couldn't stop the whirlwind of thoughts in my head. I dreaded having an honest conversation with my friend because I feared hearing her disappointment. The shame continued to engulf me.

Just a few days after returning home, I was excited to celebrate my 46th birthday. I tried to shake off what had happened and pretended to feel better, but my body knew differently. Having not attended an in-person workout class since the pandemic began, I decided to join my friends at our regular dance class to celebrate my birthday.

Surrounded by friends, listening to great music, and dancing felt liberating, yet something still felt off. I was supposed to have lunch with a friend from class, but she wasn't feeling well and had to cancel, which left me with no plans for the rest of my day. After saying goodbye, I drove the 20 minutes home, and as soon as I hit the freeway, I began to cry uncontrollably. I spent the rest of my birthday alternating between tears and silence.

An overwhelming sense of deep loneliness washed over me, reminiscent of feelings I had in high school. I was disappointed that my plans got canceled, but the intensity of what I was feeling didn't seem to match the situation. Despite having wonderful friends, a happy relationship, and many positive aspects in my life, something was wrong, and my body refused to let me ignore it any longer.

The next day, I decided to ask for help. I had been to therapy a few times, with one experience being particularly beneficial, yet I didn't feel drawn to return to her. I needed something different, something deeper. Perhaps a new therapist, or maybe a spiritual approach?

A lifelong friend had recently shared her positive experience with a medium. Based on her description, I felt this woman was legitimate. I had seen a medium twice before, both times with powerful results. Although I'm not religious, I consider myself spiritual, and my previous experiences had left a lasting impact. Since my last experience, I had avoided revisiting that path, fearing it might uncover something I was not yet ready to confront.

I also researched therapists and found one who seemed like a good fit. I reached out to both the therapist and the medium, leaving the outcome to the Universe. That same day, I heard back from the medium, while the therapist took several days to respond. It felt like a sign.

In my first session with the medium, who preferred to be called an Intuitive, I felt an instant connection. She explained that "Intuitive" was a more approachable term for her work, and I understood her reasoning—this field can sometimes feel a little "woo-woo" or unconventional to some.

During my reading, she quickly connected with both of my parents on the other side. While I won't publicly share what she revealed, there's no doubt she knew things only they could have shared. I received answers to questions that had been holding me back, the most significant being my book.

The reason I struggled to finish my manuscript was that I had been avoiding writing about the very topic I needed to address to fully heal: my family's struggle with addiction. The primary reason for my avoidance was the same reason I kept the secret hidden in the shadows for most of my life—I didn't want to hurt the people I loved. My session with the Intuitive, along with my parents' insights, helped me to realize that the silence had been the source of our pain from the beginning, and it was time to shine a light on it to end that cycle.

I had long been buried under the weight of this family secret. I knew that finding the courage to speak my truth would also mean revealing things about my family that had remained unspoken. With my parents no longer alive, I feared that me being truly honest about my experiences would somehow dishonor their memory. Then there was my sister; I knew there was no way to do so without involving her. Our relationship was already complicated, and I didn't want to make it worse than it already was.

The thought of speaking my truth and sharing how my family's addiction issues had impacted me filled me with dread. However, I reached a point in my life where I realized this was THE thing I needed to do—not just for my own healing, but to help others heal as well. This part of my story explained so much about who I am, why I feel called to do the work I feel called to do, and ultimately became a central aspect of my purpose in this world.

After my first session with the Intuitive, I resumed writing that same day and continued for five straight hours. Once I recognized that I needed the courage to explore my family's silent struggle with addiction and its impact on my life, I didn't stop until I had written 529 double-spaced pages.

I poured everything into the writing process, which coincided with some of my deepest healing work. Writing had always been cathartic for me, and this experience was no exception. I rediscovered my love for writing as I processed my emotions. I cried buckets of tears, felt frustration, anger, and pain as I revisited memories long buried. I became uncomfortably honest with myself, connecting the dots necessary to release the fear and shame that had held me captive for so much of my life.

The result of this journey is this book. While it has been pared down from the original version, I am incredibly proud of what it has become. While some of this book may be difficult for my sister to read, I sincerely hope she does so and finds something within these pages that guides her toward healing as well.

Throughout my writing process, I had countless conversations with individuals whose lives had also been touched by addiction. I realized that although our experiences may differ, many of the themes I was uncovering through writing resonated with others.

Knowing that this book could help someone else feel less alone or more validated in their struggles motivated me to finish and publish it. My hope is that my journey toward speaking my truth will inspire others to do the same, so none of us has to continue suffering in silence.

Writing this book also helped me clarify and hone in on the work I want to pursue. It is deeply connected to my mission of continuing my own growth and healing while empowering others to find their own paths toward transformation.

Thank you for reading.

Take care,
Melinda Kelly [Stewart] Velasquez

SECTION ONE

Early Childhood: When Family Was Everything

"A happy family is but an earlier heaven."
~ *George Bernard Shaw*

CHAPTER

1

My earliest childhood memory goes back pretty far—probably before I was even a year old. One of my parents had put me in the car as everyone hurried to get ready to leave. They fastened me into the car seat, and they must have thought I would be fine as they stepped away to gather up the others before we headed out.

I know I was in the front seat, because, at some point, I got curious about the gear shift—or maybe I accidentally kicked it. Suddenly, the car popped into reverse and slowly rolled down the driveway, across our quiet residential street, and into our neighbor's front yard. I remember seeing my mom and dad screaming and frantically running toward me until the car came to a stop among the neighbor's bushes.

I was completely unharmed, but the memory of being alone in that car, drifting away from my home and my parents, never left me.

MELINDA VELASQUEZ

I was born in 1975, the blue-eyed red haired second daughter of my family. My red hair quickly turned to light blonde curls with dark roots, and I was told by almost every adult how "blessed" I was to be born with such beautiful, thick, naturally curly hair. However, for much of my childhood and adolescence I thought my hair was more of a curse than a blessing. Not to mention, once my red hair turned to blonde, other than my dad's blue eyes, I didn't look like anyone else in my immediate family.

There was a running joke that I was the mailman's kid, because he also had blonde curly hair. It was a silly thing my whole family loved to say whenever someone asked where I got my curls. They could have said I had my grandmother's curls, my mom's smile, and my dad's blue eyes, but the mailman joke was more fun to them.

That joke got old really quick for me and it set the tone for so many little digs that continued to chip away at my sense of belonging, as well as my ability to celebrate any kind of unique qualities I possessed. My family had a way of "othering" me by constantly pointing out ways I was different from them.

It is only with hindsight that I can see the "othering" was just one element contributing to the perfect storm of fear and self-doubt that would rule much of my life. Like a death by 1,000 paper cuts, my family was armed with tiny ice picks that gradually eroded my self-esteem and my sense of self-worth one nick at a time. I don't think they were being malicious. I think they were just having fun. My family joked all the time. It was just what we did.

I was not the only focus of their humor; general sarcasm and self-deprecation was standard practice in our family culture. It wasn't until around age 12 that I started to notice how much I felt like an outsider within my own family. The passive-aggressive humor often used by my family, both against me, and each other, left me feeling hurt, confused and uncertain of what message I was supposed to be receiving. I was well into my adult life before I was able to name those feelings that had been buried deep within my subconscious.

Those little criticisms that started early in my life laid a foundation for how I not only saw myself in my own family, but how I fit in, or didn't, in any group or situation. An unhealthy pattern began with me wanting so much to be loved and accepted, that I continuously lost sight of my sense of self, and what I actually needed or wanted. I learned that focusing on the needs of others, rather than my own, would give me a false sense of the love and acceptance I so desperately craved. People pleasing not only became a way of life for me, but a means of emotional survival as a sensitive being in a harsh and difficult world.

One consistent focus of my uniqueness that was constantly used as a comedic weapon was my naturally curly hair. My older sister of five years, used to call me Frizzball. As a young girl I really felt as though that is what my hair looked like, a literal big ball of frizz. My hair was also very coarse, and she used to say, "Your hair feels as thick as dental floss when it gets stuck between my toes!"

All I wanted was to have hair that could feather like my sister's, or Farrah Fawcett's from the Charlie's Angels television show made famous in the 1970's. Oh I tried it, and I have the horrible school pictures to prove it!

I wished someone in my family knew how to bring out the best of my natural curls, rather than the Frizzball look! My mom used to perm her hair to make it curly, but she still didn't seem to know how to work with my curls to have them work *for* me, instead of *against* me. Back then I wanted so badly to just be like everyone else.

MELINDA VELASQUEZ

Many people think that when you have thick hair, it must mean that you have a tough head that can handle pulling and tugging in order to wrangle it. That has never been the case with me. Even though my hair was thick, I had a very sensitive head and was not happy when my mom tried to comb through the knots. This was the main reason for the short haircuts when I was little, which led to the Frizzball look.

My thick hair and sensitive head are actually a perfect metaphor for how people saw me, and how I learned to portray myself. Tough and capable of handling anything on the outside, but deep inside my soul was broken. Some could see through the cracks, but not many; not even me for a long time. I would have no idea how broken I was until my pain went from inconvenient speed bumps to roadblocks I could no longer avoid.

Frizzball or not, I actually had a really happy early childhood. My memories of my mom being home up until I was around five years old are filled with happy moments. I felt so safe and happy in her presence. She was so good at making me feel special and seen.

She always found little ways to show she enjoyed spending time with me, like setting up a cozy bed on the floor in the living room by the fireplace on cold winter days complete with a picnic. As we enjoyed our snacks and juice, she would tell me to pretend we were in some enchanted forest, and the warmth we felt from the fire was coming from the sun shining through the trees. When I was with her, I could easily be transported to the most magical places in the world through the lens of her vivid imagination and soothing voice.

My mom could not only dream up a good story, she could also create wonderful meals in her kitchen. My favorite childhood meal made by her was comfort food at its best, chicken fried steak, mashed potatoes, country gravy and green beans. I loved the smell of the garlic as I heard that first sizzle as she placed the breaded masterpiece into the hot skillet. She used round steak that she pounded and seasoned with love before she dipped it in flour and dropped it into the pan to brown it in butter and create a mouthwatering crispy yet soft coating around the steak.

As a kid I never liked gravy, except my mom's perfect white country gravy. I couldn't wait to smother it on top of the chicken fried steak and add a healthy dollop to my mashed potatoes. It was thick, creamy, and salty, with a hint of garlic and the perfect spice from the pepper. Then she would pair this meal with her signature green bean recipe. She used fresh green beans that she slow-simmered with garlic and pieces of real bacon. Having our house filled with the aromas of my mom's culinary delights always added a cherished sense of safety and warmth to my world as a child.

In the summers, before my mom had gone back to working full-time, *our* house was *the* place to be. All my friends in the neighborhood loved to hang out at my house. My mom loved having all the neighborhood kids come to play and they loved her because she just had a way of making everyone feel welcome. Whether she was dishing out snacks, or tromping through the creek alongside us as we searched for crawdads and other treasures, she had a way of making everything better. I loved to run barefoot through the wet grass and feel the mud squish between my toes as we splashed around in the sprinklers in the front yard.

One of my earliest happy memories of this time was when I was around three or four years old making mud pies in my front yard of our family's first home. It was a simple single-story home that was just a short walk from the creek and in a neighborhood filled with kids. I ran around all day with my bouncy blonde curls, in my white Minnie Mouse t-shirt, covered in mud with my big plastic red spoon I used to whip up my mud masterpieces. My mom was, of course, my best customer.

My mom was a natural when it came to being playful and engaging with me on my level when I was little. I made a mess of the front yard and myself, but she didn't care. Instead, she joined right in, visiting my make believe mud pie restaurant and letting me serve her my best mud pie. She would smile and convincingly pretend to eat, gleefully saying, "Mmmm, what a delicious pie!" When I was a little girl, I felt safer and more loved in her presence than with any other person on the planet.

We lived in that house until I was five, and then my parents bought a big five-bedroom, two-story house with a pool, and a large patio with a built in basketball hoop in the backyard. It was fantastic! This would be the house where I would start kindergarten, and make friends that I would have for life. Unfortunately, it would also be the place where the demise of my family would begin.

CHAPTER 2

The good times continued for a while once we moved into our new home. Before we moved to the new, larger house, I don't remember my parents ever fighting. I imagine they did, I just don't remember it. That would change drastically after we moved to our new home.

The city where I grew up was set up in neighborhoods everyone called sections, and in each section the names of the street started with the same letter of the alphabet. We moved from L section to B section. The new home in B section already had a pretty great backyard, and then my dad built me a playhouse where I would go to hide out and play pretend. I loved to swim, and now we had a pool too. This was the home where I learned how to ride a bike and roller skate as I bumped into our forgiving neighbors' cars while I fumbled down the street. This was the home that I most remember as my beloved childhood home.

In this new house, we had what we called a Family Room and a Living Room. The Family Room had more casual furniture and was where we gathered regularly to watch television. I always hated the carpet, this awful gold color shag that was so ugly and felt like sandpaper.

The Living Room never seemed to get dirty because we mostly used this room for larger family gatherings and special occasions. We hosted many a Super Bowl party and holiday family gathering in that Living Room, and it was where we placed our Christmas tree and opened presents on Christmas morning.

The living room was also where I held my own private dance parties, too self-conscious to ever let my family catch my solo performances. I remember loving the movie Urban Cowboy as a kid—which now seems odd considering the violence. I was really there for the dancing. I have always loved any movie with dancing in it, regardless of the plot. For me, dancing has always brought me joy.

I liked the character named Pam from Urban Cowboy because she had beautiful long, *straight* hair. I very clearly remember having an aversion to one of the main characters, Sissy, played by Debra Winger, because she had curly hair. In my eyes, the girls with the long straight hair always seemed to be the prettiest, in the movies and in real life. From a very young age I adopted the belief that people that looked like *me* were not seen as the pretty girls.

I would wear towels or pillowcases on my head to pretend I had long, straight beautiful hair like Pam from the movie. There were three arches with columns and a wrought iron piece linking each section together separating the entryway from the Living Room. When no one was around, I would pretend one of the columns was John Travolta as I tried to reenact the dancing scenes from the movie.

In the new house, my sister and I had our own bedrooms, and in addition to my parents' large bedroom, my dad had his den, and my mom had her sewing room. It was a pretty big upgrade from our little house in L section. The half bathroom downstairs was often the place I would run and hide from my sister when we fought. The door locked and it was not far from the Family Room, the perfect escape from our sibling rivalry.

It was in this home that I met my best friend, Laura. We met and became best friends in the third grade. Laura and I actually attended the same preschool, but we would not meet and become friends until the third grade. She lived down the street from me and we would meet each other halfway between our houses, singing a song called, "Who's Holdin' Donna Now" by Debarge, at the top of our lungs while pulling our Barbie cars behind us with strings we attached to them. She was silly in the best ways and no matter what we did, we always had fun together.

Laura's parents were divorced, and she lived with her mom who worked full-time. Her mom loved to get all dressed up and go country and western dancing. Laura and I loved to sit on her giant waterbed and watch her get ready. She used to teach us all the dances she learned, and we would practice them with her as we giggled through every step. At that time our home lives could not have been more different, but our friendship just worked.

When Laura and I first met, my parents were seemingly happily married and her mom and dad had been divorced for some time. Her dad lived in the same city, but she spent most of her time with her mom. Her mom always seemed to have boyfriends doting on her and taking her out. Laura's older brother lived with them too, but they didn't get along most of the time.

The hair on the back of my neck used to rise up when I heard Laura's mom yell Laura's first and middle name out, "Laura Jean!" when she was displeased with something Laura did or didn't do. When we had too many lights on she loved to bellow, "What do you think, I have stock in PG&E or something?" She was a loving and fun woman, but I would definitely say I had a healthy fear of her as well!

From the beginning, Laura and I just clicked. She knew all my secrets and never shared my secrets with others, or used them against me. My perception of Laura was that she seemed to always have the ability to be who she was without any fear of judgment from others. That is part of what made her personality so magnetic.

Laura's magnetic personality applied to boys as well. All the boys loved Laura. Even in the third grade one boy used to follow her around every chance he got and repeatedly ask her, "Will you go out with me? Will you go out with me? Will you go out with me?" In the third grade!

I was a little jealous that most of the boys seemed to gravitate towards her, but she never acted like she thought she was prettier or better than me. She was always my biggest cheerleader, and she always did everything in her power to raise me up and never knock me down. If you were Laura's friend, she was loyal to you, sometimes even if you did not deserve it. She was the kind of person everyone seemed to want to be around.

Laura and I were competitive with each other sometimes, but only about one thing…I just knew she always cheated at Yahtzee, but I could never catch her and prove it—that drove me nuts! Other than that, our issues were pretty minor. I had other friends, but Laura was the one I spent most of my time with, and we became more like sisters than friends.

Laura was always there for all major events, we went with each other on family trips, and when she was at my house she helped me with my chores, and I did the same at her house. My parents became surrogate parents for Laura, and her mom, became a surrogate mom to me. Laura was the person who I first heard use the word "Framily" to describe a friend that was not blood related but had become family. Laura was not just Framily to me; my entire family felt that way about her as well.

Even though my immediate family was just the four of us, we were close with our extended family as well. I cherish my childhood as the time in my life where we got together with aunts, uncles, cousins and grandparents for unforgettably fun holidays. I even enjoyed being "stuck" at the kids' table because I was always the youngest and that was the time I got to hang out with my big sister and my favorite cousins. After dinner we ate pie and stayed up late laughing, telling stories and playing Charades and Tripoly. To me, it didn't get much better than that.

Another family pastime was football season. Football was serious business in our house. Although my sister fought it and rebelled by choosing other teams, I never strayed from our family team, the San Francisco 49ers. My 1980s childhood also paralleled the true glory days of the 49ers.

When game day came, we would rummage through mine and my sister's stuffed animals to find one that resembled the mascot of the opposing team; throughout the game we would all take turns venting our frustrations about the game on the innocent stuffed toy. It was so much fun! It was the thing our family did together. We all got really involved and emotional about the game, so it was a form of release and just good, silly fun.

Since we were a 49er family in the glory years of the team, Super Bowl parties were a huge event, especially when the Niners were playing. We had themed food, and my mom painted all of our nails with different 49er themed art. We didn't go to church on Sundays; football was our family's religion, and I loved every minute of it. I probably loved it so much because even when my sister refused to root for the 49ers, we were all there, together, as a happy family.

MELINDA VELASQUEZ

Some of my most fond memories also include weekends at the local swimming hole with thirty of our closest friends, or, as Laura would call them, Framily. This group consisted of people I would call "aunts" and "uncles" but there was no actual blood relation. We hosted a huge block party on the Fourth of July every year, with my dad hauling the ladder into the street to put on his amazing fireworks show. Holidays and birthdays at our house were always something I looked forward to every year.

One birthday in particular my parents put together an elaborate surprise for my party. A group of family and Framily gathered around the picnic table in the backyard for hours on the morning of my birthday party. They were plotting something big, but I wasn't allowed to know what until my guests arrived.

It turned out they were planning a treasure hunt! What made it so cool was that they didn't use cheesy decorations to make it a themed party. Instead, they made it feel authentic and role-played the whole thing as if it was real and all of us kids got to be a part of the hunt.

They spent that morning tearing up pieces of paper and painstakingly burning each one to look aged. Then my mom used her calligraphy skills to write out the elaborate clues. They wrote the clues as if an old pirate was leaving them using riddles and rhymes.

They hid treasure and clues all over the backyard and that day I think the adults had as much fun planning it as the kids did participating. It was an unforgettable birthday filled with excitement and mystery as we dug through bushes and under rocks to find our buried treasure. I don't even remember who won because the hunt itself was the best part.

My life *then* felt so full and happy. While the kids swam in the pool and the adults played croquet, the soundtrack of my childhood played on vinyl on my dad's stereo—from Fleetwood Mac and The Doobie Brothers to the Eagles, Queen, Bob Seger, The Cars, Heart, and beyond. I was blessed to have an early childhood education in excellent music.

I felt lucky to have what I had. I loved being with my family so much then, it is hard to imagine how much things began to change. As I got older, things that may have started out as fun, like the sarcastic family jokes poking fun at each other, or the role alcohol took in my parents' lives began to take on a different meaning. The older I got, the harder that was to ignore.

CHAPTER

3

I was aware that my parents drank alcohol regularly, and although sometimes their drinking led to situations that didn't feel happy or pleasant, I learned to accept it as normal. One of the household norms was that we were not supposed to talk to mom or dad after they returned home from work until they had taken a few sips of their first after-work drink.

I was conditioned to understand that regardless of how excited I was to see them and tell them about my day, their needs came first. While they didn't resort to any physical harm if we didn't wait to engage until they had their first drink, the difference in their mood without the drink was palpable.

I've always been sensitive to the energy in a room. If we didn't adhere to this norm, the response we received from them felt like a looming cloud of resentment and irritation that lingered over us for the rest of the night. It became a delicate balancing act that I learned to master at a young age, as I perfected my ability to ignore my own needs and feelings to prioritize those of others.

Being born in 1975, much of my childhood took place in the 1980s, a decade characterized by excess that often felt like one never ending party. My parents were no exception—they enjoyed partying, and this was deeply ingrained in our family norms and culture. Adults drinking alcohol at a party seemed entirely normal to me, even if it was a kid's party.

As a highly intuitive child, I knew that my parents' drinking habits weren't good, but it was my normal. Moreover, it was also often mirrored in the homes of my close friends at the time, indicating that it extended beyond just our home. Even though something deep in my gut screamed out, "This is NOT good," I lacked any comparison to anything different or better.

I had witnessed someone with a "real" alcohol problem before, and my parents were nothing like that. We had been living in our new house for a few years when my uncle—my mom's only living brother—moved in with us, and HE was what I understood to be a full-blown alcoholic. He would come home late, really drunk, stumbling through the house. He had even been arrested once. I believe my parents offered to have him stay with us in an attempt to help him out after that.

My uncle had always been so much fun. He often took us to lunch and the movies, and he was always so goofy and hilarious. Together with my dad, they formed a regular comedy duo. I believe my dad liked having another male in the house, as he was always outnumbered. They loved to scare us girls, especially while watching scary movies.

I fondly recall a memory that still makes me giggle when I tell the story. We were watching a scary movie in the Family Room, and right at a terrifying moment, my dad and uncle sneaked outside and turned off the power to the house. Before we could figure out what had happened, they burst into the house through the garage door with my mom's nylons on their heads to disguise their identities, and add to our terror. They yelled out as they entered, and we all screamed and jumped out of our seats.

It's fortunate we knew all our neighbors pretty well because we all let out loud, blood-curdling screams. It was one of those moments where you are so scared you are screaming bloody murder, then you are so mad at them for pulling the prank, and then you can't stop laughing because it was genius. This was all before my uncle's drinking spiraled to a point where it couldn't be masked.

One night, when I was around eight or nine years old, he stumbled in, and I was sleeping on the couch in our Family Room. I often did that on the weekends so I could fall asleep to the television. At first, I don't think he realized I was downstairs, and I pretended to be asleep because I could tell he was drunk. By then, I had learned that when he returned home that late and drunk, he wasn't the fun uncle I loved so much.

I don't recall the exact details of what happened or what I might have said or done, but he became angry. Holding a shot glass in his hand, he raised his arm with a scowl on his face and hurled the shot glass at me.

It narrowly missed, and while I don't believe his intention was to hurt me, it scared the hell out of me. Not the good kind of scared; this time, there was no laughter, only fear. Somehow, no one in the house woke up, and I remember feeling relieved about that.

Looking back now I can clearly see that my role as the peacemaker was already surfacing. This role was nourished by my desire for harmony and balance, and my fear of conflict and chaos. Part of me feared that I would lose the uncle I loved if my parents had woken up and discovered what had transpired. Another part of me grappled with questions about what I might have said or done to provoke his anger.

After the incident, I ran up to my room and never told my parents what happened. I can't recall if he talked to me about it once he sobered up. I don't think he did, or if he even remembered doing it. That incident marked the beginning of a pattern where I stifled my voice regarding addiction-related matters within my family, and my codependency and enabling tendencies took root.

Growing up in my family, I experienced a constant tug-of-war between what I perceived as normal and what didn't feel right. There were so many things I loved about my family, but the older I got the more that internal voice of mine kept nagging at me, hinting that something just wasn't right. It wasn't until fourth grade, around age 9, that I truly began to heed that inner voice.

By this point, our family still had our really happy times, but the frequency of less joyful times had begun to increase. Mom and dad engaged in loud, passionate arguments on a regular basis. While nothing physical ever occurred, the profound intensity of the exchanges between them was scary to me. They seemed oblivious to what my sister and I could hear or the emotional toll it was taking on us; if they *were* aware, they didn't let it stop them.

Many of their arguments centered on another man or woman, which I later learned was because my parents had somewhat of an open marriage. Back then they would have been labeled as "Swingers". There were signs that some partner swapping between close friends might have been happening, but that didn't occur to me until I was much older. It seemed that when one of those relationships became too intimate, that is when the arguments between my parents reached a fever pitch.

MELINDA VELASQUEZ

I remember at least one occasion when my mom kicked my dad out of the house for a while. Suddenly, Mom began preparing special breakfasts for us during the week, which was definitely not a regular occurrence. One morning she even made us homemade crepes with fresh fruit. I don't even remember eating breakfast during the week, much less crepes.

It felt like such a wonderful and special treat to have this special breakfast, but it also brought me back to those early childhood memories before mom started working full-time. It brought back fond memories of those fireplace picnics she made for us when I was really little. It gave me a moment of happiness amongst all the confusion and chaos. It was during these times that I started to associate food with love and comfort.

My dad left our home and was staying with my uncle after this particularly bad argument. With him gone, Mom emphasized that it was a special time for "just us girls". She even made us pretty signs with our names on them to put on our bedroom doors. I remember these signs specifically because when my dad had come by the house while we were out, he ripped the signs off our doors and left them in pieces on the floor for us to discover upon our return

He acted out of anger toward my mom, but once more, failed to consider how his actions would affect my sister and me. Witnessing what he had done, I was overwhelmed with an intense mixture of confusion, anger and sadness, all swirling within me simultaneously. I didn't know what to make of it, and I remember it felt aggressive and kind of scary.

I was deeply hurt and angered by his decision to vent his frustrations with her on us. Yet, she, too, was guilty of doing the same types of things as well. During this period, it seemed everything they did was part of a painful game of emotional blackmail with my sister and I as the prize.

Dad had his chance to spoil us and win us over too, but his trick was taking us to McDonald's or some other fun place. I have a distinct memory of playing at a McDonald's play structure. This was a big deal back then because, first, McDonald's was always a treat as a child; second, I had never been to a McDonald's with a play structure before; and third, we rarely spent time with dad without mom there.

It should have been a really fun day, but even at a young age, I understood why we were there and why mom wasn't, and it felt tainted. Those poignant memories stuck with me. No matter how much time passes, whenever I see a play structure at any fast-food restaurant, it is the first memory that comes rushing back to me.

I vividly recall the exact moment I fully grasped the reality of what was happening with my parents—it was when I turned in a set of sentences using my fourth-grade spelling words. One of the spelling words was "argue," and I wrote something about my parents arguing a lot. I remember my teacher leaned over as she handed me back my work and softly said, "It's okay. It's normal for parents to argue." I waited for her to walk away, and said under my breath, "Not the way they do."

Instead of feeling comforted and reassured by my teacher's kind words, I felt a strong sense of dread in the pit of my stomach. My face started to feel warm the way it does before I start to cry, and then the feelings of shame came flooding over me. I struggled to hold back my tears, fearing embarrassment in front of class. I also desperately didn't want my teacher to come back and make a big deal out of it, or even worse, tell my parents.

In that moment, the intensity of shame and vulnerability I felt was overwhelming as I came to the realization that my family was clearly not "normal" or okay. I lowered my head onto the desk to avoid eye contact with anyone and pretended to be writing something until I could regain control of my emotions.

I don't remember how old I was when the fighting started with my parents, but by age nine, things at home had become much more unpredictable and messy. The happy times I cherished seemed to lessen, while the tense and uncomfortable moments increased dramatically. Then, when I was around 10 years old, my dad lost his job, and from that point on, nothing would ever be the same again.

CHAPTER 4

My dad worked in the parts department of a car dealership, and his job was a big part of his identity. When he was let go, it really took a toll on him.

At first, I think all of us knew it was bad, but not the end of the world. With mom still working full-time, we figured dad would find a new job soon. However, my dad had trouble finding a new job at any of the car dealerships or shops within a 40-mile radius of our home; it started to wear on him, which then trickled down to the rest of us.

He became convinced that he was fired because of one guy who was out to get him. Knowing that the automotive industry where we lived was a very small world, he started to suspect that this guy was going around to other dealerships trying to ruin his good name. As a result, he started to doubt his own skills and abilities. After he was turned down a couple of times, he really started to believe in his conspiracy theory.

MELINDA VELASQUEZ

He began to look defeated and sad. He became more short-tempered, which increased my level of anxiety immensely. I don't remember a lot of details from that time, just a heaviness lingering over our family. I have this clear picture of the change in my dad, sitting at the dining room table, stressing out while paying bills, and my mom and him arguing about money.

When I was younger, my dad and I were not close. In fact, I had come to fear him. My mom consistently portrayed him as the disciplinarian in our household. The words, "Wait till your father comes home" often reverberated through the house whenever we misbehaved. Back then, he was the one to issue the spankings, which I found out later he hated doing.

I also learned that he once spanked my sister as a form of discipline, and she refused to speak to him for a week. After that incident, he never spanked her again. However, it was not the same for me. I viewed my dad as this strong man to be respected, and even feared.

Spankings back then were the norm in a lot of families, but that didn't take away from how awful it felt <u>every single time</u>. Not every bad behavior warranted a spanking, most of the time if I didn't do my chores, I would have my allowance docked or I would lose my television privileges for the evening. However, the one thing that I distinctly remember leading to a spanking was talking back or being "smart-mouthed", usually to my dad. It wasn't something I did often, but when I did, there were strict and swift consequences. It is the earliest memory I have of suffering severe penalties for expressing my voice.

As a young child, I shouldn't have been expected to know how to sort through whatever emotion I was feeling, and find a way to deliver my message to the receiver in a respectful way. In fact, many *adults* struggle with this type of emotional regulation. But, when my emotions ran high and I felt the need to push back, or express my opinion about how I felt about something, I was often met with anger rather than empathy from those around me.

The moment those emotionally charged words rolled out of my mouth and reached my dad's ears; I could feel the tide turn against me. I would see my dad's eyes widen with shock, then watched as a deep line would appear between his eyes as he furrowed his brow in anger and frustration. It was usually at that point I would feel blood rushing to my limbs, telling me to *RUN* before he reached the next phase. Next, the blood rushed to his face, and it turned red as his frustration became more visible. Finally, his thick index finger would pop out from a clenched fist aimed right at me, loaded with invisible emotional bullets laced with anger and disappointment.

I hated the feeling of disappointing people, especially my parents. Whenever I found myself in trouble for something, my heart would race, my ears burned, my face flushed, and I felt my stomach jump into my throat. I felt so much shame and guilt when I was being spanked. Soon after that, all I felt was anger towards my dad. Then, as I sensed his remorse, I hated *that* feeling even more. The whole experience was soul crushing.

I understand that my dad struggled with the role of being the disciplinarian. It came naturally to him to expect things done a certain way and done correctly. However, there were other aspects of him that I didn't get to see early on in my life that were very sensitive. I had no idea how sensitive he truly was, how easily *his* feelings could get hurt, and how often he tried to mask his pain with humor or deflection. Up until a certain point in my life, when I thought of my dad, I envisioned a towering figure of strength that could handle anything.

He was a Marine who served in the Vietnam War, but he never talked about what he saw or experienced there. I know he joined in order to avoid being drafted and to have some kind of choice in the matter. Despite the evident impact of the war on him, he worked hard to never show it. At that time, there was little awareness surrounding the concept of Post-Traumatic Stress Disorder (PTSD) and the struggles faced by soldiers returning home from war.

The side most people saw of my dad was this gregarious, occasionally wildly inappropriate, fun-loving party guy. It is not a far stretch to conclude he very likely learned to use humor to deflect attention away from his own pain. It's also plausible he used alcohol and drugs to numb himself from the horrors he must have seen at such a young age.

Dad embodied that "pull yourself up by your boot straps" attitude, and was not welcoming of excuses as to why something didn't get done. He definitely liked to party hard on the weekends, but he always showed up for work on time, took pride in his work and seldom took a day off sick. He held himself to a high standard and expected nothing less from those around him.

That very same attitude also gnawed at him when he struggled to find a job in his field and was forced to resort to taking on odd jobs to keep our family afloat. Grace was not something he afforded himself, or really anyone else for that matter.

For a while, he worked with a family friend who owned a pool and spa business, installing pools and maintaining pools for customers. This job often demanded non-standard hours, resulting in him often returning home after we had finished school for the day. My sister and I had become "latch-key kids," so we had gotten used to being home alone after school with a little freedom between the hours of 3:00 p.m. to 5:30 p.m., but now that had all changed.

He often came home physically tired from the kind of work he was now doing, leaving him with little patience. This is when the Marine came out. There was no time for horseplay or watching television after school; chores came first. Around this time, my sister, who was now 15, and my dad started to clash frequently. It seemed as though she had gone from being the golden child in his eyes to a rebellious teen.

Before my sister's teenage years, our family dynamics were clear: she was dad's favorite, and I was mom's favorite. My sister used to be a bit of a brown-noser, always doing things to please my dad and be in his favor. She was always volunteering to help him with projects, she did her chores, and seemed both helpful and responsible. I was "the baby" and my mom spoiled me and was protective of me when I was little, which often caused friction between mom and dad. It also created a sense of distance between my dad and me.

I longed for my dad to see me in the same positive way he seemed to see my sister, Shelly. However, I was different and had no desire to do the things that seemed to make him proud. It was so much easier with my mom. I could just be me without judgment.

I was a very emotional child, feeling everything very intensely from a very young age. My dad was the kind of person that wanted to teach us to be independent, learn to take care of ourselves, and do what we were told. He lived his life by a certain set of rules and values, and he seemed to struggle if people didn't fall in line with his worldview. His way of communicating was very direct, emotionless, and succinct. As I've mentioned, he also had a very silly and fun personality, but when it came to getting things done around the house, the Marine in him always showed up.

My mom's pattern of trying to get me out of doing something she thought I was too young to do became a problem between her and my dad, and it also started an unhealthy pattern for me. If something was too hard or something I didn't want to do, I knew all I had to do was cry and my mom would step in and save me, and I wouldn't have to do it. This kept me stuck in a place of fear, preventing me from stepping outside of my comfort zone and building self-confidence by pushing my limits in a healthy way.

I remember so clearly being strongly attached to my mom. Once I started school and she started working full-time, I missed out on having her volunteer in my classroom or being there to pick me up and bring me home to feed me a snack. I felt so jealous of kids who had that.

To me, she was the most beautiful woman in the world. I was so proud she was my mom. I would get so excited when I forgot something and she would have to come to school to give it to me. I couldn't wait for everyone to see her walk in, all dressed up for work.

Her makeup was always flawless—just enough to accentuate her beauty, but not too much to overwhelm it. Her shoulder-length, dark brown hair would be perfectly done. She had a perm to make her hair curly, but she also used a curling iron to get the perfect look. She usually had it pulled back just slightly with a bobby pin behind each ear.

I always thought she looked prettiest in a dress. She had great legs and she looked so elegant in nylons and high-heeled shoes. Although she would be in a hurry to drop off what I needed and get to work, the way she carried herself never felt hurried. In my eyes, she would glide through the classroom, leaving just a hint of the smell of her perfume in her path, which washed over me like the comfort of a warm blanket.

My mom looked so different than me, with her olive skin, dark eyes, and dark hair. She even modeled for a while, but that wasn't why I thought she was beautiful. It was because of who she was to me that I saw her that way.

She was so good at seeing and understanding the way I saw the world. I can't recall a single instance of her being short or impatient with me. Instead, I remember her beautiful smile, her playful nature, her contagious laugh, and feeling so completely loved by her.

One thing that my mom did for my sister and me when I was young that I cherished so much was what she called our "Special Day." She would pick a day, leave work early, and take us out of school at lunch for our Special Day.

I would be filled with excitement as the time drew near for her to come pick me up. She would pick us up and take us out to lunch at a restaurant we liked called The Buttercup Pantry. It wasn't just any fast-food place; it was a real sit-down restaurant where servers come to your table and take your order! Back then, it was also such a big deal that we got to have lunch AND dessert! She would also give us each a little gift.

My favorite Special Day gift was my first diary. That is when I realized how much I loved to write. She started that for me. It was such a simple gesture, but it really did make me feel so special. These Special Days were a little slice of time she carved out just for us girls. They showed me that she wanted us to know how special we were to her, and that meant the world to me.

The Special Days stopped right around the time my dad lost his job. With him being home more after school, he became relentless about chores and keeping the house clean, but now my mom wasn't there to act as a buffer. I got a lot of the red face and angry dad finger-pointing about every little thing I wasn't doing right.

It seemed like nothing I ever did was good enough for him. While I had always been closer to my mom, this period of time made me want to avoid my dad even more. His way of "motivating" me to do things and "toughening me up" unfortunately only did more damage to my self-esteem. It set the stage for me subconsciously wanting to please him and desperately seeking his approval in everything I did in life.

My sister began pushing the limits, as teenagers do, and was no longer the agreeable young girl who always did as she was told. She started sneaking out and putting pressure on me not to tell on her. All I ever wanted was for her to *want* to hang out with me, so in an effort to earn her love and acceptance, I kept her secrets. Little did I know, this would not be the last time I kept secrets for her, and the secrets would only grow bigger and more complicated as we got older.

Mom was getting tired of being the only one consistently bringing in the money, which sparked new fights between her and dad, and exacerbating his feelings of failure. Everyone was spinning about something, and I felt like I was just aimlessly flying around in the mix. I was desperately searching for something stable to grab a hold of to help me feel safe and grounded again.

Eventually we couldn't afford our mortgage and had to sell our house, causing my safe little world to crumble. Although we moved less than a mile away, back to L section not far from our first home, to an eleven-year-old girl, it felt like we moved to a different country. We were in a different school district, but I refused to change schools and leave all my friends. As a result, making friends in my new neighborhood was slow and challenging, leaving me feeling isolated.

We also went from a quiet cul-de-sac to a much busier street; so, running around with friends in the street in front of our house was no longer an option. We still had a home, our health, family, and friends. We still had a lot to be grateful for; that being said, it was still a profound loss in my life.

I would ride my bike over to our old street, past our old house, lamenting over my old life. I was still able to transport myself back to a time in my life when my family was still happy, and life was good. That home was the last place during my childhood where I felt truly happy and safe.

After we lost my childhood home in B Section, I was grateful for all that I still had, but at that age, I was a little shell-shocked at all the changes. It wasn't just the move, there was a different energy between my mom and dad, and it wasn't good.

Our whole family felt different, but we never talked about it. I felt so lost and confused, yet I was afraid to voice my feelings, as it seemed like I'd be poking at a giant open wound in our family. We fell into the unhealthy pattern of not talking about the obviously REALLY bad thing happening that was affecting all of us.

Instead of discussing our emotions, mom and dad instead tried to get us excited about all the work we needed to do to make the new house feel like our home. My bedroom had this horrendous wallpaper that was wall-to-wall brown, orange, and lime green motorcycles, and the front and backyard were seriously overgrown. With a little hard work, paint, and a high-weed mower, we slowly unearthed the hidden gems in our new home.

The backyard was huge and had a bunch of fruit trees, an old greenhouse, a shed, and plenty of trees for privacy. Once the weeds were cleared, my mom and dad worked their magic to transform it into a beautiful place for friends and family to gather once more. Working together in the yard was something they both loved and took pride in; during that time, I started to see a glimmer of the connection between them begin to resurface again. It provided a much-needed break from the months of tension leading up to the move.

MELINDA VELASQUEZ

Our new backyard was quite expansive. We jokingly referred to one area as 'the back 40' because it was set back from the house, with a fence and an open walkway dividing it from the rest of the yard. There was enough space to pitch a tent, allowing me to host a really cool campout birthday slumber party with my friends. It felt like we had our own private campground!

Our bedrooms were much smaller in this house, but we still had our own rooms, with an extra room for mom and dad to share for the den and mom's sewing area. Considering the circumstances, things could have been much worse. I was grateful to have a home with a big backyard, albeit in a new neighborhood. And even though things had been difficult, at least my family was still intact, and I still had the support of good friends.

SECTION TWO

Adolescence: Queen Bees and Broken Families

"True belonging doesn't require you to change who you are; it requires you to be who you are."
~ Brené Brown

CHAPTER

5

Once I entered fifth grade, Laura and I were no longer in the same class. While we still spent a lot of time together outside of school, during school we spent time with friends from our respective classes. By the time we got to the sixth grade, Laura and her mom had moved to another town, resulting in her changing schools. Despite being just a fifteen-minute drive away from each other, I missed living close enough that I could walk or ride my bike to her house. We still spent a great deal of time together, but it was mostly only on the weekends.

In the fifth and sixth grade, my regular gang consisted of five girls. I remember us being the popular group of girls, or at least one of them in our class. It was with this group of girls that I first learned just how complicated the dynamics of female friendships could be.

When things were good, we spent our recess trying to make

it across the long span of parallel bars on the jungle gym, playing tetherball or handball, and of course my favorite, kickball! If we didn't feel like playing, we would sit on the steps of the portable building adjacent to the playground, either talking about, or flirting with boys. After school we often walked over to the friend's house that lived the closest to the school, just a few houses away.

At some point, a pattern of cruelness began within our group that left me always feeling fearful and uncertain. This was the practice of "leaving someone out" of our group. It was always temporary, but that didn't lessen the emotional pain and humiliation it caused.

It was never over anything serious; usually, it was as trivial as the way someone said something or even the assumption about someone's intentions. It was cutthroat. There was no discussion or effort to get to the bottom of the misunderstandings. One day, you were good, and the next, you would show up to school and suddenly no one would speak to you.

My first memorable experience with what I now know was adolescent female relational aggression actually started around the fifth grade. Relational aggression is widely used among adolescent girls as an indirect means of bullying. Relational aggression, or relational bullying, is the use of gossiping, excluding and withdrawing in order to cause harm to relationships.

In our group, each of us took our turns being the one who was left out, except one girl. Rosalind Wiseman would call her the "Queen Bee" (QB) of our friendship group. Leaving someone out would typically start with our QB, Jenny, having some sort of issue with one of us, and the rest of us followed suit. Alternatively, if one girl innocently mentioned how she was annoyed or wronged by another, that girl would then become the next target of the group. It would usually start when the targeted girl was not around and escalated very quickly.

It could start with something as simple as someone saying, "I can't believe she said she couldn't spend the night at my house. I think she's lying and she just doesn't want to come." Someone else would chime in, "Wow, really? What is her problem?" And the next thing you know, the group is pulling up every single moment of annoyance or hurt feelings, regardless of how small, piling it on and heightening the situation. Often, it started with one person's insecurity and quickly turned into a war.

So when that girl showed up to school the next Monday, she would discover that she was the odd girl out. I don't ever remember being told what to do, but somehow we all knew. We followed the lead of whoever was in charge, for our group it was usually Jenny. If you didn't fall in line, you could be next! That fear gripped me for the entirety of my fifth and sixth grade years.

Experiencing being left out or even having to be cruel to someone I considered my friend was a special kind of torment for me. This happened at a time when things at home were starting to fall apart, leaving me feeling particularly vulnerable and really in need of the support of my friends.

There was a formula for this kind of torture. It was subtle but extremely effective. It usually went something like this:

1. Ignore the target. Do not engage. She will wonder what is happening and possibly be confused about what she did, but don't tell her.

2. Be really nice to all others in front of the target, especially people we wouldn't normally associate with or give time and attention to. This will add to the intensity of the isolation for the target, as we will dominate any possible groups she could escape to for comfort and support.

3. Look at her, talk quietly, and laugh loudly. Even if we aren't saying anything bad about her, she will think we are. You can also make passive-aggressive comments loudly about things that she will know are about her, but no one else will, so we won't get in trouble.

4. Exclude her from all activities after school and while at school. Make sure she is picked last for team games. If the weekend comes before we have decided to welcome her back, then she doesn't get invited to sleepovers or other fun events.

Most of the time the targeted girl would only be left out for a few days. In our group, the issue was never resolved. It just suddenly wasn't a big deal anymore. It was as if "doing time" in friendship purgatory just somehow wiped the slate clean.

But the slate wasn't wiped clean for me. Especially after one time I was left out for a particularly long time. It may have only been two weeks, but one thing was for sure; it was longer than anyone else.

For me, it was one of the first instances of "not good enough" that cut me deep to my core. I just never understood it. I couldn't help but wonder, what was so bad about me that could make my friends want to be so cruel to me? Especially Jenny.

The weight of that hung over me like a cloud of shame. I began to scrutinize myself, noticing even more ways I differed from my friends, and started to internalize it all. Even though our group stayed close through the end of sixth grade as we prepared for junior high, the resentment and hurt feelings I carried from being left out in fifth and sixth grade still lingered inside me.

While all of this drama was happening at school with my friends, the dynamics of my family were also becoming increasingly complicated.

CHAPTER

6

In elementary school, my friends and I were big fish in a small pond. There wasn't much opportunity to mingle with other friend groups, but honestly, I had no desire to anyway. They were my childhood coterie. We had no idea that when junior high rolled around, everything would change.

As sixth grade came to an end, Laura told me she would be living with her dad and going to school with me again. I felt a rush of excitement and relief. Not having Laura around in school at the end of elementary school was hard for me. She was the only friend I had up until that point whom I knew I could trust implicitly. Though we had little disagreements, we never left each other out or did anything to purposely hurt one another. She would once again be at my side as we made our way through another milestone…junior high school.

Now that Laura was back, we started spending a lot more time together. We quickly befriended a girl named Naomi who attended a different elementary school in our district. Laura had a boyfriend she spent a great deal of time with too, so Naomi and I ended up spending a lot of time together. Before we knew it, Naomi and I became very close friends.

I shared a few classes with Naomi, one of which was woodshop. Our teacher was a sweet older man who had a laid-back attitude about our activities in class as long as we completed our projects. Naomi and I spent many classes up in the rafters of the shop building, talking, laughing, and learning about each other's lives.

I shared the war stories of my parents' latest arguments at a time when I felt no one could truly understand what I was going through. Naomi listened to me, offering me support and empathy, and I did the same for her when she told me about some of the troubles with her own family. I felt so lucky to have found a new friend who could relate to me on such a deep level.

Thanks to Naomi's friendship, I gained a whole new group of "popular" friends. Knowing that I was now "cool" with the most popular people in the new bigger, scarier world of junior high school gave me a sense of safety and power I had never felt before. Naomi had a keen ability of making me feel seen. She was extremely loyal and was the first to step forward and defend me or challenge anyone who dared to do me wrong.

Naomi and I talked about everything—boys we thought were cute, family issues, and life before junior high. Our conversation naturally included Jenny and the "odd girl out" drama. Naomi had an immediate and very negative reaction to Jenny leaving me out. It was comforting to have someone who wanted to stick up for me.

Having Naomi acknowledge how horrible it felt to be left out helped to unearth the feelings I had buried. I never even talked to

Jenny about it in an effort to be welcomed back into the group. With Naomi in my corner, eager to show her loyalty, combined with my newfound popularity and a grudge against an old friend, it was the perfect setup for my debut as the perpetrator of relational aggression.

My confidence began to grow, I started to feel a sense of self-worth that I hadn't quite experienced before. With everything going on at home, I found myself in a deeply emotionally vulnerable state. This newfound sense of belonging was validating, intoxicating and extremely dangerous.

Although Laura was always there for me, she was pretty distracted by her boyfriend at the time. Forming a friendship with Naomi provided me with a similar sense of emotional security that I had previously only found with Laura. She cared about me and was there for me. I began to trust her explicitly.

While I occasionally overheard Naomi talking negatively about others or say mean things to them, she was never like that with me. Even though Naomi and I became much closer, Laura and Naomi also remained friends. They had a number of classes together, one of which was P.E. with Jenny.

Knowing what I know now about relational aggression, Naomi was playing the role of my savior. It is crazy to think adolescent girls can exhibit such predatory behavior, but in many ways, it mirrors the grooming tactics of an abuser. This savior role becomes a means of survival in "girl-world" and can be more like an instinct than a strategy. It may vary slightly, but here is my observation of how it went with Naomi.

Naomi started by gaining my trust, initially through simple acts of friendliness and helpfulness. It wasn't long before Naomi became indispensable to me. My overall need was to feel that someone truly cared about me and made me feel safe, emotionally, and physically. Naomi was a good listener and loyal friend, and she also brought the added bonus of a group of friends who I believed would physically protect me.

As my trust in Naomi grew, a pattern of isolation began to emerge. Naomi was proving her loyalty to me, ingratiating herself to me in a way that made me feel I was in her debt. She became exceedingly negative about Jenny, which helped continue to break down my loyalty to one of my oldest friends. Naomi's loyalty tests started out subtly, involving simple tasks like rude comments about friends we had in common but that we weren't really close with. I believe these tests were designed just to gauge my reaction and willingness to join in or not.

What started out as me venting about being hurt by Jenny ultimately led to me unknowingly providing Naomi with the ammunition she needed to launch her attack. Throughout my friendship with Jenny, no one had ever chosen ME over her. For once I felt empowered, but it was for all the wrong reasons.

By this time, Jenny and I were not really spending time together. We had both made new friends, and while I remained close with one of the girls from our original group, the rest had basically split apart. Two of the girls remained very close, and would remain that way throughout life. When I saw Naomi's dislike of Jenny, instead of defending my oldest friend, I took the opportunity to seek revenge for all the suppressed feelings I had about our friendship. I had the power now, and I was going to give her a taste of her own medicine.

Not only did I fail to defend Jenny, but I also chose to sabotage what was left of our friendship. I betrayed her trust, feeding Naomi's fire with details that would surely humiliate her. That would teach her, right?

THE WEIGHT OF SILENCE

Even though I was still harboring the pain of how I believed Jenny had abandoned me in elementary school, I felt torn. Naomi's campaign against Jenny was like a runaway train, and I didn't feel like I had the power to stop it. Naomi had begun to escalate things to a level that made me uncomfortable, but I was terrified.

If I stood up to Naomi, I feared she would see it as a betrayal, and I'd risk losing the one person who had made me feel truly seen and valued in a way I desperately needed. Even though Laura was still my best friend, our bond hadn't changed in essence, but it had evolved. We didn't have any classes together, and I knew I had to share her with others—her new life living with her dad, new friends, and especially her boyfriend, who took up much of her time and attention.

Even though Laura and I had been drifting, I still felt the weight of her absence—of the friendship we used to have. It was during this time, when I was grappling with the changes in my relationship with Laura, that Naomi stepped in. She quickly became my trusted confidant, the one who made me feel important and safe in a way that no one else did at the time. Deep down, I knew what we were doing was wrong, but I was blinded by the rush of my newfound popularity and the overwhelming fear of being left out again. I wasn't just afraid of Jenny's rejection anymore; I was petrified of Naomi's.

I had never told Jenny how deeply hurt I was that she left me out all those times—in fact I was afraid to tell her. As a young girl, I had learned to suppress my feelings if it meant that expressing them would risk destroying my place in the social hierarchy—a place I believed was essential to avoid loneliness and isolation. I believed it was a necessary evil in "girl-world", but I was wrong. Some girls are not afraid to speak up and stick up for themselves; unfortunately, I was not one of those girls. Jenny, on the other hand, was.

Naomi's dislike of Jenny soon turned into an all-out campaign against her, and the ammunition I initially provided was a key factor adding to Jenny's humiliation. The things I told Naomi about Jenny weren't deep, dark, earth-shattering secrets, but they were the kind of things that could easily humiliate an adolescent girl if taken out of context.

Naomi was a master at twisting what I told her into a shroud of shame as she stalked Jenny on her way into the cafeteria, shouting about it so everyone could hear it. She would yell out things like, "Look at that bitch," as we gathered by our lockers and Jenny had to pass by on her way to her next class. Any chance she got to yell out something embarrassing or mean so everyone would turn and take notice, she would do it.

I continued to play the role of the coward, standing behind Naomi as she taunted Jenny any chance she got. As far as I knew, this was Jenny's first time as the target of relational aggression, and at first, I admit, it felt good to not be on the receiving end. However, that feeling didn't last long.

I started thinking of all the slumber parties and giggles Jenny and I had together and I didn't like how all this felt. Moreover, the verbal attacks directed at Jenny were far worse than I remembered them being against anyone in elementary school. Junior high was a different world altogether; here, the social stakes were much higher.

Unfortunately, it was too late to stop the runaway train of relational aggression. The campaign against Jenny became Naomi's main focus, and sadly, I was not courageous enough then to do anything to stop it. I could not undo what I had done, and my fear of damaging my new friendship with Naomi kept me silent. I didn't want to be seen as a wimp, and the delicate game of social status was one I was too afraid to lose.

THE WEIGHT OF SILENCE

A couple of weeks passed, and Jenny finally snapped—she fought back. Naomi was walking behind her, yelling and taunting her during P.E. class one day, and Jenny turned around and pushed Naomi with what appeared to be all the anger and frustration that had built up over the past weeks. They both got suspended for a day or so and that was pretty much the end of it.

Naomi and Jenny never made peace, but their hatred of each other never reached the explicit level of daily torture again. Naomi still called Jenny names in my presence and in my yearbook, but things never escalated again. I felt secretly proud of Jenny, admiring her for sticking up for herself. I wished I had been able to do the same, rather than cowering to her like she was some sort of friendship dictator.

Jenny and I were now definitely in different camps. Laura and I remained very close, while Naomi and I spent even more time together and became very close friends. As the school year came to an end, Naomi and I spent more time talking in shop and less time working. Just as my friendships seemed to stabilize, things at home continued to worsen. I was so grateful to have such loyal friends like Laura and Naomi at such a difficult time in my life.

CHAPTER 7

My desire to hang out with my sister and be accepted by her only grew as she entered her teenage years. She had grown into a beautiful girl, and I began to admire her in the same way I admired our mom when I was a young child. Although we still fought, it wasn't like when we were younger. I think that suffering the ups and downs of our parents' marriage had started to bring us closer together. We bonded over the shared experience of our family's dysfunction.

Dad was still more likely to respond with anger when conflict arose, while my mom would shut down and disengage. Many of the family friends we had spent so much time with when I was younger seemed to fade away as the years passed, and we eventually lost touch. The older we got, the less we got together with extended family as well.

We had a family friend who had a house in Truckee, California, and our family often went up there to stay with her. On one particular trip when I was eleven or twelve, my sister didn't want to go and she was allowed to stay behind. I was excited because I loved it up there and was happy to pretend to be the only child for a couple of days.

All the adults went down to the only bar in town, and I stayed behind alone at the house. I was pretending to be asleep on the couch when my parents returned, but I soon wished I really were asleep, or just about anywhere else. They were fighting, and this argument was particularly bad. It had something to do with another person —a woman my dad was flirting with, from the sound of it. Things went from bad to worse very quickly.

Mom and dad argued for what felt like forever, and it got pretty nasty. The discussion of ending their marriage came up. My mom then told my dad she was going to leave him and that my sister and I would choose to stay with her over him.

At that moment, it felt like I could hear my mom slam a dagger right into my dad's heart. I didn't know the full details of what led to the fight, but I instantly felt bad for him. Then my dad began to sob uncontrollably, his vulnerability a sight I had never witnessed before. It was gut-wrenching hearing my dad sobbing. My heart felt like it had been torn out of my chest and ripped it into a million pieces; the worst part was realizing that my mom had suddenly become the source of my pain.

My dad had become a mess of raw emotion, something I had never seen in him before. This man, whom I always saw as the enforcer of the rules—the one who gave the spankings, the one who could simply wave his finger and send me to my room in tears—was now being emotionally crushed. The woman I had always seen as fun, loving, and caring was the one delivering the emotional blows.

She was being so mean to him. It didn't really matter what he had done, they were both obviously very drunk. Mom was relentless with her verbal assaults, refusing to let up on him. It was a side of my mom I had never seen before, and one I didn't like. At the same time, my dad was showing a more tender side of himself, one I had always wanted to see.

This seemed to go on for hours, and the whole time, they were aware that I was there on the couch. Were they so drunk that they actually believed I could sleep through all of that? Did they even care? Instead of sitting up and asking them to stop, I just lay there frozen, forcing myself to listen to every horrible word.

The next day we packed up and drove home. For the whole ride, I felt as if I had been gutted. Still, I said nothing to either of them about what I had witnessed. There was a dull ache in my stomach, unlike any feeling I had experienced before. It was dread —my body's way of warning me of the impending doom that lay ahead for my family.

I kept reliving the argument, and that trip ultimately helped me realize that my parents should not be together. Two people who could make each other so unhappy and be so cruel had no business being married to each other.

Once we got home, my empathy for my dad went into overdrive, and I didn't want to leave his side. Suddenly, I was eager to help him with anything around the house, regardless of the task. I vividly remember helping him assemble a wheelbarrow in the middle of our living room that very day.

After what my mom said to him in Truckee, I desperately wanted and needed him to know how much I loved him. The thought of him believing I didn't love him as much as I loved mom was not something I was willing to let happen. Witnessing the traumatic argument and seeing him express such deep vulnerability made me view him in a different light.

It also changed my perception of my mom. That sweet, loving woman who had always been on my side had revealed a darker side. I couldn't forget how it felt to hear her talk to him that way. She sounded like a bully kicking her victim while he was down.

I had no idea what was truly going on between them. All I could see was that she had the capacity to be incredibly cruel, which deep down felt like a betrayal of who I thought she was.

My mom had been right—if forced to choose, I would have stayed with her. But after that night, I began to question everything.

CHAPTER

8

It wasn't long after the Truckee incident that my dad finally found a full-time job as Parts Manager at a Ford Dealership. It was a promotion from his last position and a great opportunity he couldn't turn down. Almost instantly, his confidence seemed to return.

Unfortunately, the job was a little over an hour away from our home. It didn't take long before the commute began to wear on him. He would come home so tired, and soon the tension returned during the workweek and eventually spilled over into the weekend.

Mom felt neglected by my dad, and Dad was exhausted and frustrated when he couldn't meet expectations. Once it became clear that my dad was quite an asset to the company, his boss wanted to help. His boss let my dad use one of his houses during the week instead of commuting home. At first, Dad would come home mid-week and on the weekends. Then he started staying there all week and coming home only on Fridays.

I remember my parents taking a weekend trip to try to reignite the spark. It seemed to make things temporarily better, but it didn't last long. My mom started to feel her marriage slipping away, so she drove up to the town where my dad was working to look for a new job.

She had been working for the county where we lived and was able to find a similar job up there. She came home and announced that she got a new job and that we would be moving so Dad wouldn't have to commute anymore. My sister, who was a senior in high school, absolutely refused. It was a big argument that ended with doors slamming. It was decided that since it was Shelly's senior year, it wasn't the best time.

After my mom turned down the job, things continued to deteriorate. With my dad hardly ever home, my mom and my sister started arguing more. My sister started partying a lot, drinking more, and experimenting with drugs.

I began to feel more and more isolated and lonely. I spent a lot of time with friends, especially my new friend, Naomi. Her family was also having problems, so she could relate to what I was going through with my family.

My life had changed so drastically. Every day, I would wake up with a feeling of dread, uncertain of what would happen next. Everything felt upside down, and my family was not even recognizable to me anymore.

My stomach constantly felt as if it was a taut rope and there were people twisting and pulling it from both sides. Everyone seemed to be so angry, and loud arguments became the new norm. Home, once a safe place filled with joy and love, transformed into to a toxic and uncertain nightmare in a pretty short amount of time.

MELINDA VELASQUEZ

By the end of my seventh-grade year, my parents legally separated and began the process of a very difficult and emotionally draining divorce. They had been married for nineteen years. While I understood that their divorce was not a mistake, enduring it was extremely stressful and painful for me.

I constantly felt trapped in the middle of an emotional battlefield, with my mom on one side and my dad on the other. With my sister legally an adult by then, I was the only minor. Whether my parents realized it or not, I often felt more like a bargaining chip than a daughter.

My dad was now permanently living hour away from us to be close to work. He also had a girlfriend, whom we found out he had started dating before Mom and Dad separated. His girlfriend also had two daughters, one slightly younger than me and one a little older than me. At times, I felt jealous of the time he spent with them, especially once he moved in with his girlfriend. It seemed like he was there for them when I needed him to be there for me. It felt as though he had replaced his old family with a new one that fit into his new life.

Dad had a whole new wardrobe, a newly pierced ear and a new attitude to go along with it. Suddenly, he seemed overly concerned with what other people thought of him and us, especially his new girlfriend. She was a very critical person, and it was starting to rub off on him. He would say things to my sister and me that just came across as hurtful, judgmental, and just plain rude.

In junior high, I went through a phase where I just wore black and white all the time. It was a style at the time, just a normal adolescent phase as I figured out my own sense of style. Dad picked me up for the weekend, and on the drive-up, he took it upon himself to comment on my fashion choices.

THE WEIGHT OF SILENCE

It's pretty normal for parents to comment on their nearly teen children's fashion choices, but this conversation was particularly hurtful in how it landed on me at the time. He compared my clothing choices to that of his girlfriend. He talked about how his girlfriend always wore colorful outfits and often even had the perfect shade of lipstick to match. The message I got was: you would be so much prettier and more likeable if you were more like her.

My sister hated my dad's girlfriend and appeared to be angry with my dad all the time. True to form, I did my best to accept her and, of course, wanted her to like me. She was nice enough, but she was extremely judgmental and elitist. It wasn't until I got to know her better that I realized why my dad seemed to have changed so much, and that his new attitude most likely stemmed from her.

She was very different from my mom. Even as a 12-year-old, I could sense her strong sexual energy. She drove a flashy sports car with a personalized license plate, and she had a very strong personality. It was clear that if she didn't get what she wanted then no one was happy.

My dad's girlfriend became his main focus. I often felt like she controlled him and wouldn't hesitate to let him know who held the power in the relationship. I knew she genuinely cared for my dad, but there was always this sense to me that she had the upper hand, and she knew it. It was a weird energy to be around.

I never felt comfortable relaxing or being myself in her presence, and eventually, I began to feel the same way around my dad. I found myself constantly seeking his approval. As he spent less time with us and became more involved in helping raise *her* daughters, my feelings of not being good enough just keep growing and festering.

Dad did show up and spend time with us, but it often felt more like a box he had to check for the divorce lawyers than something he genuinely wanted to do. Everything was on his time table, and the time he would block out for us seemed to continue to shorten in length. During that time, neither of my parents seemed to give much thought to what Shelly or I needed or wanted. It was all about them.

Everything they did seemed to come down to getting the upper hand in the divorce. For my mom, it was about getting my dad to pay more, while for my dad, it was finding ways to pay mom less. Despite not wanting my parents to get back together, I was still angry. I was grieving the life I once knew. Once the divorce proceedings began, my emotions were all over the place.

I vacillated between being angry with my mom one week and my dad the next. Most of the time, I was unable to explain why I was angry with either of them —I just was. Then my tender heart would start to feel guilty for making them feel bad, and my anger would turn to guilt.

I was living with my mom and my sister in the same house in L Section we had lived in prior to the divorce. When the initial break-up happened and my dad moved out, my mom was consumed by anger. One day my mom was playing music loudly throughout the house. She wasn't crying or yelling nor was she expressing much emotion at all. However, her lack of communication about what she was doing felt ominous.

She had taken down all the pictures we had around the house of family and friends and brought them into her room. After a few hours, she came out and began hanging them up again. I figured she might be just updating the pictures, or rearranging them, but as I got closer, I realized she had cut my dad out of every single picture. She closed everything back up and then hung them all back up again.

THE WEIGHT OF SILENCE

My heart sank. The hole that now existed within our family had become a sad spectacle on the walls of our home, casting a dark shadow over our once happy family. I didn't say a word or share my feelings with my mom, fearing it would make things worse. This was part of a toxic pattern that I would develop. Inside, my emotions were screaming, *Say something! This is so painful!* But on the outside, I just put up a brave front and tried to suppress the pain of what had just happened.

I felt like I couldn't say anything or do anything to challenge what was happening. I lacked the courage to use my voice and let her know how deeply this affected me. I was always more concerned about hurting someone's feelings or making them displeased with me than about speaking my truth.

We lived like that for a very long time, with our memories chopped up and displayed on the wall for everyone to see. I felt like she was trying to erase him from our lives. At the same time, my dad was taking steps to disappear from our lives in real time. I just wanted him to fight harder for us. No matter how difficult things got between him and Mom, I didn't want to hear negative things about either of them, I just wanted to feel safe and loved again.

That kind of anger only seemed to increase between them, and they appeared completely incapable of seeing the impact it was having on my sister and me. The anger and hostility just loomed over our family all the time. For me, it was torture. It felt like I was treading water in a toxic sea of negativity, with no sign of shore in sight.

Every little thing turned into a battle between Mom and Dad—it was exhausting and incredibly stressful. It seemed as if they were incapable of acting like responsible adults or putting their children's needs first. To thrive, I desperately needed to live in a home filled with love, not anger. I didn't understand what was happening to my family. This was not the life I knew and cherished.

MELINDA VELASQUEZ

I went from having a close family that joyfully celebrated birthdays, holidays, and special occasions together, to one that could barely manage to be in the same room together without an argument erupting. Even after the incident in Truckee had rocked my view of my mom, she was still someone who made me feel loved and cared for. But before long, that version of her became a rare sight.

Once Dad moved out, Mom started going out all the time, even during the week. She began dating men that she met at bars, and would bring them home without regard for how it made us feel. There was no conversation about it, just some random guy I had never met hanging all over my mom, who could care less about us.

It was not uncommon for the bar to close and the party to move to our house. My house would be filled with 20-30 people — some I came to know, but many I had never even met. It felt very different from the parties my parents used to have with close friends who were like family to me when I was younger.

My life became completely unrecognizable to me. I hardly saw or spoke to my dad anymore; he was living his best life with his new girlfriend and his replacement daughters. Meanwhile, my sister and my mom were always either out partying with friends, working, or sleeping it off. At 12 years old, my life was in turmoil, and I felt utterly abandoned by my entire immediate family.

CHAPTER 9

The summer between seventh and eighth grade was extremely difficult for me. Not only were my mom and dad fighting about the separation and divorce, but my mom and sister also had a volatile relationship —fine one day and at each other's throats the next. It was during this time I learned from my sister that my mom was addicted to the narcotic, methamphetamine or meth as it is commonly called.

As I mentioned previously, both of my parents were heavy drinkers who liked to party. Looking back, I now understand they were both functioning addicts. What I didn't know as a child was that they both also experimented with cocaine and marijuana on the weekends when they partied with friends. Recreational cocaine use in the 80's was quite common.

Years later, my dad told me that my mom eventually started using more, and moved to meth because it was cheaper and the high lasted longer. She started spending a great deal of money on it and had moved from partying on the weekends to daily use. He also told me that this was one of the things that eventually pushed him away and pulled them apart.

By the time she was 17, my sister also became addicted to meth, and she was a pretty heavy drinker as well. I think she started using similar to my mom and dad, just partying with friends. But it didn't take long for the addiction to take hold of her, just as it did with my mom. She started a pattern of running from her emotions and then using alcohol and drugs to numb or escape her emotional pain. Around the time of our parents' separation and divorce, she also developed an ulcer.

Although my mom never admitted it to any of us, my sister showed me where she found drugs in my mom's purse, along with the remnants of a powdery substance left behind in a small baggie. Despite my sister being in the throes of her own meth addiction, she and her friends were also walking, talking examples of how to spot the signs of meth addiction. She was open with me about her use of meth, and, strangely, we shared a weird bonding experience around the harsh reality of my mom's meth addiction.

I'm not sure if she was in denial about her own dependency on meth, but I wasn't. At age 12, it was clear to me that both my mom and my sister were meth addicts. My sister seemed completely oblivious to the fact that the very things she was angry at my mom for doing because of meth were the same things she was doing herself.

At that time, her addiction seemed somehow more manageable than my mom's. My mom was the emotional landmine we both had to tiptoe around daily, never knowing when or how we might trigger an explosion.

THE WEIGHT OF SILENCE

My whole life, I had longed for my sister to want to connect with me and to share a closeness that I believed only sisters could have. I never imagined that the bond we ended up creating would come from her educating me about our mother's meth addiction. She even revealed to me that Jane, my mom's close friend of many years who had attended countless fun gatherings at our house, was essentially my mom's drug dealer.

I was shocked at first, but then I realized that Mom had stopped taking me on her magical trips out to Jane's house in the country as I got older. When I was little, I used to love to go on those fun adventures with mom to see Jane. Mom and Jane shared a love of gardening, and mom would often spend time gathering clippings of Jane's plants while they talked. I would roam the property, playing with the baby goat and the other animals.

As I got older, I noticed that on the days Mom went to "see Jane," she would drag herself out of bed, practically snarling at anyone that came close to her. She would leave the house with a dark cloud over her head, but upon her return, she would be full of energy and exuberantly happy. She would affectionately dote on me the way she did when I was little, and suddenly feel motivated to do a deep clean of the entire house.

Before I knew about the meth and Jane's role in it, I thought mom's shift in energy came from welcomed time with a good friend doing something she loved. When I learned the truth, all of it made a lot more sense. I learned a lot about meth and the behaviors people on the drug exhibit, mostly from my sister, and the more I learned, the more Mom's behavior made sense.

She and my sister both had constant mood swings, going from extreme highs to extreme lows. They would have tons of energy and then suddenly crash, spending an entire day or sometimes multiple days in bed. This is commonly referred to as "coming down" as the high starts to wear off.

They would go from barely eating anything to eating everything they could as they were coming down. Meth addicts often lose weight and become very thin. My mom and sister's weight would fluctuate, but there were many times when I noticed a significant difference in their weight.

If you look up a picture of a meth addict, you will most likely see a rail thin person with bad teeth, sunken cheeks and possibly covered in sores. While there were times when both my mom and sister were thinner, there were also times when they put on weight. There was NEVER a time when they fit the mold of a "typical meth addict" when it came to their weight. This was another thing that messed with my head and made me question if and when they were still using.

There were plenty of times I witnessed my sister and her friends stay awake all night drinking alcohol and snorting meth. They often wouldn't sleep at all; they would just snort another line of meth in the morning before they went off to work. My mom did not usually stay up all night, but she would go out, close the bar, stay up until three or four in the morning, and then, I imagine, hit up the meth in the morning to get herself off to work.

This pattern could go on for days until they eventually crashed and came down hard. It was not fun to be around either of them when they were crashing or coming down. They would be extremely moody, short-tempered, and sometimes just downright mean.

My mom was what is often called a high-functioning addict. She held the same county job for 26 years until she retired. Despite her addiction, she was able to mask it with the turmoil of the divorce, kids being sick, or whatever excuse she could use to make sense of her missing work. She had worked there so long that she had built up a lot of paid time off she could use for those mornings when she didn't have drugs or she was coming down.

Her boss also allowed her to come in late, and sometimes bring work home. She was good at what she did too, so I'm sure that helped. I often wondered what her colleagues really thought, and if they had any clue about her addiction.

Another reason my mom and sister fought had a lot to do with my sister refusing to move when my mom got a job near where my dad had been working. After my parents separated, my mom even told my sister that the divorce was her fault because she wouldn't move.

Most children of divorced parents feel like their parents divorcing is somehow their fault; my mom actually came right out and told my sister she blamed her for it. I don't know if my mom ever apologized or took it back, but the damage was done. It was right around that time that my sister started abusing meth.

Throughout my life, I have always wished for a close relationship with my sister. I always looked up to her and wanted to be with her, but the feeling never seemed mutual for her. To her, I was just her "bratty little sister". Growing up, we fought a lot because my parents gave her the job of looking after me after school until they returned home. We both had chores to do after school, and she was always nagging me to do them.

"You're not the boss of me!" I would yell at her, sitting as close as possible to the television, most likely watching *The Great Space Coaster* or, as I got a little older, the soap opera *Days of Our Lives*. She would get so mad at me, but I would just check out in front of the television and ignore her.

One day, she got so mad at me ignoring her that she threw a stick at me! It was an old broom handle my dad had fashioned into a wedge to lock the sliding glass door. I don't think she meant to hit me with it, because it was quite large and heavy, but it struck me right on the head!

I screamed in pain, clutching my head as I ran to hide in the bedroom from her. I was crying and saying, "Wait 'til mom and dad get home! You are so busted!" As she is apologizing and pleading with me to open the door where I was resting my injured head, I pulled my head away and saw a huge smear of blood!

"I'm bleeding!" I exclaimed.

"What?!" she yelled in a panic. "Open the door right now! I need to make sure you are O.K.!"

I had never seen so much blood, and it coming from my head only heightened the situation. I started to feel woozy, so I opened the door. She rushed me into the bathroom to tend to my wound.

I was crying, and she was apologizing as she held a towel to my head wound, "I'm so sorry, Minna. I didn't mean to hurt you. I never thought the stick would go that far. I just got so mad at you, so I threw it."

She called me by my nickname, Minna, a name I had given myself as a child when I couldn't say my whole name. It had stuck over the years and was something only my family and close childhood friends used, and still is to this day. I could tell she genuinely felt bad, but I also took the opportunity to milk it for something I never got enough of…quality time with my big sister where she was being nice to me.

It turned out the wound was just a small cut that had bled a lot. The scene in the bathroom became somewhat comical because neither one of us could stand the sight of blood. Whenever I see a lot of blood, especially my own, I can feel my face get warm and I start to get tunnel vision. My ears start to ring, sounds become muffled, and I feel like I might pass out.

My sister hates the sight of blood too, so as she was tending to me, I thought we might both pass out. It would have been quite a sight for my parents to come home to! We made it through without passing out, but she knew if I told Mom and Dad, she would be in big trouble.

I mean, she did throw a large stick at me, and it had hit me in the head. To keep me from telling Mom and Dad, she decided to spoil me for the night. She took me out to ice cream, and we hung out all night playing board games. I was in heaven. This was the sister time I always craved but rarely got. It was worth every drop of blood I shed that day.

My parents knew something was up, but they didn't ask too many questions. The way she was acting with me, it was clear she was repenting for something. With my hair being so thick, there were no signs of my injury. The chores were done, and everything seemed well, so they were probably happy to not engage in more of our sibling rivalry drama.

After Mom and Dad separated, Shelly and I grew closer, especially as mom became more selfish and focused on her own needs rather than ours, we bonded even more. However instead of my mom and dad having intense arguments, I now had to deal with the intensity of my mom and sister's verbal battles.

They would yell and slam things around, and their fights almost always ended with one of them storming out of the house. As things got worse, my sister made sure not to leave me alone there, so she started taking me with her. I don't remember my mom ever trying to stop her; in fact, this gave my mom the freedom to leave the house and do what she wanted.

My sister, like my mom, was filled with anger, but also so much sadness. All anyone could see on the surface was anger, but I knew her sadness ran deep. She turned 18 before the divorce proceedings began; as a result, it created a weird dynamic in the family, especially between her and Dad.

He still had to put in effort to show he was showing up for me for the divorce proceedings. Since Shelly was technically an adult, he didn't *have to* do the same for her. Over time, I watched the divide between them widen, and saw how it chipped away at her self-esteem. She tried to act like she didn't care about what Dad thought of her, but I knew how much it hurt her.

What my mom had said to my sister was awful, but I believe her feelings of betrayal and abandonment by my dad far outweighed anything my mom had said. It was hard to not feel somewhat discarded by Dad; I even felt that way at times, especially after he moved in with his new girlfriend and her two daughters.

My sister was always on the go, hanging out and partying with her friends, never slowing down long enough to really feel anything. I believe that for her, actually feeling all that pain was just too hard and a dangerous road to go down. On the surface, she acted indifferent, but I read some of the poems she wrote at the time, and I could see how much she suffered in silence.

At that time, I wasn't sure how much my dad knew about what was going on with my mom. It wasn't until I was an adult that I found out he was well aware of her drug use; regardless, he knew mom's behavior had become increasingly erratic. Our home life had grown chaotic and unhealthy, yet he chose to leave us with her. Sure, I always had the option to uproot what was left of my life in the midst of dealing with the demise of my family to go live with him, but why was that the only other option?

Option #1: Live with your alcoholic, meth addicted emotionally unstable mother in constant chaos.

Option #2: Leave your home, your school, your friends, and everything that is left of familiarity and comfort in your life during this traumatic time to go live with your dad.

Both choices felt impossible for me. I desperately wanted to feel safe, loved, and care for by the two people who were *supposed* to do that, ALWAYS. Even though I didn't fully understand addiction back then, I knew enough that my mom was not capable of putting her kids first. What I couldn't understand was why my dad couldn't put in more effort to make us feel like he was there for us?

Many times, it seemed as though he would use me to gather information he could use against her in the divorce proceedings. Whenever I was with him, he had so many negative things to say about her. His girlfriend never held back her opinions about my mom's behavior either. They were the adults, yet they constantly spoke ill of my mom around me and directly to me.

They both had such strong opinions about her and never seemed to hold back from sharing them with me. At the same time, it didn't seem like my dad was willing to sacrifice any part of his new life to make sure we were safe and cared for, or to help the mother of his children get the assistance she needed. At the time, it felt like all he cared about was looking good on paper for the judge and not disrupting his life or new lifestyle by making his kids his priority.

Not only did I feel caught in the middle of my mom and dad, but I also often felt torn between my sister and both my parents. I was angry too, but my people-pleasing nature and role as the peacekeeper kicked into high gear, complicating things for me in a different way. I struggled to actually express my anger because of my deep desire to be liked and loved by everyone. My extreme aversion to not want to hurt people's feelings left me floating in what I can only describe as a form of emotional purgatory.

MELINDA VELASQUEZ

Life during adolescence was already confusing and frustrating enough, but the divorce drama just made everything feel worse. The tension between everyone in my family was palpable. I have always been the kind of person who wants everyone to get along and be happy, so for me, the emotional rollercoaster we were living on was gut-wrenching.

The divorce hit right in the middle of my adolescence. As a pre-teen girl held captive by crazed hormonal changes, everything felt incredibly intensified. The life I loved ceased to exist. With things so out of balance at home, I was grateful to have school as an escape, providing some respite from the chaos and drama that had taken over my home.

CHAPTER

10

I continued to feel like I was caught in the middle of the fights with my mom and dad, as well as the arguments between Shelly and each of them. Shelly and I had finally built a closer relationship where she spent time with me, and I didn't want to risk losing that. When she was angry with mom or dad, I would side with her, even if I didn't agree, out of fear of damaging our relationship.

Many of the fights between my mom and sister, where I felt compelled to choose sides, took place in the summer between seventh and eighth grade. Even though my sister had revealed my mom's meth addiction to me, she assured me that she herself wasn't addicted. Shelly reassured me that she and her friends only did it when they were "partying" and that she didn't need it like Mom did. However, what I witnessed told a very different story.

When the fights between my mom and sister got really bad, Shelly would leave and take me with her. Many times, when we left, she and her friends would rent a room in the creepiest hotel in town, nicknamed Hotel Hell. It was known around town that on any given day you could find both drugs and sex workers there. It was an older, run-down hotel where no one cared what you did as long as you paid for your room and didn't completely trash it.

The hotel was also right next door to a really great hamburger place I loved, where one of Shelly's close friends worked. She used to bring me burgers and fries after her shift ended, and it quickly became my favorite. The burgers were huge and loaded with all the fixings, topped off with their special sauce. I either had it with their steak fries or beer-battered onion rings. It was a lot of food, but I had no trouble devouring every bite. Once again, I found myself in a stressful situation with my family, and I used food as a comfort.

Once my sister and her friends got the hotel room, they would fill up the bathtub with ice and beer, and party all night with me in the room. There were only a few times when my mom didn't allow me to go with my sister after they fought, but most of the time she didn't protest.

I had to call and check in with my mom to reassure her that I was okay. Most of the time I would lie and say we went to the burger place for dinner and then told her we were spending the night with one of Shelly's friends. This was long before caller ID, so she had no clue I was calling from a hotel. She never checked.

Most of the time, Shelly and her friends used drugs in my presence, but I never drank or did drugs in those situations. My sister made sure no one gave me drugs or alcohol. I always wanted Shelly to take me with her because I didn't want to be left behind to deal with Mom, who was often angry after a fight with my sister, or my dad. I'm pretty sure my mom had no idea what I witnessed every time I hung out with Shelly and her friends, and I certainly wasn't going to tell her.

There were also times when my sister had parties at our house too. They would let me join in on the drinking game, Quarters, where the object is to bounce a quarter into a glass and then pick someone to make them drink. My drink of choice was a big pitcher of Kool-Aid.

Shelly's group of friends also used to buy a large amount of meth that they would then "cut" with some other similar substance to increase their supply and make a profit. I witnessed this process enough times that I could have written a how-to manual on it. Any white powdery substance would do. They would mix it in a ratio of about three parts meth to one part other powder such as corn starch or baking soda. I think they even used baby powder once.

For me, it wasn't so much about what they were doing as it was about finally being allowed to hang out with my sister and her friends. I had craved her time and attention since I was a little girl, and now that I had it, I wasn't going to risk losing that privilege. No matter how uncomfortable I felt or how wrong I knew it was, I just kept my mouth shut and pretended it was no big deal.

Within a year or two, my sense of normalcy had completely shifted. My life went from fun family gatherings and Charades to a house full of anger and bitterness. By the age of 12, I was receiving weekly lessons in how to use and sell drugs, as well as playing drinking games. This lifestyle became my new normal, and I continued to normalize this behavior for many years to come.

To normalize behavior is, in a way, to excuse it or not give it the weight it deserves. Throughout my childhood and much of my adulthood, my parents and sister engaged in activities that were extremely damaging to my development. However, it took me a long time to understand the impact it had on me because it was just the way things were in my family.

MELINDA VELASQUEZ

As a young child, I had friends whose parents also partied a lot, so what was being reflected back to me at a young age made sense with what was happening in my home. This made it easier for me to minimize the damage occurring around me. Additionally, I had never been physically abused by my parents, which made it simpler to overlook the emotional toll. There were no external bruises to reveal the depth of my suffering. All the pain was buried deep inside of me, hidden even from my own comprehension.

But throughout my life, my wounds began to ooze out and rear their ugly heads. They manifested as lack of self-esteem, envy, pride, self-loathing, depression, anxiety, desperation and many other negative attributes or emotions. Now, I refer to them as my shadow side. I look at them the way I do biases —we all have them, but they only have the power to affect how we present ourselves in the world if we don't know what they are and learn how to combat them.

Witnessing my sister and her friends snorting lines of meth multiple times a night became a part of my new normal. On any given day, I would watch them start with a pile of meth on a mirror or the glass from a family picture frame. They would use a razor blade to separate it out into neat little lines for each person. Then, they would use a straw or, in a pinch, a rolled-up dollar bill, or take apart a ballpoint pen and use the outer shell to snort it up one nostril while holding the other closed. After everyone snorted their line, someone would yell out "numb-ers" as they gathered up the remaining powder residue and rubbed it under their top lip for a numbing effect.

Once the drugs had made their way into their bloodstream, I watched as their high began to take hold. I had a front-row seat to watch the energy shift among all of them. They all exhibited a jittery energy that was both annoying and slightly overwhelming to me. I witnessed them talking faster, louder and more assertively. Most of them also became far more emotionally aggressive. All of their feelings and emotions seemed heightened, and their reactions to things became highly exaggerated.

I noticed that a few of her male friends became more belligerent and agitated, which made me nervous. They were all smokers, but the number of cigarettes they smoked increased immensely when they were high. Often, they would barely put one cigarette out before they were picking up another one to light it. They had no desire to eat until they were coming down, and then they would suddenly have voracious appetites. Sometimes, it took days for them to come down from the high.

For many kids my age, witnessing all of this, combined with the pedestal I had my big sister on, could have easily led me right down that same path. Fortunately for me, the only benefit I saw was that they were able to stay awake all night. Thankfully, my 12-year-old brain rationalized that I could stay awake with them just by drinking Kool-Aid, which seemed like a much more enjoyable experience to me.

I had suffered from severe sinus infections and allergies for years by the time I had my weekly "Intro to Meth Use and Distribution" sessions with my sister and her friends. The idea of snorting something up my nose and having it drain back down my throat just to stay awake seemed like more of a nightmare to me than a good time. Fear was a dominant force in my life, and in this case, it may have actually saved me. This was one of the many times in my life where witnessing someone else's experience instilled enough fear in me that instead of running toward it, I ran in the other direction.

Fortunately for me, the thought of meth truly disgusted me, the same way cigarettes did. I decided to try cigarettes one day at age 10 when my parents were at work and my sister wasn't around. I was curious about them because every adult I knew smoked them.

I always hated the smell of cigarettes when my parents or their friends smoked, but I wondered if it might be different being on the other end of the cigarette. I decided to try my dad's pack of cigarettes instead of my mom's. Dad smoked Camel cigarettes, which didn't have a filter. With nothing between my mouth and the tobacco, one puff and I knew it would never be for me. It was the most disgusting thing I had ever tasted! The pieces of tobacco got into my mouth and stuck to my tongue, and the smell was just as bad as the second-hand smoke.

Having a strong physical aversion to cigarettes and meth was definitely helpful in avoiding that path, but I also consider myself very lucky that somehow the addiction gene in my family didn't have the same hold on me as it did on my mom and sister. I have always had the ability to learn not only from my mistakes but from the mistakes of others as well. I think being a people-pleaser and looking for approval for most of my life was what drove that, and it did save me from going down the wrong path more than once. However, it also created a pattern that eventually would lead me further from my authentic self than I ever imagined possible.

As the summer after seventh grade came to an end, I looked forward to school starting because it was a distraction from what was going on at home. In addition to the fights my sister and I would get into with my mom, my mom started dating and bringing home men that I found creepy and weird. At times she would also have loud sex with them while I was in the house, many times while I had friends over. It was humiliating.

Another big change was that Laura moved back in with her mom and planned to attend a different school for eighth grade. Over the summer,

Naomi got an opportunity to travel out of the country and visit relatives. With Laura in another town and Naomi in another country, I felt trapped in the chaotic world of my family, with no escape or refuge.

I had other friends, but the limited access to the two I trusted most made my family drama even more unbearable. When Naomi returned, we became inseparable. The time apart seemed to make both of us appreciate our friendship even more, and she started spending a lot of time at my house. Having her there eased my fear and loneliness.

By the time eighth grade started, aside from Laura, Naomi had become my closest friend. We had shared so much about our lives and our families with each other, and I knew that nothing could ever break that bond. Naomi and I were so excited to be big eighth graders together; we were ready to rule the school.

SECTION THREE

Adolescence:
A Simple Misunderstanding

---

*"The less we talk about shame, the more we have it.
Shame is the most powerful, master emotion.
It's the fear that we're not good enough."*
~ Brené Brown

CHAPTER 11

The beginning of eighth grade was everything I had hoped for and more. Unfortunately, I did not have any classes with Naomi, but we would hang out at break, lunch, and after-school. I had friends in every class, and there were rumors that the boy I liked actually might like me too. While things at home were still up and down, my life at school was the best it had ever been.

One day, I got permission from my mom to walk home with Naomi and spend the night on a school night. We walked home with a group of girls, mostly the popular ones Naomi had gone to elementary school with, as well as a new girl who played basketball with them. Her name was Courtney, and my initial perception of her was that she was kind of quiet and pretty. I often found something to admire in almost anyone who looked different from me, especially if they had a different body type or straight hair that was not puffy like mine.

MELINDA VELASQUEZ

I was in eighth grade from 1988 to 1989, and the truly *must-have* hairstyle of the time was a big "wall" of bangs on top with the sides of the hair blown and hair-sprayed straight out, resembling wings. My naturally curly, extremely thick hair made this particular hairdo nearly impossible to wear. While I could do the bangs, my hair was too heavy for the side "wings." Back then, I never wore my hair down because I had no idea how to manage it well.

I did feel pretty good about wearing my hair half up in a ponytail. My sister came up with the great idea to wrap it with a piece of fabric so it sat nicely on the top of my head, which was a popular style at the time. We actually cut the leg of a pair of white tights, wrapped it around a few times, and it worked perfectly. It wasn't the wings, but I finally felt like I found a hairdo that made me feel pretty for once.

Courtney managed to get the "wings" to stick straight out, and I once commented on it to Naomi out of jealousy and admiration. I said something about her hair looking like a rainbow because of the way it was styled — a look I wished I could achieve but couldn't. I had no idea how much that one comment would come back to haunt me.

This was the first and only time I went to Naomi's house, which was notable since she had spent a great deal of time at my house. We sat up in her room, and her mom made us popcorn with some sort of special seasoning on it. Naomi's mom seemed really nice, though a little timid.

I was shocked at how short-tempered and bossy Naomi was with her mom as she took the popcorn and forced her out of her bedroom. I couldn't imagine getting away with treating my parents, or any adult, that way. But her mom just put her hands up and quickly backed out of the room.

THE WEIGHT OF SILENCE

After her mom left, Naomi and I began talking about everything that mattered to us, like we always did. This was the moment when I broke the cardinal rule of friendship. Naomi was asking me about Laura since Naomi had not seen her since summer. Laura had gone through a rough time over the summer while Naomi was away, and I foolishly shared something Laura had shared with me. I had no right to share anything Laura had told me with Naomi.

My intention was not to hurt Laura or betray her in any way. Naomi's questions seemed to come from genuine concern for Laura, and I mistakenly thought that since they were friends, Laura would trust Naomi with that information too. I wasn't the first adolescent girl to make this mistake, and I certainly wouldn't be the last.

I had no right to share anyone's secrets, especially Laura's. She had always been such a good friend to me. Even though Laura never explicitly told me not to say anything, I should have known better. It was not my story to tell.

Immediately after I told Naomi, I felt regretful because I realized Laura hadn't shared it with her. I wished I could take it back, but it was too late. I swore Naomi to secrecy, trusting that she would not tell anyone. Given everything Naomi and I had shared with each other, I had no reason to believe she would ever betray my trust.

We had been in Naomi's room for a while when we heard yelling. Naomi had mentioned before that her dad and brothers fought often, but until that night, I had no idea how bad it could get. The yelling we heard was in fact her dad and one of her brothers. The two of them got in a really big argument that spilled out into the street and escalated into a physical altercation. I was completely shocked by the whole situation.

MELINDA VELASQUEZ

Things at my house were chaotic and tense; what I witnessed at Naomi's house felt so different from my family's brand of chaos. The drugs, Hotel Hell, and the constant arguing and emotional ups and downs had all become some sort of twisted norm in my life. Despite hating how my life had changed, I had learned to adapt and cope with my situation, even though it was undoubtedly causing me emotional damage.

What I witnessed at Naomi's house was different, and it scared me enough that I never wanted to spend the night there again. I had never witnessed family members being physically violent with each other in real life, and it was traumatic. The whole family seemed caught up in it, and I found it equally terrifying and sad. I felt so bad for Naomi, but I didn't know what to do, and my immediate response to the trauma was to get the hell out of there as quickly as possible. I pretended to be sick and had my mom come pick me up.

I felt bad for leaving Naomi, but I couldn't stay there. When we talked the next day Naomi seemed embarrassed and apologized for the craziness. I told her it was fine, but in the back of my mind, I knew I never wanted to go to her house again. Despite that, I still wanted to be her friend — nothing had changed and as far as I was concerned, I would always be her friend. I didn't judge her for what went on with her family; if anything, it made me feel closer to her.

Even though what happened at Naomi's house was different from what was happening in my family, it somehow validated that families are messy and that bad things can happen in homes that can go unnoticed by the outside world. This was certainly true for my situation too. The teachers and counselors at school had no idea exactly what was happening in my home. I never brought it up because the thought of not being with my family seemed far worse.

THE WEIGHT OF SILENCE

My life seemed pretty crazy back then, but the fear of people finding out just how crazy it was firsthand was even worse. As crazy as things had become, the last thing I wanted was for my mom or sister to get in trouble, or for me to be forced to leave my home. I was learning to compartmentalize the craziness and ignore the emotional toll it took on me.

Regardless of what happened at home, I always felt physically safe; I don't think Naomi would have been able to say the same. My heart broke for her when I thought about all she had to endure. This was around the time I began minimizing the impact of my traumatic experiences on my emotional well-being whenever I considered someone else's experience to be more tragic than my own.

I compared my experiences to others', which seemed far worse than my own. It was a way for me to lessen the negative impact my experiences had on my life, and a strategy I adopted as a way of not appearing weak. I didn't want to see myself as a victim. I wanted to see myself as strong and resilient.

The fact that there was physical violence present in Naomi's situation was part of what made it so much more intense and scarier to me. The idea of facing physical harm or injury was entirely unfamiliar and frightening. Little did I know that silently enduring the impact of numerous unseen emotional wounds could be just as damaging to one's soul as physical violence— the key distinction lies in the visibility of the scars.

Prior to that night at Naomi's house and afterward, whenever I got into arguments with my mom, Naomi would tell me that I should just move in with her. At the time, I didn't actually take her seriously. To me, it was just one of those things friends say to each other when they are young.

Regardless of the indiscretions taking place in my own family, I knew my parents would *never* allow me to move in with a friend. I also knew I could never live there after what I witnessed. I chose not to tell Naomi how I truly felt about being at her house because I didn't want to hurt her feelings. For me, keeping silent about how I felt was much easier than potentially hurting someone's feelings by speaking my truth.

The pattern of avoiding conflict that occurred in my family primed me for avoiding difficult conversations. While there was plenty of conflict in my family, after the initial emotional outbursts, there was never any discussion or debrief about what happened. Things never got resolved; they just festered.

I have always had a very difficult time confronting or saying things to people I care about that might hurt their feelings. This often led me to make comments about people behind their backs, especially during adolescence. The concept of talking *to* someone rather than *about* them was foreign to me. In girl-world talking about people behind their backs felt like a survival tactic, or at least that is what I believed at the time.

In junior high, social survival was a daily battle. At any given moment, someone could pull the rug out from underneath you and life, as you knew it would change before you hit the ground. At home, my own "rug" had already been pulled out, and I was flailing around in the air trying desperately to grab hold of something to help manage all the stress. Little did I know, more was coming and nothing would ever be the same again…

CHAPTER

12

It was a Friday at lunch when the first domino fell, setting off the chain of events that would seal my fate for the rest of my eighth-grade year. Candace, a girl I had met in the seventh grade, approached me. I knew her as an acquaintance and we had a class or two together, but beyond that and mutual friends we had little contact. On this particular day, out of nowhere Candace came up to me with a group of people behind her and started making passive-aggressive comments toward me. Her posturing and the way she spoke felt threatening, catching me completely off guard.

I don't recall exactly what Candace said or why she suddenly had a problem with me, but I just stood there in shock. One of the popular girls I had made friends with through Naomi stepped in and told Candace to back off, which she did immediately. Unfortunately, Candace was in my next class, where the taunting continued. She somehow drafted a few people in the class to join in with her, and for the entire class, she spewed rude comments at me loud enough for everyone but the teacher to hear as we worked in our small groups.

Finally, school ended for the day, and I decided to go to my friend Morgan's house to hang out. Morgan was one of the original five girls from elementary school. We still spent time together after school, but not as much during school. After the horrible day I had at school, I just wanted to be around a friend.

Even though I had people stick up for me, I just felt so alone. I wasn't afraid of Candace per se; my real fear was that I would return to school on Monday and once again find myself to be the odd girl out. After all, that was how it happened in elementary school.

When we arrived at Morgan's house, I called my mom to let her know where I was, and we got in a huge argument. I asked her to pick me up on her way home from work, and she just blew up at me. I told her I would find another ride home and hung up. Later, when she returned home from work, we talked again over the phone and had the worst fight we had ever had. The argument culminated with me saying, "Fine, I'm moving in with dad!"

I had grown so tired of arguing with my mom, because it seemed as though that was all we did lately, and I had finally had enough. The drugs made her moods completely unpredictable, and the divorce proceedings only intensified her mood swings. My mom was mad at my dad all the time, and my dad seemed to find new ways every week of pushing her buttons; unfortunately, Shelly and I were often on the receiving end of her anger and frustration with Dad.

Between the drinking, the drugs, and the divorce, I constantly felt like I was walking on eggshells around my mom. I could never predict what kind of mood she would be in, and living like that was emotionally draining. Any little thing could set her off and I never felt like I could truly let go and trust or enjoy even the good moments when they happened. I learned to keep my guard up with her, because it was too painful when those moments would abruptly turn bad.

Both of my parents were so cruel and spiteful toward each other that they even had a huge battle over who would pay for the lawnmower on the Sears credit card. They resorted to purposely costing each other money by getting the lawyers involved in the pettiest of arguments. Living in this environment, being pitted against one parent or another, and also my sister, felt like my own personal hell.

After the day I had at school, the fear of once again being the odd girl out and the chaos at home became more than I could bear. I was hanging on by a thread and my friends and school were my only escape and solace. The sheer stress of thinking I could now be losing that too finally boiled over during that fateful fight with my mom.

I felt completely overwhelmed, unable to navigate the emotional chaos that had consumed my life. What I craved was harmony, and at that time in my life, my dad's house seemed to offer just that. Even with his comments about how I dressed or the judgments he and his girlfriend passed on my mom, his home provided structure, calmness, and a sense of control. It sounded like the perfect sanctuary to me.

From the minute I hung up the phone with my mom, everything moved so fast. That night, we argued a little more at home. I was being stubborn and completely unwilling to change my mind, even though I was already having second thoughts. I called my dad, and he said he was surprised but agreed to come pick me up the next day. Before I knew it, I was all packed up and ready to go.

On Saturday morning, my mom tried to reason with me. She seemed so sad now that she knew I was really leaving. I felt really bad and suddenly, whatever we argued about no longer seemed important. I had a gut feeling that I should change my mind, but my dad was already making the hour-long drive. I felt like I had made too big a deal to go back now. In that moment, I didn't want to disappoint my dad, or hurt his feelings; it didn't matter how I felt.

I also didn't want my dad to be angry for driving an hour to pick me up only to turn around and go back alone. It never occurred to me that seeing his daughter on a Saturday morning, especially when I was going through a difficult time, shouldn't have been an inconvenience; but that was how it often felt. He would always make comments, sometimes indirectly, other times directly, about the long drive. Just little comments here and there that left me feeling it wasn't something he really wanted to do.

From the start of the separation, I just wanted him to fight for me. I wanted him to *want* to spend time with me regardless of what he had to deal with in order to have that time. Instead, it felt like he thought his life would be so much easier and better if he didn't have to disrupt his perfect little world by being my dad.

All of this was running through my head as I packed my things and prepared to leave with him. Deep down, part of me felt that if I rejected him, I might lose him for good. I was afraid this would be the thing that pushed him further away from me than he already felt. Maybe he would just stop trying to see me altogether and leave me there with Mom and her erratic, drug-induced behavior.

As I waited for him to arrive, I began to feel a wrenching in my stomach, a pressure in my chest and the heat of my face as I tried to hold back my tears in an attempt to be strong. Instead of realizing that

I was disappointed in his failure to protect me during this traumatic time, I just internalized those feelings, and they once again manifested in me a belief that I was not enough.

Despite feeling unworthy of his love and attention, the thought of hurting his feelings was unimaginable to me. I recalled the night in Truckee when my mom said, "I'm going to leave you, and the girls will want to live with me." I witnessed that moment break him in a way I didn't think was possible.

If I changed my mind at that point, I truly believed I would break him again and completely destroy what was left of our relationship. The thought of doing that made me feel sick to my stomach. I had lost so much already. I couldn't stand to lose him too.

In the end, my desire to be loved and accepted by my dad, and my desperate need for him to not be disappointed in me, overshadowed everything else. My intuition screamed at me, urging me not to go, but in my mind, there was no turning back. The fear of letting people down was my kryptonite, and I just couldn't bear the thought of failing in front of the one stable parent I had, regardless of how inadequate and flawed I felt in his presence.

It all happened so fast, I didn't even have the chance to tell Naomi before I left. Morgan was the only one who knew because she was there during the argument my mom and I had on the phone. I tried to call Naomi but could not reach her. By the time I told her I was moving an hour away with my dad, I was already at his house unpacking my stuff. It was already too late to change anything or talk me out of it.

I finally got a hold of Naomi Sunday night, and as I unpacked my things while we talked on the phone, I knew I had made a huge mistake. She was crushed, and I was miserable. As soon as I heard

Naomi's voice, I realized that she had no intention of siding with Candace and leaving me out. She pleaded with me to come back, but I told her it was too late; I had already moved.

My dad lived in a nice house, free of the kind of daily drama that had become the norm at my mom's house. However, he lived outside of town, and there were no people my age around. To make matters worse, I had no friends and was going into a new middle school.

I already felt that I had put my parents through so much by making this big decision to move, but I had no idea how to tell them I made the wrong decision. Now I was an hour away from everything I knew, except my dad. But even he felt like a different person compared to the dad I remembered from my childhood.

My dad had this whole separate life away from us at that point, and I felt I had interrupted his new life. *Living* with him was very different then a fun rafting trip down the Russian River on the weekend. Even though my mom and I fought a great deal, I felt different around my mom compared to my dad. As a child, I could only sense this difference; it wasn't until I became an adult that I was able to name it.

My dad had a way of saying or doing things that triggered feelings of insecurity in me, causing me to question who I was, what I looked like, how I dressed, and whether I was ever good enough. I know he loved me and was proud of me, and I believe he did his best. However, the way he spoke, acted, or reacted to things really triggered emotions in me that fed my low self-esteem. I wanted so much for him to be proud of me that I could not see how little pride I had in myself.

I desperately wanted a closer relationship with my dad. I still carried those childhood feelings that he viewed me as the spoiled child my mom let get away with everything. I yearned for his respect and approval. At the time, I believed I would never have that if I shared my true feelings with him about my decision to move being a mistake.

Feeling like I didn't want to let my dad down only made me feel more isolated and alone after moving in with him. I was set to start school the next week, and all I wanted was to go back to my old school with all my friends. I was terrified to start a new school, but I did everything I could to hide that from my dad. The thought of hurting his feelings or disappointing him drove me to keep moving forward with this new life.

It took some time to get everything set up, so I didn't start school until Friday that week. I was really scared. I had NEVER been the new girl before. The whole reason I chose not to change schools when we moved before was because I was afraid I would not make new friends.

For a thirteen-year-old girl with deep self-esteem issues, starting over in a new school with no friends felt like a fate worse than death. All I wanted was to turn back the clock and be back in my hometown with my mom, my sister, and my friends. I had missed my chance to voice my desire not to move, and there was no going back now.

The morning of my first day at my new school, I put on my favorite outfit and felt pretty confident that I might be perceived as a girl people would want to befriend — at least, I hoped that would be the case. My dad took me to school in the morning so he could fill out paperwork and get me started. After he left, I started my classes, and the time during class wasn't bad. A few girls started talking to me, and a cute boy even flirted with me a little.

During break, the girls who talked to me in class just smiled and looked away, giving the impression they didn't want to welcome me into their clique. To avoid the humiliation of being seen sitting by myself, I decided to walk around and find all my classes.

When lunchtime came, the anxiety in my stomach had reached my throat. As I went to the cafeteria to get food, it seemed as though everyone was staring at me, and not in a good way. I felt exposed, lonely, and unsure of myself. The newfound self-esteem I had at the start of eighth grade suddenly seemed non-existent.

I decided not to eat because then I would have to sit down and hope that someone would let me sit with their group. I knew how it felt to be the odd girl out, and I would do just about anything to avoid feeling that horrible feeling again. Unfortunately, in my rushed decision to move, I didn't think through that I would have to go to a new school and start over with no friends if I lived with my dad. I just knew that living with my mom had become too difficult.

I walked through the quad again where all the groups gathered, smiling at the girls I had met earlier, hoping they might call me over, but they didn't. It never occurred to me to have the courage to ask them if I could sit with them. Back then, I believed that being rejected was just as bad, if not worse than being alone.

After my last unsuccessful attempt to be invited into a group, I walked to the furthest corner of the school and spent the rest of lunch hiding out and crying. I was stuck, wallowing in self-pity, and I asked myself: *How did I get here? How soon can I go home again?*

I had plenty of time to think on the bus ride home, as my stop was one of the last stops on quite a long trip. By the time I made it back to my dad's house, I had made up my mind — I was going home. I knew I would need to talk to my mom and dad about it, which I was not looking forward to, but I knew I had made a huge mistake.

When I got home, Naomi called and told me how much she missed me and how the whole week really sucked without me being there. I told her how bad my first day was, and she urged me again to just come home. Some of the popular girls were with her, and they got on the phone telling me I should return home too.

One of the girls told me that Candace, the girl who bullied me on my last day at school, was bragging about me leaving, saying I left because I was afraid of her. Honestly, I was not a girl who handled confrontation well; however, my fear was not just about Candace having a problem with me, but also about everyone else siding with her.

In my experience, if you angered one influential girl, soon everyone else would follow suit. It was bad enough in elementary school when your whole class ignored you, but junior high was so much bigger. With seven classes a day and different classmates in each one, I was certain that if my fear of being left out came true, soon the whole school would turn against me.

None of this really mattered anyway because the main reason I left was because of the horrible argument I had with my mom. Candace played a tiny role in how vulnerable and frustrated I felt the day I decided to move, but she was nowhere near the deciding factor. I wanted to tell Naomi that day on the phone that I was coming home, but before I could tell anyone, I had to talk to my mom and work through our issues.

CHAPTER 13

After talking things out with my mom and dad, I was back home with my mom by the end of the weekend. I think my dad was disappointed that I did not give the new school a fair shot, but back then, bravery and embracing change were not my strengths.

I felt really stupid about the whole ordeal, but I was eager to move forward and get back to my normal life. I called Naomi and let her know I was coming home; she told me how happy she was. She seemed a bit off on the phone, but I figured there must have been something going on at her house.

I was back at my school by Monday, and the first thing I did after checking in at the office was look for Naomi. I couldn't find her anywhere, so I asked a few of the girls that she sometimes drove to school with if they had seen her, but they just shrugged their shoulders, rolled their eyes, and kept walking.

I found it strange that they didn't seem surprised to see me back; in fact, they appeared annoyed by my presence. I felt confused by their response to me, and I felt a pang of anxiety creeping up my stomach.

These were the same girls who were on the phone with me the previous Friday, urging me to move back. Yet now, they seemed to care less that I was here. Since I wasn't as close to any of them as I was with Naomi, I decided to let it go and focused on finding Naomi.

When I finally found Naomi, she gave me the same look as the other girls and would not even talk to me. It was a look I had seen before, one she reserved for someone she didn't like, and it immediately began to set off alarm bells. The feeling I had in my stomach had now spread up through my chest, neck, and ears like fire in my body, and the panic and anxiety reached my brain, and the message was clear: WARNING! DANGER AHEAD!

I knew this hot feeling in my body well. It usually came when I felt vulnerable and was often a precursor to tears. I desperately wanted to believe this was all a mistake and that whatever was happening wasn't about me at all. I worked hard to fight back my tears, which only intensified the heat in my body. By now, my neck, face, and ears were surely turning red with the combination of fear, panic, and anticipation of what was to come next.

Naomi used to light up with joy and with a smile on her face when she would see me; now, all I saw was a cold and angry stare that chilled me to the bone. But I still couldn't fathom what I might have done to make her so angry with me. Admittedly, she did seem a little off on our last phone call, but this still just didn't make sense.

She was standing next to the new girl Courtney, the one with the perfect rainbow hair, who seemed to be staring me down, as she stood confidently at Naomi's side. Naomi acted like she hated me, and she had never treated me like that before. Desperate for understanding, I asked with sincerity and desperation, "What's wrong Naomi? Are you mad at me?"

She seemed to glare right through me with a contempt I'd never seen before from her and said, "Oh like you don't know what you did," as she turned to walk away, she dismissed me with a hand gesture and a flick of her hair.

As Naomi turned to walk away, Courtney smirked at me with what I can only describe as an evil smile and snapped, "Bitch." As if to finish the sentence for Naomi before she turned to follow Naomi away from me. I thought Courtney might hit me or even spit on me in that moment, but she didn't. Her face said it all, the message I received loud and clear was, *Watch out, bitch! You're out and I'm in and there is nothing you can do about it now!*

I couldn't believe what I was hearing. Before Naomi walked away, I tried to reason with her, but it was as if a switch had been flipped, transforming her into a completely different person. The eyes of my friend, once filled with kindness and empathy, now held only cruelty and indifference.

It felt as though the last year never happened, and we were meeting for the first time, but instead of becoming close friends, she seemed to be repulsed by the very sight of me. I was devastated, bewildered and overwhelmed with sadness. Frozen in place, I stood there feeling completely dumbfounded.

Could it be possible that the very thing I feared had now happened? Had I once again become the odd girl out? It felt like a cruel joke or a bizarre twist of fate —some might even call it a self-fulfilling prophecy. The thing I had feared most, which had consumed my thoughts with an unrelenting obsession, now seemed to be unfolding before my eyes.

I assumed that, like in elementary school, this too would pass and Naomi would soon forgive me. I couldn't wait to see the look on Courtney's face when Naomi and I became friends again; she would feel pretty stupid for being so rude to me for no reason. While I had many other friends I could hang out with, I wasn't ready to give up on my friendship with Naomi. Determined to find out more about what was really going on, I turned to my good friend, Morgan.

All of what had occurred so far had taken place within the first few weeks of the school year. After my unsettling encounter with Naomi and Courtney, I sought out Morgan. She had been there during the phone call with my mom that had led to my moving out, and she knew what I went through that day. However, as soon as I began talking to her, I noticed that even Morgan seemed cold and annoyed with me.

My level of sadness and anxiety went up a notch knowing that one of my oldest friends seemed to be upset with me too. A sense of dread weighed heavily on me. Even though I thought Naomi was taking things a bit too far, I could understand why she felt hurt by me, but why was Morgan acting this way towards me?

I wanted to get to the bottom of things, so I made a mistake many adolescent girls at the time made: I wrote Morgan a note. This was before the era of texting or Snapchat, we communicated through handwritten notes on actual paper. We even had fun ways of folding them, turning the delivery and opening of them into part of the process. It never occurred to me that it was written proof of whatever I said, nor did I anticipate that it could be used as future ammunition to humiliate me.

MELINDA VELASQUEZ

I don't remember the exact words I wrote to her, but I believe I asked her if she was mad at me and why everyone was acting so weird toward me. I also shared how no one would talk to me or let me hang out with them at the other school, and how stupid and alone I felt. I completely expected her to tell me that she was not mad and that we were still friends. Instead, what I got was a note telling me exactly what she and others thought of me, and it was not good.

I used to save notes from my friends, and as I looked back through my childhood keepsakes the original copy of this note was among the ones I saved. The following is an exact replication of the note, except I changed the names of the others named:

Melinda,

I don't know if I'm really mad or not but it seems like you are using excuses just to get away from everything. Like when you first left, it started out that you were going to leave because of your mom. Then, it seemed like it was because of Candace, and that you were just using your mom as an excuse. And when you went to your dad's, you only went to that new school for one day. You didn't even give the new school a chance! Besides, if you come to a new school after the school year has already begun, you shouldn't expect to make all new friends on the first day. And when you left [name of our city abbreviated] R.P., you only told 3 people you were leaving, so you made it seem like you didn't even care.

Why did you even come back if you were having so many problems at home? If your problems were as bad as you say, then you would have stayed with your dad and given things a chance for once instead of running away every time you don't like something.

I'm not going to tell you any names because they asked me not to say anything, but I'm not the only one who feels this way.

Morgan

As I read this note, I remember feeling like I was in one of those movie scenes where the character receives the worst possible news, and the world around them blurs like a kaleidoscope. Everything seemed to spin out of control, and the sounds around me became muffled and distorted. I felt lightheaded, and for a moment, I feared I might actually pass out.

I had already felt so incredibly embarrassed and stupid for what I saw as impulsive decisions and emotional actions. But now, the people I had hoped would empathize with my actions and forgive my mistakes had seemingly turned their backs on me. Not only did I feel ashamed about what had happened, but I was also devastated to realize that my friends thought even less of me than I did of myself.

It felt like everyone was quick to pass judgment on me without even taking the time to listen to me or try to understand things from my point of view. While I had my moments of insensitivity, I have always been an emotionally sensitive person and easily hurt by other's negative words and actions. Many times throughout my life, this sensitivity would prove to be my Achilles heel.

My thoughts shifted to Jenny and I began to consider how she must have felt about me. It was in that moment that I decided that all of this was my fault, and that it was some form of karmic retribution for what I had done to Jenny. I felt like I was being made to pay for deliberately hurting Jenny in retaliation for what I believed she had intentionally done to hurt me.

Regardless of what I had done to Jenny, she had new friends now and seemed really happy. I recalled the physical confrontation between her and Naomi and couldn't imagine things between Naomi and me ever escalating to that point. Naomi hated Jenny, but I knew in my heart she could never feel that way about me.

MELINDA VELASQUEZ

Morgan and I had been through this before in elementary school, but we always managed to reconcile and become friends again. I tried to reassure myself that this might be terrible for a week or two, but eventually everyone would move past it, and things would return to how they were before I moved. I never imagined that I was about to endure one of the most painful and lonely years of my life.

CHAPTER 14

My first mistake was believing that Naomi's newfound contempt toward me would pass. Unlike in elementary school, all was not forgiven and forgotten within a week or two. One day I ended up in my counselor's office to settle some things related to switching schools, and our conversation shifted to what had happened with Naomi. She could tell I was upset and offered to have Naomi come in so we could talk it out with her help. Desperate to find out what I had done to make Naomi turn on me so quickly, I agreed.

I was convinced that away from everyone else, Naomi would come to her senses. The counselor pulled Naomi out of a class to come and talk with me. When I asked her what I had done to make her so mad, she responded coldly, "First, you moved away and didn't even tell me, even after I told you that you could live with me. Then, even though I had asked you so many times to move back, it was not until the other girls asked you to move back that you finally did!"

MELINDA VELASQUEZ

I was a little shocked but slightly relieved because clearly it was just a simple misunderstanding. Her words were masked by anger, but I could see the pain beneath them. She felt hurt and abandoned by me after we had built such a strong friendship and shared the solidarity of dealing with dysfunctional families. I was certain our bond was strong enough to survive Naomi's misinterpretation of my actions, and that we could clear it all up pretty easily with the counselor's help. I could not have been more wrong.

The counselor acted as a mediator, allowing each of us to share our side of the story, and what was going on for each of us. Naomi tried to reign in her emotions and adopt a more neutral stance, but I could feel the shift in her energy towards me. Sitting so close to her in that room, I noticed something in her eyes changed when she looked at me or talked about me. A wall of protection had been erected between us, and the care and empathy that used to be in her eyes when she looked at me had turned to anger and contempt.

Naomi did what was necessary to satisfy the counselor's belief that she had helped ameliorate the issue, but she still made it clear that she no longer wanted to be my friend. Unfortunately, this little intervention only seemed to escalate Naomi's anger, leaving me feeling even more weak and vulnerable.

I was still upset about the loss of our friendship, while Naomi behaved as if she couldn't care less. My counselor assured me that all of this was normal and that if I just waited it out, "it would pass." I had been telling myself the same thing, but after witnessing Naomi's behavior that day, I started to fear that things would only get worse.

Prior to the misunderstanding with Naomi, I always looked forward to break, lunch, and after- school gathering in the quad. The quad was the courtyard at the center of the school, where the cafeteria and walk-up snack bar was located. Around the perimeter of the quad were benches, and on the side closest to the snack bar were the front of the school and the main administrative office. The quad was the social hub of the school—it was *the* gathering place for my friends and a place where I once felt very comfortable.

Different groups or cliques gathered in different areas of the quad, while some groups gathered at other areas of the school. The popular crowd I was once a part of always gathered in the quad; their group was the largest and hung out closest to the cafeteria.

After the morning of my return to school, everything changed. The friends I thought I had in every class had been turned into adversaries. Many of them had been friends with Naomi first, so it was not completely surprising that they would take her side. Now instead of talking *to* me, they were talking *about* me.

As I walked through the halls to get to my classes, they would shout mean things at me, talk loudly, saying negative things about me, block my path, and even purposely bump into me. It was hurtful and scary, especially since my perception was that some of these girls carried themselves in a way that conveyed toughness I was afraid to challenge. I had never been in a physical fight before and had no idea how to defend myself. I was terrified of being beat up by someone, and that fear paralyzed me.

Not only had my new friends turned on me, but my old friends abandoned me as well. I suppose if they were not angry with me, they were likely trying to protect themselves from the wrath of Naomi and her crew. As things progressed, they made it increasingly difficult for me to have any friends at all.

If someone were brave enough to talk to me during a class or let me hang out with them during break or lunch, Naomi, Courtney, and their group of followers would quickly put an end to it. They would approach us, acting extra friendly to the people I was with while simultaneously saying cruel things about me and to me.

Sometimes they were explicitly rude and obnoxious, but other times they were more covert, making gestures or underhanded comments. It felt like a form of emotional blackmail. Naomi was the Don, and her crew was the school mafia, making it clear to everyone that you were either with them or against them. If you went against them, there would be serious consequences.

No one wanted to risk becoming the next victim of their social torture, so whenever they saw the opportunity to secure my position as the outcast, they seemed to jump at the chance. No one wanted to get caught in the crossfire. Like a series of enemy ambushes, they picked off my allies one by one, pushing me further into total isolation.

In the beginning, there was a group of girls I would hang out with on the weekends at the roller skating rink, but during school, we moved in different circles. They were nice to me and didn't join in on what quickly became daily torture sessions that took place, but they kept their distance whenever Naomi and her crew were around. Self-preservation is a necessary evil in the world of adolescent girls, and even those who try to stay neutral have a hard time avoiding all the blowback from the daily bombs that went off around me.

Each day, as the bell rang for break or lunch, I was filled with anxiety, dreading the impending doom awaiting me in the quad. *Maybe today they won't notice me in line for food,* I thought to myself as I walked cautiously into the quad. But like clockwork, I was surrounded by a mob of people eagerly awaiting my daily torture and humiliation.

THE WEIGHT OF SILENCE

Most days, Courtney was the one standing at the front of the pack, hurling insults and threatening my physical and emotional safety. It seemed like she knew all my secrets —everything I told Naomi in confidence was now being used as a weapon to torment me. This girl I barely knew had taken my place in the social hierarchy and swiftly became my nemesis.

Very rarely did Naomi stand before me and address me directly. Much like the previous year with me, Naomi, and Jenny when I was in the background and Naomi was in the foreground, it was all playing out again, only this time I was on the *receiving* end. Every day, at least twice a day, sometimes more, I was subjected to unrelenting harassment.

The regular daily torment usually consisted of the main crew of the most popular girls, along with many of the popular guys, who would stand by laughing or pointing as they witnessed my suffering. Occasionally, even the guys would join them spewing their venomous insults at me as well.

If the people around me were not saying things about me or to me, they were usually cheering on or further provoking those people who were verbally attacking me. They certainly didn't do anything to stop it or help me. The bystanders among the students were integral to the highly antagonistic nature of the bullying, contributing to the heightened emotional atmosphere that fueled my bullies to continue.

In the beginning, it felt like the whole school would gather around to witness the drama. There were times when at least 20-25 people stood around me, often right outside the Vice Principal's office. Someone told me to yell as loud as possible, "Leave me alone!" so that the noon aide or someone would know that I needed help. It seemed absurd that a single girl surrounded by a mob wasn't already an obvious sign of a problem, but I was desperate, so I tried it.

MELINDA VELASQUEZ

I yelled repeatedly at the top of my lungs, "LEAVE ME ALONE!" but no one came. Instead, the group mocked me, by repeating my words as if I were a whining child asking for her mommy. Unfortunately, even my mom could not help me. I felt angry, hurt, and completely defeated.

When I went to my counselor, she told me again that "it would pass." When things got so bad that I could no longer hide it from my mom, she called the school for help, and my counselor told her the same thing. The same thing happened to my sister in the eighth grade at the same school, and my mom was beside herself with concern. Later, I found out that my mom told my counselor about my sister's experience, but the counselor told my mom that she knew more about it than my mom, and she should trust her advice.

My mom was really concerned about what was happening with me, and as a result, we fought less. I think part of it was because she knew how awful things were for me at school. However, even though things were a little better at home, they were still not good.

By this time, my mom had met a guy named Dan who seemed to be a better choice than some of the men she had spent time with over the summer. He had a good job and two young kids. Dating him regularly seemed to have a positive influence on her; she seemed happy again. Dan took her on dates, bought her gifts, and did a good job of making her feel special.

Dan's presence also seemed to make her less angry with my dad, and less crazed about needing money. Before I was ready, mom invited Dan to move in to our house with his kids, Rex and Carrie. For the first time in our lives, my sister and I were now sharing a bedroom, which I secretly loved because I got to spend more time with her. During that time, we grew closer as we formed an alliance in solidarity of having to share our home with another family. Rex and Carrie left to spend time with their mom sometimes, but most of the time they remained with us.

Since dad moved out, there always seemed to be people at our house, either our friends or mom's *new* friends. At first, it was nice to have a feeling of family again under the same roof. We had to figure out new routines and bathroom schedules, but things started out pretty well. However, it would not be long before that familiar tension I felt with my own family would return and disrupt this new blended family dynamic.

Rex was eight and Carrie was six years old. It was an adjustment, and one that I didn't foresee being as difficult as it was. Rex and Carrie's dad and mom fought as much, if not more, than my mom and dad. Having two dysfunctional families coming together in the same house was a recipe for disaster.

Carrie bonded with my mom very quickly, and soon my mom began the same pattern with her as she did with me when I was a kid. My mom became very protective of Carrie, spoiling her and letting her get away with anything. Seeing my mom treat Carrie the way she had treated me when I was little was really difficult. We no longer had that kind of bond. Things had gotten a little better since I moved back, but not like they were when I was little.

I know that those feelings of envy for the relationship I missed with my mom hindered my ability to become close with Carrie. It wasn't her fault, but it created feelings of animosity within me that I'm sure she felt and didn't understand. I was starving for the motherly love my mom had once showered on me, and it was extremely painful to feel as though another woman's child had been brought in to take my place.

Rex, on the other hand was a total hellion! I was convinced that one day I would come home to find our house in flames. Mischievous didn't even begin to capture his personality. He was feisty and full of energy, often at odds with his dad. We bonded over the Super Mario Brothers video game, which he would play for hours.

Shelly and I had been raised very differently from Rex and Carrie. We both felt they were spoiled and got away with way more than we ever did. My mom also spoiled them both, and it made me crazy because I was desperate for my mom's love and attention. Our relationship had become strained and unpredictable, and it seemed like once Rex and Carrie arrived, I became even more invisible to her.

Despite my feelings of jealousy and frustration, I couldn't help but empathize with Rex and Carrie. Their dad, Dan, seemed to be very laid back about some things but also could completely go overboard with anger at them. Dan could be very silly and fun to be around, reminding me a lot of my dad's energy when I was younger. However, the longer he lived with us, the more I saw him become increasingly short-tempered and occasionally explosive with anger.

Most of the time Dan's anger was directed at Rex, but eventually he and my mom started to fight, and there were occasions when he even lashed out at me. Once again, my home felt extremely chaotic and stressful. The tension was thick and oppressive. Once things started going bad, I don't recall a day when there wasn't yelling or doors being slammed by kids and adults.

There were many times I felt sorry for Rex and Carrie, witnessing their dad react to something they did with such anger. Even when they were being disciplined for something they did to me, I couldn't help but feel guilty when seeing the wrath he would unleash on them. Later on, I learned that he was also using meth. The longer he lived with us the more his behavior seemed to mirror my mom's erratic mood swings. Towards the end, it seemed like he was angry all the time.

THE WEIGHT OF SILENCE

All of this was happening at home while I was facing daily harassment at school. Since my parents' separation, my home was no longer a sanctuary for me, and the challenges with the blended family only amplified that feeling. My emotional safety in the two environments where I spent most of my time —school and home — had completely eroded.

Eventually, Dan, Rex, and Carrie moved back into his house in a nearby city, and he and my mom just started to drift apart. Before he moved out, he had told my mom that someone should have taught me how to fight so I could defend myself against those girls. He offered to show me a couple things, but it wasn't enough to give me the confidence to stand up for myself. Instead, the torture continued.

Part of the problem at school was that many of the girls who took part in some, or all, of the bullying were the supposed "good girls". Naomi, for instance, was the Vice President of Student Council, and many other girls were also members of student council. Most of them were very good students who played sports and participated in school activities, and many of them were even allowed to go on a special eighth grade trip to Washington D.C., despite holding a key role in the daily emotional torture inflicted upon me. It was as if they were untouchable, and they had everyone fooled to believe that *I* was the problem and *they* could do no wrong.

As things deteriorated, my grades began to drop and my attendance rapidly shifted from good to poor. I found myself wishing I could get sick just so I didn't have to go to school. But, even on days I stayed home, the girls would gather together at someone's house after school and call me, leaving messages calling me a chicken and a loser for not coming to school.

MELINDA VELASQUEZ

This was during the time of answering machines and before caller I.D., so we just stopped answering the phone altogether. We had to turn down the volume on the answering machine to avoid being tormented by the numerous awful messages they would leave.

Because we had the answering machine, we would record the messages so we would have proof on tape, but a voice was not enough proof, even though I could easily identify the caller's voices. The messages they left varied from threats and insults to immature pranks. Even once I got home, I couldn't escape the harassment, and things were stressful enough there as it was.

My mom was once again struggling to pay the bills after her boyfriend moved out. Despite having a well-paying job at the county, and money coming in from my dad, she also had that nagging drug habit that was becoming quite the drain on her finances. To alleviate the strain, she decided that since my sister and I were already sharing a room, she would take in a couple of roommates to help with the monthly bills.

Two women moved in with us, and I later discovered that both were drug addicts, with meth being their drug of choice. My mom had met them at the bar she frequented, and they became friends, though I don't think she knew much about them before they moved in with us. Surprisingly, I became very close with one of the female roommates. She at times felt like a surrogate sister, and sometimes even a mother figure to me.

She had been dating a married man and she got pregnant. She ended up moving out when she had the baby and we lost touch when she moved to another city. One day, I received a letter from her out of the blue. In it, she confessed to me that she was a meth addict, and she was writing to me to apologize. I didn't realize it at the time, but she was making amends, a crucial part of a 12-step recovery program. She admitted to stealing money from me when she lived with us and wrote to apologize and repay what she had stolen.

THE WEIGHT OF SILENCE

When I was thirteen, I had a job cleaning up and restocking at a video store, earning me around $60 a paycheck every two weeks. One time, a check I usually kept in my nightstand drawer went missing. I had always thought I lost it, but it turns out she had stolen it from me and used the money to buy drugs.

Reading her letter, I felt shocked, hurt, and confused. I couldn't imagine doing something like that to someone I cared about. This was the first time I truly understood what a drug addict is capable of and the lengths they will go to get what they need — even stealing from a child.

The chaos at home and school was really starting to wear on me. I no longer had to fake being sick to stay home because the stress had begun to wreak havoc on my body. I became extremely depressed and chronically ill. I had a recurring case of strep throat and started legitimately missing school quite often.

The strep throat led to tonsillitis, and although tonsil removals were less common than they used to be, the doctor decided my case was an exception. This was the first time I realized that feeling powerless in a situation, unable to stand up for myself and speak my truth, would severely impact my health.

In addition to the students, there were times when it seemed even certain teachers and administrators turned against me. One history teacher in particular, seemed cruel and insensitive. She had no patience for my absences and appeared to favor my tormentors. She had a rule that if you were caught passing a note, it would be taken away and displayed on the wall at the end of the quarter.

One day, a few of the girls in the class decided to write horribly mean and embarrassing things about me in a note and purposely get caught passing it. Their plan worked, and as promised, the teacher put it up on the wall for everyone to see. Unbeknownst to me, they had also passed the original note I wrote to my friend Morgan when all of this started. In that note, I had chronicled how pathetic I felt at the new school because no one wanted to be my friend.

I felt humiliated and dehumanized. I was forced to sit there while my classmates eagerly lined up to read the cruel and mortifying words written about me, and by me, as my bullies basked in the glory of my degradation. I was always pretty well-liked by my teachers, but it felt like this teacher was colluding with my bullies instead of protecting me from them. I began to dread her class the most every day.

She was married to a popular coach who was also the other school counselor, and many of the girls in my class played on his team. She sat by and watched them point and laugh at all the things *they* wrote about me, and I had no escape. I hadn't even done anything wrong. I didn't write *or* pass either note in this class, yet I was the one being attacked. By allowing my suffering to continue, it only added to my isolation and loneliness.

As the constant harassment at school and at home led to physical illnesses that caused me to miss a lot of school, many of my bullies appeared to be far better students than I was. Even when I did go to school, I found it extremely difficult to concentrate, and I was terrified to participate in class. Besides fearing that I might ask a stupid question or give a wrong answer, asking an insightful question or providing a correct answer would also give my bullies just as much ammunition against me. It was during this time that I learned to just fly under the radar, and make myself as small as possible.

I stopped asking questions in class and only participated when a teacher forced me. With no one else stepping in to help, I had to find some way to minimize the opportunities they had to publicly ridicule me. Though my peers shamed me into silence, many of the adult faculty and staff were complicit by not doing anything to change the toxic environment in the school and classrooms.

All of this only compounded my feelings of abandonment. I couldn't trust the people in my home including my mom, to keep me safe. My dad was rarely around, and when he was, it seemed like he'd rather not be there. Lastly, the people at school, whose job was to create a safe learning environment for *everyone,* either didn't take the situation seriously or actually contributed to my trauma.

By that point, my counselor, teachers, and the administrators were fully aware of the trouble I was having with these girls, but nothing was being done to help me or punish them. Not a day went by without one of these girls taunting me in some way. Whether it was before or after school, during break or lunch, or even in class, I could not escape them.

I stopped going to school dances, something I once loved, after they cornered me at the first school dance. It was early on in the bullying, before I fully grasped the extent of their cruelty. I was having fun dancing with a small group of people, when about five or six of them surrounded me. They corralled me out of the multi-use room and away from the chaperones' view.

They began to close in on me, careful to not be detected by any adults, as their verbal bullets flew at me from all directions. They taunted me with threats and insults: "Why would you even come here tonight? No one wants to be around you, and all the guys think you're ugly. You can't dance —everyone was laughing at you. You'd better watch your back. The first time we see you walking alone off school grounds we're going to kick your ass!"

My stomach jumped into my throat, and I felt trapped. A teacher came outside and said, "Hey, what's going on? You know you're not allowed to be outside during the dance unless you're leaving." I was so petrified of what they might do to me that the only memory I have after I heard the teacher's voice is of me running along an outdoor corridor lined with classrooms and lockers, crying. I don't remember how I got home, but I know I somehow made it back safely.

That night taught me that school dances were now off-limits if I wanted to avoid getting physically assaulted. Thankfully, Naomi and her crew never went to the skating rink, making it one of the few safe places for me. Even though Laura had moved to a different school, she was still close with that group of people, and I often felt like they were cool with me because I was Laura's best friend. I was just grateful to have a safe place to escape all the drama.

One night, I was at a skating rink friend's house for a girl's sleepover and some boys showed up to hang out with us. The girl hosting the party was a grade below me, as were the boys, which was a relief since they didn't seem to know that I had become persona non grata with the popular group in my grade. The girl's parents had gone out for a while before the boys showed up, leaving us with the house to ourselves.

Things got exciting for me when one of the guys started flirting with me. I thought he was cute, and it seemed like we might even end up kissing that night. I hadn't kissed a guy since my first French kiss in the fifth grade. I was nervous because I didn't have a lot of practice, but excited at the chance to try it again. He seemed to be completely into me, giving me his full attention. It felt so good to feel like a "normal" thirteen-year-old girl again.

He and I had been alone in one of the rooms, talking and flirting, when we heard a bunch of noise in the other room. We looked at each other inquisitively, trying to figure out what was happening, when I heard the familiar voices that filled me with dread. They called out with the type of malice used in horror movies, "MAAA-LIN-DAAAHH, where are you? We know you're here."

I felt my heart sink, and my throat tighten as Naomi, Courtney, and some of their regular crew busted into the room where we were. They burst out laughing and said to him, "What are you doing with HER?" He quickly jumped away from me like I had an infectious disease, and suddenly acted like he was not interested. I think he even made it into a joke, acting like he never liked me and that he was just messing with my head. And just like that, I was once again drowning in a pool of humiliation and isolation.

The same ruthless tactic they used at school with people I was hanging out with were now unleashed here, without any mercy. They made it abundantly clear to the guy I was flirting with that if he had anything to do with me, he would be the laughing stock of the whole school. Naomi and her clique stormed in like a wrecking crew, and once again my hopes were destroyed and I was crushed. The next week at school, the flirty guy from the party acted like he had never even met me. How that boy treated me that night when Naomi and her crew showed was pretty devastating; unfortunately, how it felt remained imprinted on my heart for a very long time.

The incident at the party dealt a significant blow to my self-esteem. The hits had been coming for a while, some less noticeable than others. This incident had a massive impact on me that would last a lot longer than I could ever imagine. From that point on, I really began to feel as though I had been branded as an outcast.

What happened that night made me believe that if I showed any interest in any guy, whether inside or outside of my school, then somehow my bullies would find a way to sabotage it. Even worse, was the common knowledge that anyone, male or female, who dared to show interest in spending time with me would be labeled a loser and made to suffer the same persecution I was forced to endure.

As the school year progressed, their spitefulness became unrelenting, and it seemed like nothing and no one could stop them. The school administration appeared to vacillate between turning a blind eye and applying tactics that either changed nothing, or made things worse for me.

My bullies seemed unyielding in their quest to make me suffer. The lengths they would go to and the intensity of their focus on me seemed to worsen with each passing day. I reached a point where my self-esteem had been so savagely diminished that I could barely leave the house without overwhelming fear and anxiety about every aspect of myself. Every detail—from how I talked, what I said or didn't say, how I walked, what clothes I chose or how I styled my hair, every part of me had been brutally picked apart and ridiculed.

They scrutinized everything about me on a daily basis. Emotionally, they tore me apart like tigers tearing into fresh meat, while the crowd of bystanders cheered them on from outside the invisible cage of my humiliation. I struggled desperately not to give them any ammunition, but my fear and sensitivity to their harassment only made them crave more.

On a particularly bizarre and scarring day, halfway through the year, I wore a dark green sweater my mom had given me for Christmas. I walked into school that day with a sliver of confidence, having always been told how that color green was such a great color for me with my blonde hair and blue eyes. During break, as I walked to the cafeteria window to buy food, I heard Courtney yelling so loudly behind me that it made my very thick hair move, "Why in the **FUCK** are you wearing a *green* sweater?"

THE WEIGHT OF SILENCE

    I don't remember if I responded, but instead of brushing it off as an empty, pathetic insult, I took it personally. I went home that day, put the sweater away, and never wore it again. Not only did I not wear the sweater again, but it would be a long time before I could bring myself to wear anything green again. I had become severely traumatized by their constant social torture, but like what happened with my family I just stuffed it down and tried to avoid all my feelings about it.

    Shortly after that incident, a flurry of irrational thoughts raced through my mind. *Was that color green not a cool color? Was it the style of the sweater? No, she specifically stated a "green" sweater.* Despite trying to shake off the ridiculously unwarranted insult, for the rest of the day, all I could think about was that everyone was in on the joke except me.

    Everyone in my school but me seemed to have some guide telling them how to dress, how to wear their hair, what colors and patterns were good and bad. That had to be it; otherwise, why is it that no matter what I wear or how I look, I am ridiculed in front of everyone, and no one says anything to dispute it? In my mind, I came to believe that everyone, both at school and outside of school, looked at me and judged me harshly. As a result, I became my own worst critic.

    I was not completely naïve to the fact that the green sweater itself was not really the issue. It was more symbolic of the kind of negative propaganda that I had internalized about myself due to being bullied. It wouldn't have mattered what I wore that day—she would have found a reason to yell at me regardless.

    Unfortunately, the alternative to focusing on the green sweater was to confront the reality that these people just seemed to hate everything about me. Not only that, they also appeared to have the power to influence how other people felt about me as well. This was my harsh reality for almost that entire school year, and it seemed like there was no end in sight.

MELINDA VELASQUEZ

By that point, I was so broken down that I had given up any hope that things would ever get better. Years later, I found out that by the time of the green sweater incident, many people had grown tired of bullying me. On that particular day, when Courtney saw me coming, she asked her group, "What should we yell at Melinda for today?"

Someone replied, "I don't know Courtney, why don't you yell at her because she is wearing a green sweater."

I didn't know how to feel when I found that out. Their relentless attacks had inflicted so much emotional pain. By the time of the green sweater incident, I was already so completely shattered by their endless torment. That incident was another moment that made me fundamentally question my sense of self-worth and belonging in the world. To them, it was just another thoughtless act.

At first, I felt vindicated at the idiocy of the moment; at the same time, I felt extremely disappointed and hurt. To know that even when people were over it, they couldn't find it in their hearts to stop it and show me just a little bit of dignity and respect.

No matter what I said, did, or wore, they seized every opportunity to publicly shame me. I internalized so much of their hurtful words. At thirteen, any glimmer of self-esteem I had built was obliterated. The people in my school who had all the power—my peers—were telling me I was ugly, fat, stupid, that I did not know how to dress, and that no boys would ever like me.

Adolescence is a time when approval from your peers feels like the only way to survive, let alone thrive in such a toxic environment. With all the chaos and inconsistency I was dealing with at home in *Addict Land* and the trauma from my parents' divorce, it just felt as if nowhere was safe for me. The worst part was that none of it made any sense. Whatever friendship crime I had committed certainly didn't warrant this seemingly never-ending punishment.

Everything I said or did was used against me whenever possible. It was as if Naomi had been keeping a log or recording our conversations to use every little tidbit to her advantage. I take responsibility for the things I said and did; I definitely made mistakes and confided in the wrong people. It was a harsh lesson in trust to learn at a young age that I would never forget.

Besides, I did the same thing to Jenny. We had known each other since we were six years old, and many of the things we said or embarrassing moments we shared could only be used against each other if taken out of context. The secrets and bonds shared between girls can turn into ticking time bombs once they reach adolescence. Jenny could have blown me out of the water at any time during seventh or eighth grade, but she never did.

Even the simple comment I made to Naomi about Courtney's hair came back to haunt me with a vengeance. Early on in the bullying, Courtney came up and told me I had no business making fun of her hair when mine looked like a mop! The half-up hairstyle I wore, the one that made me feel pretty, had now become a school joke.

For all I know, this was the one piece of information Naomi used to get Courtney to think I was talking about her behind her back. It was a comment, a mere observation, and one I made because she had the kind of hair I could never have and always wanted.

The constant scrutiny I experienced led me to question every little thing about myself. I was desperate to have just one day of peace. Each day, as I stepped out of the car to enter the school, it was if I triggered a bomb or pulled the pin from a grenade. As soon as the car door closed, I could feel my heart beat faster, the sound of it resonating through my ears.

Walking into school each day felt like a scene from an action movie just before an explosion happens. As the car drove away, there was a few seconds of slow-motion silence where people scatter in all directions to avoid getting hit or becoming collateral damage right before the actual explosion. Most of the time, I could see it coming, but other times they would stealthily creep up on me.

With every step I took into school after being dropped off, I would wonder how far I would get before I felt the sonic boom of the next attack. I had been reduced to a timid mess of a girl who walked through school with my eyes on the floor, hoping that would make me invisible to all who relentlessly tortured me. Between the bullying, my parents' volatile divorce, and my mom and sisters' addictions, I felt lost, alone, sad, filled with fear, and consumed by anxiety as I did my best to make it across the tightrope that my life had become.

Things had gotten so bad that unless absolutely necessary, I avoided using the restroom at school before, after school, or during break or lunch for fear of being cornered by Naomi and her crew. The restrooms were the only place on campus that were mostly unsupervised. When the girls couldn't cause too big of a scene in the quad without being interrupted, they would take any opportunity to isolate me where they could spew their venom.

One day during break, I walked all the way to the back of the school to use the restroom, and they followed me. There were always different groupings of girls, but Naomi and Courtney were the two constants. When they cornered me like this, they always seemed to bring the girls known for being tough.

It was a cold day that day, and the restrooms at school were not much warmer than outside because the doors were always left open. About five of them gathered around me in the small restroom.

As usual, Courtney stood in the front, her breath visible in the cold air, as she said to me in a sinister voice, "What are you gonna do *now*, Melinda? Nobody is here to come to your rescue."

Once again, I felt trapped, fearing that if anything happened to me, no one would know I was there. I imagined them beating me up and leaving me in a bloody mess on the cold, dirty bathroom floor like a piece of trash. Paralyzed with fear, I stood there, unsure of what to do. Then, the sound of the bell ringing cut through the tension in the bathroom, snapping me out of my terrifying vision.

Thankfully, being the good students they were, they didn't want to be late for their next class, so they all scattered at the sound of the warning bell. As they dispersed, Courtney yelled out, "You got lucky today, BITCH!"

Just like at home, there was never any physical violence against me, but unlike at home, the fear that there would or could be every second of every day was my reality. In my mind, it was only a matter of time and the right circumstances that could leave me beaten by the side of the road or in a cold and dirty restroom.

Instead of going to the restroom during breaks, I would often go during class, which also annoyed my teachers. When things got particularly difficult during class or throughout the day, I would ask for the bathroom pass and go see my counselor. Everyone knew I talked to my counselor a great deal, which was another sign of weakness to many; as a result, things would be even worse for me when they thought I was telling on them for something.

Although my counselor seemed frustrated with what the girls were doing, at times it also felt as though she was tired of hearing me complain about it. But the problem was not going away—it was only getting worse. It seemed as if nothing and no one could or would help me. I felt so alone and helpless, and it seemed like this daily torture was never going to end.

It is difficult to imagine, but I found myself constantly oscillating between hating the girls for how they treated me and desperately wanting to be accepted and liked by them again. I didn't care about being popular anymore; at that point, I would have settled for being invisible or insignificant just to have some peace. I wanted them to be punished for what they had done; at the same time, I was afraid of what would happen to me if they *were* punished.

I lived in a constant state of fear and anxiety. The anticipation of being physically attacked wore me down emotionally and mentally. I couldn't help but wonder if I had been brave enough to fight them like Jenny did with Naomi, maybe it all would have ended before it really began.

It felt like these girls found ways to infiltrate every part of my life and do all they could to ruin it. If I had one minuscule moment of happiness, they would quickly swoop in and stomp it out. I felt betrayed by Naomi because we had been friends before, but I had grown to despise Courtney.

Although, much of what Courtney knew about me and used against me must have come from Naomi, since Courtney and I were never really friends, it was easier for me to direct my anger at her. Looking back now, it is clear to me that Naomi was probably playing us both against each other like puppets.

Courtney might have felt the same way about me; all she knew was that I was just some girl who made fun of her hair. Who knows what else Naomi said to Courtney to fuel her fire? Sadly, for what felt like a long time, if Naomi came to me and wanted to be friends again, I probably would have said yes. I just felt so lonely and missed my friend.

When eighth grade started, Courtney was the new girl in school, but unlike me she had succeeded where I failed—by staying and making friends, quickly becoming one of the most popular girls. Like many girls, including myself, Courtney was probably willing to do whatever it took to avoid losing her prized position at the top of the social hierarchy.

By the end of the year, Naomi and her crew managed to diminish my circle of friends down to two brave girls who were unaffected by the scare tactics of the powerful people. There were others who were friendly to me in class if the popular crew was not around, but outside of class, they seemed to politely steer clear of me.

One of my really good guy friends was still my friend, but he even told me he was not able to really talk to me during school. Even guys were worried about their social standing. Laura was really the only friend I felt I could completely trust, but she went to a different school. Escaping to her house on the weekends was one of the places I felt safe, one of the only things that kept me sane.

CHAPTER

15

As sad as I was when Laura moved 20 minutes away and changed schools, it turned out to be a blessing. It gave me a place to be and feel somewhat normal. I used to hang out with her a lot on the weekends and even went to one of her school dances when I no longer felt safe at mine.

When Laura brought up the idea of me going to her school dance, I was really nervous at first. Even though no one at Laura's school was aware of what was happening to me at my school, I couldn't shake the feeling that everyone there would somehow know and turn against me. If what happened to me had occurred now, with social media as a weapon of mass destruction, my humiliation would have reached far beyond my school. I honestly believe that if social media had been around back then, I might not be here today.

At a certain point, the pain, isolation, and humiliation can become too much to bear. I felt as if the whole world knew the horrible things they said about me. It was like a scarlet letter, stamped across my forehead for everyone to see. With social media now playing such a huge role in our cultural landscape, that fear is a very real possibility.

A huge part of how I felt about myself at that time had a lot to do with how I felt about my outer appearance. Most of the insults from my bullies were about my appearance or my body, and in the eyes of my peers I did not measure up to their standards. As long as they continued with the relational bullying, I felt like I never could.

For a minimum of six hours a day, five days a week, and many times on the weekend, the harsh messages kept coming at me with a vengeance. For almost my entire eighth grade-year, it felt like a recording playing on a loop, constantly screaming at me, *"NO ONE WANTS TO BE YOUR FRIEND! IF THEY DO HANG OUT WITH YOU, IT'S ONLY OUT OF PITY!" "YOU'RE SO PATHETIC! OH ARE YOU GOING TO CRY AGAIN? WHY DON'T YOU RUN TO YOUR COUNSELOR OR YOUR MOMMY AGAIN SINCE YOU CAN'T STICK UP FOR YOURSELF!" "NO GUYS WILL EVER LIKE YOU. YOU ARE SO UGLY! NO GUYS WANT TO KISS YOU, MUCH LESS DATE YOU!" "YOUR HAIR LOOKS LIKE A MOP. IF A GUY TRIED TO RUN HIS FINGERS THROUGH YOUR HAIR THEY WOULD GET STUCK!"*

That was what it was like every single day, and those are just the insults I can remember. Once they reached my adolescent brain, all hurtful words could be summed up in five simple words… "YOU ARE NOT GOOD ENOUGH!!" And that became the lens through which I viewed myself.

No matter where I was or what I was doing, I believed that regardless of what anyone said or how they acted, this was what they truly thought; therefore, it must be true. Even though Laura assured me I would have fun at her dance and that there were a few guys she thought I might like, I was more than skeptical.

I always felt emotionally safe with Laura, so I decided to go for it. I knew she would not abandon me if we got to the dance and no one wanted to have anything to do with me. We got ready at Laura's house, and her boyfriend and his dad picked us up and drove us to the dance. He seemed very nice, but the real test would be the rest of the people at the dance.

We arrived at the junior high school gym, and I could hear the music playing from outside. I LOVE to dance, and in seventh grade, I was out in the middle of the floor with everyone. But eighth grade was a different story. I flashed back on the last dance I went to at my own school, where my bullies had forced me outside and taunted me; I thought for sure I was going to be jumped and beaten up that night.

There I was, standing outside Laura's school dance, my heart racing. I was afraid to breathe and terrified to take another step into potential disappointment and emotional agony. Laura grabbed my arm and, without a care in the world, excitedly said, "C'mon, let's go!"

We walked through the doors of the gym, and I held my breath, bracing for the worst. The music was loud, and as I looked up, I saw a group of people come running over to us. My stomach tightened, and I clenched my jaw, preparing myself for my nightmare to continue in a new setting.

A large group of girls and guys rushed over, yelling excitedly and hugging Laura. Laura introduced me as her best friend, and the girls turned all giddy and excited, hugging me as well. They all said they had heard so much about me and were so happy to finally meet me. Overwhelmed by their acceptance and kind treatment, I let my guard down for one night and had a blast.

Laura's eighth grade experience was a stark contrast to mine. She was one of the most popular girls at her school, and her friends had no fear of committing social suicide simply by talking to me; their kindness seemed genuine. The proverbial scarlet letter that could be seen by all at my school was invisible here. The girls were some of the nicest people I had ever met, and there were even some boys who thought I was cute. One guy, in particular, danced with me for most of the slow songs and even some of the fast ones. It had been so long since I felt this good that I didn't want the night to end, but when it did, I was on a natural high.

I couldn't imagine what my life would have been like without Laura's friendship during that year of darkness. I would have been completely lost if she had chosen not to be my friend. There were days when the bullying and isolation overwhelmed me so much that I even considered suicide. I never attempted it, but the thoughts ran through my head more than once. I'm absolutely certain that having Laura as my friend that year saved my life.

If Laura had lived in the same town, transferring to her school might have been the obvious choice—it was a place where I felt emotionally safe. But the logistics made it impossible. Laura's school was twenty minutes south, while everyone in my family who had a car worked twenty minutes north, and public transit options were limited. Even though Laura did everything she could to include me in her new life, I couldn't shake the feeling of being an outsider. When it was just the two of us, everything felt easy. But I saw the strong bonds she'd formed with her new friends, and I didn't want to disrupt that. She never made me feel like a burden, but I feared I might become one.

Even on days when it seemed there was no end to my pain, it was Laura's friendship and loyalty that kept me sane. She was *always* there for me, and even when she had every reason to be angry with me—more so than those who had already abandoned me—she once again proved to be a true friend.

CHAPTER

16

Laura called me and said she had tickets to the New Kids on the Block concert and asked me if I wanted to go. This was when they were at the height of their popularity, so of course I jumped at the chance. The day before the concert, while I was at Laura's house, she decided to tell me what was really going on with the concert.

At some point, Naomi had called Laura and revealed that I had shared with her what Laura had confided in me. Laura was crushed and had every right to feel completely betrayed. Even though I knew that what I had shared with Naomi wasn't done with malintent, or just an excuse to gossip, it didn't change the fact that I was wrong. Naomi told Laura in an effort to turn her against me as well, and it almost worked.

Instead of throwing me under the bus and our friendship out the window, Laura rose above it all and talked it out with me. I explained what happened and apologized profusely, and in typical

Laura fashion, she graciously chose to forgive me. She then proceeded to tell me all about Naomi's sinister concert plot.

The plan was for Laura to take me to the concert while Naomi, Courtney, and their crew would be there, ready to "jump me" or beat me up. I couldn't believe it when I heard Laura telling me the plan. The thought of what could have happened made me feel sick to my stomach.

At this point, I no longer cared to be Naomi's friend. What I had done to Laura was wrong, but I had nothing malicious in mind when I foolishly shared that information with Naomi. It was clear that Naomi was out to hurt me and she did not care who she hurt or who she used to do it. I couldn't fathom that this entire nightmare with Naomi, Courtney, and their crew had started from a simple misunderstanding, which now seemed so insignificant. This was long before I understood the concept that hurt people *hurt* people.

Laura and I didn't end up going to the concert. Even though Laura had disclosed the plan to me, we didn't feel safe. Naomi had proven she would stop at nothing to inflict pain on anyone who went against her, and I didn't want Laura to be put in harm's way. The thought of being off school grounds, in a crowd full of people with loud music and screaming people, felt like the perfect setup for me to be beaten up or— worse.

I had already felt the wrath of these people, and I was terrified that being physically attacked by them would be just as relentless as their verbal and emotional attacks. My experience with bystanders at school, who often fueled the fire, made me believe that the same would happen at the concert. The thought of that kept me petrified of concerts for many years to come. The fear of what might have happened to me at that concert became imbedded in my central nervous system, and it was something my body would not soon forget.

As the year progressed, the taunting did not end, but the group effort seemed to wane, much like with the green sweater incident. Courtney, however, never gave up on taunting me. I truly believed she took pleasure in seeing me miserable. I couldn't help but wonder if I would ever get my life back. Would I ever complete my penance for the friendship sins against Laura and Jenny?

As the end of the school year approached, Naomi seemed to be growing increasingly reckless. She had become completely unrecognizable to me, and I no longer saw any trace of the girl and friend I once knew.

I heard stories about her and other girls drinking and smoking pot, and she began to show a complete lack of respect toward teachers and other school staff. She started getting into trouble, but not for anything she or the other girls had done to me.

At one point, in an incident that had nothing to do with me, Naomi was removed from the Student Council. It seemed to be the result of a build-up of various issues, and perhaps it finally made the school acknowledge what I had been saying all along.

On one hand, I felt slightly vindicated that something was finally being done; on the other hand, I feared that any punishment for them might lead to retaliation against me. Additionally, even though I knew I could never trust Naomi as a friend again, I still felt sorry for her seeing her life heading in the wrong direction.

I held my breath, bracing for backlash, but it never came. The bullying continued, but it was really limited to Courtney and a few others. They also seemed to be much more careful about when and where they said or did anything to me.

There was clearly a shift in the school's attitude toward what had been going on. It seemed that many of the girls who were more academically focused were no longer willing to risk what might happen if they continued the bullying. Or perhaps, like with the day of the green sweater, they were just over it.

Shortly after Naomi was removed from the Student Council, things got even better for me. One night, Naomi and Courtney were drinking and partying with a couple of boys, and they made a mistake that changed everything for me.

They decided to take Courtney's mom's car for a joyride. Courtney, a thirteen-year-old girl who had been drinking, got behind the wheel with Naomi and the two boys. At some point, they crashed the car. Everyone was okay, but immediately after this Courtney was sent to live three hours away with her dad.

When I heard the news the next day at school, I didn't believe it at first. Once I confirmed that Courtney was actually gone and the story was true, it felt as if the clouds had parted and the sun had reappeared. With Courtney gone, the bullying I had endured almost the entire school year seemed to come to an end.

The girls who had been a big part of the bullying did not instantly become my friends again, not by any stretch of the imagination. However, it went from daily emotional torture and humiliation to occasional dirty looks and nasty whispering in a much smaller group. Slowly, a sense of peace began to return to my life.

As my eighth-grade year was coming to an end, I was both nervous and excited about being in an entirely new school. I have no idea where I got the courage, but I decided to try out for the freshman cheerleading squad at the high school I would be attending.

Laura and I had done Pop Warner cheerleading as kids, and I really liked it, so I decided to try out. To my surprise, I made the squad. Through the tryout process, I also became friends with a girl from another school on my squad, and I was hopeful for a new beginning. It was one of many small victories on my journey back from the hell that was eighth grade.

When the eighth-grade graduation dance came around, I decided to put on a brave face and go. I went with the two girls who had been my friends throughout it all, along with a few of their friends whom I knew as well. I wore the pink dress my sister had worn to her Sweetheart dance the previous year. Aside from a small group of girls who still felt the need to sneer at me, many people complimented me on my dress.

I had one more major hurdle before I was free from eighth grade hell: the promotion ceremony. Even though the bullying had downgraded from explicit to covert, I felt the anxiety bubble up in the pit of my stomach right before they called my name at the ceremony.

Would everyone boo me? What if someone tripped me on my way up to the stage? Will anyone clap for me at all? The fear of persecution and exclusion that had gripped most of my peers might have stopped people from clapping for me, even if they had started talking to me again. I felt a tremendous sense of relief as they called my name and people actually cheered and clapped for me. I made it to and from the stage unscathed!

I was so happy and excited to start fresh at a new school; at the same time, I couldn't let go of the nagging fear that my reputation as the odd girl out would follow me to high school and I would be doomed to four more years of hell.

CHAPTER 17

On the first day of the ninth grade, all the lingering fears from my eighth-grade nightmare that had faded over the summer break came rushing back. Over summer break, I had made friends with the girls on my cheerleading squad, as well as some junior and senior girls on the varsity and junior varsity (JV) squads. We bonded at cheer camp, and none of what had happened in the eighth grade seemed to be an issue.

The cheerleaders were responsible for handing out class schedules to all the returning students, so we were required to arrive at school early and be in uniform. Although wearing my uniform removed the anxiety of choosing what to wear on the first day, it also brought back the all-too-familiar fear of being ridiculed again by my old tormentors.

The feeling that at any given moment someone else had the power to control who liked me stayed with me for a long time.

Although that fear eventually began to fade, it had rooted itself deep in my subconscious and central nervous system. It was always there, whether I was aware of it or not, and it had the power to affect every part of my life.

I survived day one—and many days after that. Laura was still a part of my life, though she lived in a different town and attended a different high school. We kept in touch and saw each other when we could, but our time together was mostly limited to weekends. It became easier to see each other once we could drive, but until then, we relied on our parents to transport us.

High school social life was much busier than junior high, and I quickly made new friends in my classes. I was doing well in school again, and I started to realize that while many people knew about what happened to me in eighth grade, it wasn't as widely discussed as I had feared. Most people didn't judge me for it, and many didn't agree with what had happened at all.

Even though it was still early in freshman year, things were going pretty well, and I was actually starting to feel somewhat settled and safe. The freshmen team played during the day and didn't draw nearly as many people as the JV and Varsity teams that played on Friday nights. Our first chance to cheer at a night football game finally came at the Homecoming game, and once again I was excited and nervous.

The feeling that the whole world would somehow single me out to make fun of or find something wrong with me never really went away. I was certain that no matter where I was or what I was doing, someone would look at me, ridicule me, or pick me apart. The trauma of being bullied ran deep, and I learned to develop ways of coping with the anxiety, and control was one of them.

THE WEIGHT OF SILENCE

Despite my fears, I was excited to finally cheer at a night game at home. I felt so grown up standing with the JV and varsity squads on sidelines of the high school football field. This was where my big sister went to school, and where I had attended many games as a little kid in Pop Warner. The lights were on, and the announcers were being broadcast over the loud speakers—being so close to the action, after growing up watching NFL football on TV was exhilarating. It was autumn, and the air was cool and crisp enough to see your breath.

As I looked around and took it all in, I finally breathed a sigh of relief. In that moment, I allowed myself feel happy. I was a high school cheerleader who loved football, standing next to my new friends, full of school pride, and having a great time.

Before I could fully appreciate the moment, I looked up at the bleachers and saw my nightmare walking toward me —it was Courtney. The thunderous roar of the crowd seemed to dissipate into to a muffled background noise, and everything started moving in slow motion. The sound of my breathing grew louder and then stopped as my whole body tensed up when I saw her coming closer.

She was looking right at me as she walked along the walkway at the bottom of the metal bleachers, the clanking of her footsteps growing louder with each step. The sounds of the crowd seemed to disappear as I focused on her walking toward me. She stopped directly in front of where I was standing with my cheer squad all around me. I was on the ground level while she was a few feet up, only about 20 feet away. With a malevolent smile, she leaned over the railing and, in a spiteful tone said, "Remember me, Melinda?"

I stood there in disbelief. *Was this <u>really</u> happening all over again?* I had just barely started to rebuild my life, and there she was again, my nemesis. The questions swirled frantically around in my head. *What the* heck was she doing there? Did she move back? Was she going to be attending **_this_** school too?

I rolled my eyes and turned my back on her. She lingered by the railing, talking to people and making sure I could still see her, all while continuing to give me dirty looks and randomly taunt me. At first, I couldn't hear what she was saying, but then I heard her yell out in her nasally voice, "I'll be waiting for you in the parking lot after the game, BITCH!"

I wondered if anyone in the crowd had heard her and for a minute feared the whole crowd might start chanting something horrible at me. One of my friends noticed I was scared and asked what was going on and I told her. She was kind of feisty, so she was ready to stand up for me right away, since I still didn't know how to stand up for myself.

Amid all the emotions running through me, I also felt a surge of anger. I was still scared, having never fought anyone before, but I was just so mad that she had the nerve to come to *my* school and try to threaten me once again.

After the game ended, we walked out to the parking lot and, as promised, Courtney was out there with Naomi and a few others. My friend's brother and sister-in-law had come to drive us home. Courtney yelled out at me again, saying the same kind of things she'd said earlier. I just kept walking, while my friend yelled back at her.

My friend was fearless and very tall. I had grown taller over the summer too, but height didn't mean much without confidence to go with it. My friend wasn't about to let this girl get away with talking badly about me, but her sister-in-law told us to just be quiet and get in the car. Thankfully, I later learned that Courtney was just back to visit her mom. I guess she figured she could get another chance to mess with me while she was there. Thankfully, that was the last time I ever saw Courtney.

I rarely saw Naomi at school during freshman year, and sometime that year, I heard she got involved with drugs and dropped out. I wouldn't see her again until long after I graduated from high school, and by then, it was clear that addiction had a hold on her as well. I couldn't help but wonder what direction our lives might have taken if we had remained friends.

Once high school was well underway, quite a few people who had played a part in the bullying came up to me and apologized, though others never did. I reconciled with old friends like Morgan. Although we would never be as close as we once were, there would always be an unspoken bond with my friends from elementary school. I chose to forgive, or at least let go of things, because I wanted more than anything to just keep moving forward.

That year, I met a girl named Leisa, and the two of us instantly clicked. Leisa and I remained close throughout high school, and I even became close with her family. Her mom became another surrogate mom to me. While we both had other friends, the bond we had was always something I cherished.

As time went by, my anxiety slowly began to decrease. However, the doubts about not being pretty enough, skinny enough, or good enough always remained in the back of my mind. At that time, I wasn't really aware of the huge emotional toll my eighth grade year had taken on my self-esteem, and I would not grasp the extent of the damage until I was well into my adult years.

As I continued through high school, I remained fixated on my body issues and feared that no guys would ever want to date me. Even though I was no longer being bullied, I still felt as though I had some sort of warning stamp on my forehead that kept boys from dating me.

I did date a little, but during all four years of high school I think I only went out on one "date" with a guy from my high school, and that was at the end of my senior year. Most of the time, I dated guys who were older and not associated with my school. The fact that no one from my school seemed interested in dating me, or even asking me to a school dance, only added to my deepest fear that no one would ever forget the negative eighth grade perception of who I was and how I looked.

I ended up losing my virginity to my best guy friend, though he was never my boyfriend. I foolishly believed that if I had sex the first time with a really good guy friend that I would not get hurt; consequently, I spent the better part of my senior year allowing him to use me and abuse the trust I had in him as my friend.

All of the emotional wounds I had endured in the eighth grade didn't suddenly heal when the bullying stopped. I carried all of it with me, embedded in my subconscious and my body. Each time things didn't go my way or if a guy or a friend hurt me, I would retreat to that place, drowning in a sea of self-loathing.

It was as if on one shoulder I had the angel telling me to believe in myself and that I *was* good enough; but, on the other shoulder was my nemesis Courtney still reminding me that everyone thought I was ugly and fat with fluffy hair, and that no boys would ever like me.

My sense of self-worth was practically non-existent. I think people would agree that I was a good friend and a fun person to be around, but I was also very self-deprecating. I was so used to people saying bad things about me that when they stopped, I just kept running that same story in my head. Subconsciously, I figured that if I made jokes about myself before anyone else could, the pain would be easier to endure. Yet, regardless of how many friends I had, I could never shake the deep feeling of loneliness that gnawed at me.

On the outside, it seemed as though I had truly become a happy person again. My circle of friends expanded, my grades improved, and I actually began to look forward to going to school again. I also made a vow to myself that whenever I came in contact with a new person in school, I would go out of my way to make them feel welcome.

When I saw a new person, I would introduce myself and ask them right away if they had someone to hang out with at break and lunch. I knew all too well what it was like to feel isolated and alone, and I didn't wish that experience on anyone.

After my experience in eighth grade, I thought much more about how I treated people. However, the thought of any kind of conflict still completely freaked me out. Unfortunately, the effort of trying *not* to be mean to anyone led to the unintended consequence of being conflict avoidant, at times passive aggressive, and terrified of standing up for myself. Fear became a thread that connected many pieces of my life for a very long time.

By the time I started high school, things at home were slightly less chaotic. There were no more visits to Hotel Hell, and while my sister was still doing drugs, I witnessed only a limited amount of her drug-related activities. My mom, my sister, and I had moved into a condo right down the street from the high school, and for a while, the tensions between us had calmed down a little.

I think the craziness of eighth grade brought us a bit closer together. There were still plenty of flare-ups between my mom and my dad, but I found new ways of coping with that drama—one of which was still walking on eggshells, and the other was avoidance.

I realized that money seemed to be the weapon of choice for both parents to use in their seemingly endless game of emotional cruelty. My dad had it, and my mom needed more of it. My dad had his own ideas about exactly how much money my mom needed every month, and he was determined to find a way to avoid giving her more than that.

Once, my dad even wrote the child support check out to *me* instead of my mom because he didn't agree with how she was spending the money. The moment my mom opened the check led to another angry phone call to my dad, and there I was put right in the middle again.

Money in my family always seemed to bring conflict, so I did my best to find a way around it. I was so tired of the reactions I received from either of them whenever I asked for anything. By age sixteen, I got a job to avoid having to ask either of them for money whenever possible.

Anytime there was a sign of conflict with anyone, I always avoided it. The only time I seemed to chase after conflict was when a guy was involved. That was when my abandonment issues would rear their ugly head. Feeling abandoned by my dad when he and my mom separated was no doubt the reason for that.

I had worked so hard for my dad's approval for so long that I began a pattern of morphing myself into whatever a guy wanted me to be. I would get a crush on a guy, and it wouldn't take much for me to cling to some sign that he might be interested. Before I knew it, he was all I could think about.

I was so desperate to be noticed and loved that I often became clingy and needy. Most of the guys I was interested in would either cut and run early on or string me along. I clung to the hope that there was something between us, even when it was never their intention. I have an entire book of poems I wrote in high school, filled with heartache from boys I never even dated.

When my relationship with my best guy friend turned sexual, I was on a runaway train to heartache and drama. He had been dating a girl in the grade below us, but like many high school relationships, theirs was off and on. I found out later from her that they were on a lot more than he led me to believe.

They eventually ended things permanently, but he kept *me* on the hook for far too long, dating or just having sex with other girls. He took advantage of my trust and our friendship in the worst ways. I was so desperate to be wanted and loved, so I kept going back for more. Since he was usually hiding his exploits with other girls from me, I became his dirty little secret, which only added to my shame spiral.

It took me right back to eighth grade when he told me he could be my friend in private, but not at school. This person who was supposed to be my friend ended up using me relentlessly to suit his needs, and I allowed it. Time and again he chose someone else over me to hold hands as they walked through school together, take to dances, and publicly proclaim to be his girlfriend. I remained hidden in the shadows, waiting for him to choose me, while my belief that I wasn't good enough was validated over and over again.

CHAPTER

18

Dealing with painful boy drama in high school was bad enough, but my home life was still filled with plenty of ups and downs as well. During my senior year, my sister met a man she began dating seriously, and he ended up moving in with us in our two-bedroom condo. Since my sister and I were sharing the second bedroom, when he moved in, they just kind of made the living room into a bedroom. It was weird, but I assumed it was just until they could save up to move out.

Throughout all this time, my mom's addiction made life at home extremely unbearable and unpredictable. I stayed at friends' houses frequently, especially after my sister's boyfriend moved in—I just didn't feel comfortable being at home. Between my mom's rapid mood swings and the lack of space, I tried to stay out of the house as much as possible.

I was still working at the retail store, and because I was in a work experience class at school, I only had four classes and could leave at lunch. Most days, I went straight from school to work, where I had a 12:30-9:30 p.m. shift. I was nearly working full-time while still attending my senior year of high school.

A bunch of my friends, including Leisa, worked at the same place. Most nights, I was happier going to work than I was going home. It provided a good distraction and gave me a sense of control and independence that I desperately craved.

At this point, I paid for everything except for the roof over my head and the food in our house. I chose to do this not only to avoid hearing my parents fight about money but also because I believed that it was easier to earn the money myself. While I didn't make enough to fund any fun class trips or anything big, it gave me a sense of freedom from the financial drama that had become a constant in my family.

By this time, my mom was consistently late with the rent and frequently complained about not having enough money. Despite her full-time job and the money my dad was ordered to pay her, being late with the rent had become a regular occurrence. I think Shelly and her boyfriend were helping with groceries and a little bit more, but their goal was to save up so they could move out.

We had very understanding landlords, but I was always worried they might grow tired of my mom's excuses and evict us. My mom used to take me with her when she went to ask them in person for an extension, I'm sure to appeal to their good nature. It was extremely uncomfortable to stand on their front porch, witnessing their understandable frustration with my mom, while also feeling their compassion and pity for both of us.

Mom's addiction was now putting the one thing at risk I didn't have to worry about before, our home. I could always go back and live with my dad, but I was now in my senior year, and all I could think of was my eighth-grade nightmare happening all over again. We had to do something.

Shelly and her boyfriend were driving the decision to conduct an intervention with my mom. We planned to confront her about her drug use and try to get her to come clean and get help. Interventions often don't go well even with a professional interventionist, but this one involved just the four of us. Moreover, Shelly and her boyfriend were both heavy drinkers and meth users themselves. It was a recipe for disaster.

All four of us sat down at the dining table, shoved into the furthest corner of the small living room. The floral tablecloth was draped over the small wooden table, which was cluttered with random papers and one of my mom's signature dried flower arrangements in the middle. We all sat in a semi-circle around the table, as it was pushed up against the wall, leaving space for us to sit around about two thirds of the table.

The stakes were high and the energy was extremely tense. I felt terrified of what might happen, but I never imagined how this moment would impact me and the future of my family.

Shelly's boyfriend started the conversation by saying, "Linda, there is something important we need to talk to you about because it effects all of us."

Mom looked confused and anxious as she replied with urgency, "What's going on?"

He continued, "Linda, we know that you're doing drugs, and we aren't going to act like we don't know, or that it is not a problem anymore."

The look of shock and confusion on my mom's face was something I will never forget as she quickly adopted a defensive stance and said, "How **dare** you accuse me of something like that? Who do you think you are?"

Shelly chimed in, "Mom we're not stupid. We have known for a while. We have dealt with your mood swings, staying up all night partying then sleeping all day the next day. And you are always struggling with money because you are spending it on drugs!"

Mom's confusion was now quickly turning to anger. She pointed her finger at Shelly and said, "Show me what money has gone to drugs. I spend my money on rent, bills and groceries while your father is living on easy street with his new girlfriend! Every penny I get from him is a battle!"

Shelly quipped, "That's because he knows you are spending your money on drugs instead of things you *should* be spending it on!"

Then I jumped in with, "Why do you think dad tried to write the child support check out directly to me, mom? He didn't want you to spend it on drugs!"

Bringing my dad into it only intensified her anger and she went for the jugular, "I can't *believe* this! Shelly, you are 22 years old and you and your boyfriend are living here RENT-FREE! What gives you the right to question anything I do with money? You have some nerve to judge me for anything!"

Shelly clapped back with, "Mom it's so obvious, every time you go to the grocery store you write the check for $100 extra or something so you can get cash back and use that cash to buy your drugs!"

Mom stood up and shouted, "This is *crazy*! I don't have to put up with this!"

By this time, I felt a fiery pit burning in my stomach, and my chest, neck, face, and ears turned red hot from the anxiety over what was unfolding. Things went off the rails, and it happened so much quicker than I had anticipated.

I had been so hopeful that confronting her about her drug use would work and that it would give me the chance to have the mom I loved so much back in my life again. Unfortunately, the beast that is addiction had her in its grasp, and it wasn't going to give her up that easily.

I was desperate to find and connect with the mom who had once made me feel so loved and cared for as a young child. By this time, I was crying and I called out to her, my voice cracking, "Mom we are just worried about you! We don't want something bad to happen to you, or for you to get in trouble! I don't want to lose you!"

Mom was also crying, her voice rising as she delivered the coup de grace to my soul, "I can't believe you would all be so cruel to accuse me of something like this. How could you say such awful things to me? Why are you all making up such awful lies about me?"

I must have blocked out exactly what my mom said next, because all I remember is how quickly she went from hurt to anger and began to attack. I have tried to recall her words, but I have never been able to remember it. Some words you never forget, others are too painful to remember. All I know is that it was extremely hurtful. She knew exactly what to say to each of us to shut us down and end this confrontation; not only did she end it but also found a way to completely turn it around on us.

I felt as if *I* was under attack, even though I didn't believe I was doing anything wrong. All I was trying to do was help her; I just wanted my mom back. I was crying and so upset, but she just kept coming at me with horrible things.

In that moment, I was thrust back to the horrible night I had witnessed that awful fight between my parents while I pretended to be asleep on that couch in Truckee. I once again saw a side of my mom that scared me and made me want to get as far away from her as possible. I felt hurt, overwhelmed, and extremely vulnerable. What we had just gone through was awful. I felt a deep sense of dread as the walls of that small condo began to close in on me. Every fiber of my being urged me to find a way out of the tangled mess my home had become before things spiraled further.

Openly defying or talking back to my parents was not something I did often; yet somehow, what we had just done was being twisted into us being disrespectful and insubordinate towards our mother. Fear began to creep in, gripping me as I wondered what would happen now that I had been part of this dumpster fire of an intervention. One of my biggest fears in confronting my mom was that my sister had it wrong. What had just happened only added to that fear.

I definitely saw behaviors in my mom that lined up with what I knew about meth addiction, but how could I be sure if she was denying it so fervently? And, I had actually *witnessed* my sister doing meth, but I had never seen concrete proof that my mom did it. All of this just sent my head spinning in a million different directions, none of them good.

I definitely knew my mom at least had issues with alcohol, as I could see that with my own eyes. Since drinking is often normalized and very socially acceptable, the fact that she was still very functional and capable even sometimes made *that* confusing. That sliver of uncertainty, combined with the fear of being iced out of my family, fueled my fear of confronting the very real problem that was slowly and methodically eating away at my family.

After she spewed her venom onto all of us, Mom went upstairs to her bedroom. Every cell in my body screamed at me to get out of there, so I took that opportunity to plan my escape. This was before cell phones, but I knew my best guy friend had a pager, so I ran to the phone in the kitchen to page him.

I paged him with "911", to signal that he needed to respond quickly. Despite everything he had put me through, I vowed that what happened with us wouldn't hurt our friendship. He could be an ass, but that night, when I needed him most, he showed up for me.

Within just a few minutes, he called back and told me he was nearby at a mutual friend's house. When he called, Mom picked up the phone too from her room. She waited until she heard me ask him to come get me, then interrupted the phone call and made me hang up.

My closest friends knew what was happening with my mom, but not many others did. He knew what was going on and could hear in my voice that I was not okay, so he ignored my mom and came to get me.

As a child of an addict, I was used to keeping secrets. As unhappy as I was in my home, I was even more afraid of being taken away from it. As unpredictable as my home life was, it was still my home, and, in my mind, it was better than the alternative. I also feared that my mom might be arrested and sent to jail. I didn't want my family to be addicts, but I didn't want them in jail either. I was so close to graduating high school and becoming an adult; if I could just get to that point then I would figure out the rest.

Within minutes of my phone call, my friend was there to pick me up and take me back to where he was. When I arrived at the mutual friend's house, I was extremely upset. I didn't want her parents to ask questions, so I pulled myself together and pretended I was okay. By then, I had perfected the art of feigning that everything was okay.

My mom started calling around to find out where I had gone. It didn't take her long to get the number to the house I was at. She told the parents that I was in trouble and needed to come home immediately. I felt humiliated, angry, and terrified. I had no idea what to expect when I returned home. I hadn't run away; I just needed some space.

Shelly and her boyfriend could leave and go wherever they wanted, but not me. I was still a minor stuck in the house, dealing with the blowback from the emotional bomb that just went off. I already felt like collateral damage in the war between my mom and dad; after that night, I felt like I had become a pawn in the battle between my mom and my sister.

When I got home, Mom grounded me for "leaving the house without permission". But I knew the real reason why I was being punished. I had learned my lesson, and from that point forward, I *never* confronted my mom about drugs or alcohol again.

The beast that is addiction became the elephant in the room within our family. That beast continued to grow, change shape and take up space, eroding almost every piece of love, trust, and joy our family once had. Before the end of my senior year, Shelly and her boyfriend finally moved out into their own place. The intervention might have been what finally made that happen, but I can't recall for sure.

My family became masters at conflict avoidance. Take the intervention, for example: It started with a confrontation, which led to a *huge* emotional argument and upset within the family. Then came a period of uncomfortable ignoring, and then like clockwork everyone was talking again like nothing happened.

We never discussed it, ever. This became the norm within our family after my parents separated, and the bullying I experienced in school only compounded it. What I didn't realize until much later in life was that I was not only experiencing emotional bullying at school,

I was experiencing it at home as well. The intervention, in particular, was a major factor in the continued silence of my voice.

Not long after Shelly and her boyfriend moved out, Shelly got pregnant. She stayed completely clean from drugs and alcohol while she was pregnant, and it was so nice to have my sister back during that time. She hadn't been this person since she was 17. Toward the end of my senior year in high school, a little ray of light came into my world: my niece, Kayla.

Once my niece was born, she became the most important person in my life. I discovered a different kind of love I had never felt for another human being. I spent a lot of time at Shelly's apartment when Kayla was little.

My mom and dad still didn't get along, but they were at least able to be in the same room without huge drama erupting. About a year before I graduated high school, my dad and his girlfriend broke up. This was the same woman my dad left my mom for when I was in junior high. Although they had been living together for years, she had never finalized her divorce from her children's father. After the breakup, dad bought a small two-bedroom house and settled in on his own. Although my dad tried to remain strong, it was clear he was deeply affected by the breakup. Becoming grandparents also seemed to soften my parents toward each other a bit. It was a shared joy that helped build a small bridge between them.

For the first time in a long while, life with my family didn't feel completely chaotic. I still struggled with my mom a lot, but after Kayla was born, I often went to my sister's place to escape. Shelly also stayed off the drugs for a while after Kayla was born, and I took full advantage of having my sister back.

My mom loved being a grandma and she was pretty good at it too. I think the first couple of years after Kayla was born, some of the joy that had ceased to exist since my parents separated returned to my family. Even my dad beamed with pride and happiness when he looked at little Kayla. She became the most important part of our family, and we all felt compelled to protect her.

Before long, the time was fast approaching for me to graduate high school. I was getting nervous. Although I had a lot of friends, my best friend went to a different school. With graduation drawing near, I feared that while everyone else walked out arm-in-arm with their best friends, I might have to walk out alone. Suddenly the fear of humiliation began to creep back in once again.

Towards the end of senior year, Jenny and I reconnected and started spending time together again. We never addressed the issues that caused the rift in our friendship, but when we both realized we had no one else to walk with at graduation, it felt like a full-circle moment for us to choose each other.

At that time, I felt very uncertain about what life held for me. Even though I should have been relieved to be released from the social prison that was my adolescent school years, and to finally escape the drama at home with my mom, I also feared having to start from scratch in college. I had made a handful of very good friends, but many of them would be moving away to go to college while I stayed behind to attend junior college locally.

A school counselor once told me that I could avoid taking the SATs by going to our local junior college and then transferring to a four-year school. I hated taking tests and was terrified of taking the SATs, so I set my sights on junior college. It was another decision I made out of fear —fear of not doing well on the test, fear of going away to college and being too far from home, even though my home was unstable, the general fear of the unknown guided most of my choices.

MELINDA VELASQUEZ

Maintaining harmony in my relationships, regardless of the personal cost to me, became my main focus. The trauma of being bullied, the horrific divorce, and the dirty family secret of addiction had left my nervous system and my sense of emotional safety barely intact. What I didn't realize at the time was that my internalized fear of speaking my truth would be the cancer that eroded my self-esteem far more than I could ever imagine.

I endured so much emotional trauma within my own family, as well as other important relationships in my life, but hadn't taken the time to reflect on it all, much less heal. I just stuffed it all down and kept moving forward. It never occurred to me that these unresolved issues might have lasting effects, trapping me in a place of fear and forcing me to walk on eggshells in nearly every aspect of my life.

CHAPTER 19

I turned eighteen a few weeks after high school and knew I would need to find a place to live. My dad's child support checks would come to an end, and my mom told me that, if I planned on staying at home, I would have to pay half the rent.

Since graduation, I had been working full-time at my retail job, but there was still no way I could afford to do that.

Even though I was so tired of the drama that came with living in my mom's home, I was hurt that she would expect that of me when I planned on attending school full-time and working full-time as well. Also, she never expected it from my sister, so her setting that expectation with me was another crushing blow to my self-worth.

Maybe if I had stayed, she might have changed her mind. Perhaps that is what happened with my sister. I never even tried to talk about it with her, partly because I was avoiding the conflict, but also because deep down I knew I needed to leave her house.

Leisa's mom, Sandy, found out about my mom's expectations and invited me to stay with them. When I asked her how much rent I would need to pay, she told me to just pay whatever I could afford.

Sandy was not a rich woman living in some big fancy house, but she knew I needed someone in that moment, and she stepped in without hesitation. That's just who she was. I will be eternally grateful to her for that kind gesture. She made me feel seen and cared for in a way that I hadn't felt from my own mom in a long time. She made me feel like I mattered and loved me unconditionally.

Leisa and I spent less time together in our senior year, but our bond stayed intact. After I turned eighteen, I moved in with Leisa's family, and Leisa and I shared her room. It was great at first—like having a sister my own age. Summer was a blast! I was now an adult and we still checked in with Leisa's mom, but we could come and go as we pleased.

During the summer and afterward, Leisa began spending a great deal of time with other friends. Living with her might have also taken a toll on our friendship, as I felt us slowly drifting apart. I started to worry that me being there was putting her in a difficult position, and the last thing I wanted was to become a burden to anyone. As usual, I avoided discussing it with her, but around the same time, I began to feel a strong need for change myself.

I was finally ready to step outside the comfort zone of the one place I had ever lived. Though I had very little money, I did have a car. For my graduation present, my dad managed to buy a used car from a friend. My options were limited, but I knew there was one place I could go that was safe, rent-free, and would provide the change of environment I was craving. My dad always told me I was welcome to live with him anytime I wanted, and this time I was ready.

THE WEIGHT OF SILENCE

I thought through everything and made a plan. On my day off, I decided to put that plan into action. I woke up early and headed out to make the one-hour drive to the town where my dad lived. I didn't tell *anyone* what I was planning to do, including Leisa or my dad. I wanted to avoid repeating the same mistakes I made in junior high, so I wanted to be sure my plan was set before I told anyone. I had a deep fear of failure and I figured if no one knew, I would be the only one who knew that I was not successful. What I was really afraid of was being rejected by my dad and feeling abandoned once again by him.

I prepared clothes for my trip that were suitable for job hunting and placed them in my car the night before, so no one would ask questions. My dad was at work, and I had a key to his house, so I went there to change and headed out to search for a job. My role of "the capable one" was in high gear, because it never occurred to me to ask my dad if I could move in without first securing a job. It was my way of seeking his approval. Being capable and responsible was how I tried to earn my dad's love and acceptance.

I figured I would stick with retail jobs since I already had a good amount of experience. A well-known clothing store was hiring for the Kid's Department. I turned in my application and they interviewed me on the spot. I had a good feeling about the job, and by the time I made it back to my dad's house they left a message saying they wanted to hire me. It was that easy. The universe had spoken, and I was ready to listen. Now all I had to do was tell my dad.

For what felt like the first time in a long time, maybe ever, I made a decision for myself. When I walked into my dad's workplace, a look of shock came over his face, and he said in a happy tone, "What are *you* doing here?"

I smiled and walked confidently over to him and said, "I drove up here today and got a job. I am going to move back here and live with you. This time for real."

His eyes lit up, and a warm smile spread across his face as he said, "Well okay…when is this happening?"

I firmly stated, "I will drive home now and give my two weeks-notice at my current job. I will be back up here after I pack up and finish my last day of work there."

He paused to take it all in, then said, "Well alrighty then, I guess I will see you in two weeks. Do you need help moving your things? I have a bedroom set for you already in my guest room, so you won't need to worry about that."

I took a deep breath feeling relieved that he didn't get mad for not asking him first or act as if I was disrupting his new life. "All I have is my clothes, make-up, hair stuff and some small items, but I will let you know."

He enthusiastically clapped his hands together loudly, as he always did when he was in planning mode and said, "Great!" He gave me a big hug and said, "I love you, honey. I look forward to having you here with me."

My heart felt like it might explode from joy right there on the spot. After spending so little time with my dad over the past five years, there was so much we didn't know about each other, and I was excited to have the chance to change that. I was so ready to start a new chapter, and it seemed he was ready for it too. This felt right.

On the drive home, I was so excited and I couldn't wait to start my new life. There was a community college in the town where my dad lived, and I planned to work and get to know my new home before I registered for the spring semester there. It was a much smaller school and felt like a less overwhelming transition into college than the junior college back home.

    Now that high school was over, I had the chance to start over in a place where no one knew me. At that time in my life, being the new girl in town was exactly what I needed.

CHAPTER 20

Being the new girl in town was a bit lonely at first, but the upside was that the pressure to make friends and be cool no longer existed. Before long, I made a few friends at work, and soon after, it was time to register for school. My dad came through, paying for my registration and books, and I was able to get all the classes I needed.

The car my dad bought me for graduation turned out to be quite a lemon—a very embarrassing one that left me stranded at intersections and broken down on freeways. My dad worked at the Ford Dealership in town and he told me he would co-sign for a used car for me if I could handle the payments and insurance.

I didn't have to pay for food, rent, or anything else, so I could afford the car. We got it just in time for my first day at school, and I felt great driving into school in my cute, sporty little red car. For the first time in a long time, I felt cared for by my dad and excited about who I was and where I was headed. As the new girl in a small town, it did not take long for me to get noticed.

I figured out the right products to use and how to work with my curly hair, learning what NOT to do to it. I finally felt good about wearing my hair down. No one there knew me as "Frizzball" or "Mophead". Instead, I started receiving compliments on my hair rather than being made fun of for it.

The change of environment made me feel like I was reborn. I left behind all the memories that had haunted me since the eighth grade back in my hometown. Living in the new town, I began to regain a sliver of self-confidence and did everything I could to hide my low self-esteem.

My fresh start allowed me to project a different energy out to the world. No one there knew who I was, and this time around I liked the way that felt. My irrational fear of being branded as the girl who was shunned in eighth grade no longer existed in this new place.

When I started school, I dated a few guys, which was a new experience now that I was living with my dad. It was weird at first because, since my dad left when I was only twelve, he missed a lot of me growing into a young woman. It was a bit like reliving my teenage years. He would always say, "If a guy calls after 10 o'clock at night, he only has one thing on his mind." He was probably right. He was right about a lot of things.

Eventually, we got to know each other and we became very close. It was nice. I started to realize how similar we were in personality, which was comforting because, after living with my mom and sister for so long, I had often felt like an outsider. The joke that I was the mailman's kid was many times more real to me than a joke. I longed to feel like I truly belonged somewhere, with someone.

Besides living with Leisa's family, all I had known for at least five years was what it was like to live with addicts. I began to question what truly was normal. Where did I fit in? Who were my people?

Living with my dad brought a sense of peace and calm that I so desperately needed. My mom and dad were polar opposites—my mom's house was chaos, while my dad's was order, both literally and figuratively.

I used to describe my dad's way of living with one word: ANAL! After his relationship with his girlfriend came to an end, he had been living alone for a while, and he became even more set in his ways. That Marine taskmaster who would come out at times when I was little, wanting everything neat and orderly, was now ever present.

He was very particular about everything, even more so than I remembered as a kid. Control was very important to my dad. He battled his own demons with addictions. His addictions were just more socially acceptable like alcohol, food, and yo-yo dieting. He was a Marine in Vietnam and never spoke about his experience with me, but I'm sure he faced his share of trauma at a young age. I think he used control of his environment to maintain a sense of calm in his life, a pattern I would later adopt myself.

At Dad's house, everything was clean all the time, and everything had its place. This had a calming effect on me, but it could also be anxiety-provoking. My dad's house was the complete opposite end of the spectrum from my mom's, which was good and bad.

One of his biggest pet peeves was the towels in the bathroom. He told me, "Honey, after you take your hair out of the towel, make sure you rub out the indentations your hair made in the towel before you hang it up to dry. Otherwise, the towel will dry like that, and it looks ugly hanging up in the bathroom."

THE WEIGHT OF SILENCE

The concept of this had never occurred to me, but I knew how much he cared about appearances. He liked the natural light coming into the hallway from the bedroom window, so he always wanted my bedroom door left open. Having my home feel light and bright during the day was something I liked as well.

At age 18, keeping my room perfectly clean and my bed made so you could bounce a quarter off of it was not my priority. To combat this, I promised I would at least make my bed every day and shove anything out of order to the other side of my bed or into the closet. That way, when you walked by my room, it at least *appeared* to be neat and clean. The messiness still drove him crazy, but it was a good compromise.

He kept his small appliances put away in cabinets—one time, I forgot to put one away after using it, and I came home to find it sitting on top of paper towels on my bed. Message received! I found it funny that as anal as he was, he had this toaster he left the bread bag next to while it was hot, and a piece of the yellow bag melted onto the toaster; everything else in his house was perfect except that. As cheap as toasters are, I found it so odd that for some reason he didn't buy a new one.

Growing up as a little kid, I remember my dad being stern and a neat freak, but my mom being the opposite of that seemed to soften him. He was also a complete goofball who would run down the hallway naked, jumping in the air and farting. However, living alone for a number of years and dating someone who was VERY focused on appearances, only seemed to amplify his anal tendencies.

I have no idea how my dad managed to live in the same home with my mom for 19 years, given his need for neatness and order. A part of him must have died inside every day. They could not have been more different in this realm. I'm certain it must have been the source of many arguments I don't remember hearing.

MELINDA VELASQUEZ

I used to think I was a complete slob, given how much my mom complained about the house being a mess when I was a teenager. It wasn't until I moved out that I realized it wasn't me at all. While I was not the neat freak my dad was, I did like it when things were kept relatively clean. I used to hate cleaning up the kitchen after my mom cooked—it looked like a bomb went off in there! She was a great cook, but the idea of *clean as you go* was lost on her.

My mom's house always looked lived-in, and her bedroom was usually the worst—a mess of piled up clothes, shoes, and dirty dishes. She had a habit of spending the day in her room when she was coming down, or she was out of drugs. Those days were the worst.

She would eat all day, and only come out of her room to get more food. The dishes would pile up in her room, and then at some point, she would bring them all down, filling up the kitchen and expecting me to clean up after her. If I didn't, I would get yelled at.

Living with my dad was definitely an adjustment—now I was walking on a *different* set of eggshells. My dad was hyper focused on outward appearances and making everything look perfect. In contrast, my mom loved thrift stores and filled her house with lace doilies, tablecloths, dried flowers, and walls stenciled with flowers and ribbons. She had a hodge-podge collection of glasses, silverware, and dishes from different sets that came and went over the years. Her house usually had that comfortably messy and lived-in feeling most of the time.

My dad's home was full of new furniture that all matched, along with a few well-placed antiques and a modern color scheme. He had one set of matching dishes, glassware, pots, pans, and silverware. While his furniture was comfortable, leaving anything even slightly messy for the day and coming back to it later wasn't an option in his home.

My mom had a one-car garage filled to the brim with keepsakes and items she hoarded from thrift stores and garage sales. When I was in high school, she had this really weird boyfriend who liked to go dumpster diving, so she accumulated even more stuff from that as well. It got to the point where you couldn't even walk in the garage anymore because it was packed full of random stuff.

My dad's garage was immaculate. As a Parts Manager for Ford, he stored everything in Ford Motorcraft boxes, which all matched and were similar in size and shape. He labeled each box with a black Sharpee pen in his perfect penmanship. He even tried to buy the same brand of power tools so they all matched in color, and his pegboards were organized to perfection. He even had outlines of the tools so they would be sure to be placed back in their rightful home. Even his garage floor was spotless.

I knew my style and way of living didn't match my mom's, but there was a sense at her house that I could plop down on the couch and just be myself regardless. Despite her blaming me for every mess ever made in the house, it always felt like it was a space where everyone was welcome.

Although my dad's anal tendencies did create a sense of calm that I desperately needed, I also felt constantly judged by him. I never really felt comfortable in his home unless he wasn't there, and even then, I had to be careful to not mess anything up.

There was no "plopping" on the couch! He would say, "You will break down the furniture, and then it won't be comfortable anymore." Like mom, my dad was also a great cook, and man could he grill! But he was always battling his weight and cholesterol so he often projected those concerns onto me as well.

MELINDA VELASQUEZ

As a young college student, I would often buy fast food on my breaks from school and eat it at home. Afterward, I would bury the trash at the bottom of the outside garbage can so he wouldn't know I ate it. A lot of my shame issues with food came from the time I lived with him.

When my parents were married and created a home together, they brought together the best parts of both of them. Now that they were apart, I struggled to find balance in either of their homes. The happy medium where I was most comfortable, the blend of their best parts no longer existed.

My dad and I definitely had our differences, especially when it came to core values and political views. However, getting to know him as an adult helped bridge a gap I had felt for a long time. On the other hand, I was so happy to be a part of the life my dad had built away from all of us that I let my desire to earn his approval interfere with my own journey and goals. I was so eager for him to be proud of me and to present myself as strong, capable, smart, and responsible that I often ignored the part of myself that was more like my mom.

My mom strongly believed in service to others, empathy, and a more liberal point of view. Despite being a high-functioning addict, she held a high-level administrative role in a county department that helped people in need for over 26 years. She was involved in the funding process for many non-profit organizations, and played a key role in organizing events like the Day of Caring, where the community comes together to help other members of the community with different projects in homes, parks, and other community-based organizations.

My dad, on the other hand, was a very opinionated staunch Republican. He made good money and wanted to hold onto it. He enjoyed traveling, fine wine, and good food. He often passed judgment on people he didn't know, and I believe he was quite ignorant when it came to the issues of society. His *new* life was one of entitlement. He had rich friends and made good money for the area in which he lived.

One thing my dad instilled in me that I will forever be grateful for, is the importance of hard work and taking pride in my work. Living with him taught me how to set and achieve goals—even if at first I was doing it to gain his respect, it is a value that I'm grateful stuck with me.

Living with my dad was vastly different from living with my mom, but one thing remained the same: I was still subjected to the lingering resentment they had for each other. The negativity, frustration, and shame he felt toward the way my mom lived her life began to seep into my subconscious, leaving me even more confused about my own feelings about her and myself. As a result, I began to suppress the parts of me that were like my mom, which only pulled me even further away from her.

The longer I lived with my dad, the more I craved his approval, and that began to bleed over into every aspect of my life. I wanted him to be proud of me and to believe that, regardless what influence my mom had over me, I had become the kind of person who made good choices. I chose to attend a school where I was earning top marks, I always had a job, worked hard, and took care of my responsibilities.

The one area where I struggled with making good choices was in the guys I dated. I had developed a pattern of picking guys who strung me along or treated me poorly. When it came to intimate relationships, my low self-esteem would go into overdrive, making me needy and clingy. This inevitably drove guys away and left me heartbroken.

I rarely shared details about the guys I dated with my dad because I couldn't stand to see the look of disappointment on his face. Knowing how judgmental he could be, I was very careful not to introduce him to guys I dated unless I believed they would meet his approval. I was keenly aware of how much my relationship with my dad influenced my dating choices. However, it took me a long time and a lot of heartbreak to recognize the powerful influence my mom had on my intimate relationships.

The emotional trauma I experienced from my family issues and the bullying showed up in all of my intimate relationships, there are three that stand out. These three significant relationships, which spanned seven years from age 18 to 25, perfectly illustrate how codependency affected my intimate relationships. Each relationship triggered my deepest insecurities plunged me into the deepest depths of shame. One of them was extremely emotionally abusive, and another exhibited emotionally abusive behaviors. All three of them at one point revealed a toxic pattern that I had to break in order to heal.

SECTION FOUR

Young Adulthood: Drowning in the Mess

"If you don't value yourself, you'll always struggle to find someone who will."
~ Unknown

CHAPTER

21

Liam

Liam entered my life just before I turned 19 years old. We met through a mutual friend while I was living with my dad. Liam had just graduated with a Bachelor of Science degree when we decided to date exclusively. His family lived near my dad, and he was moving back to the area to work for his dad for a year before taking another job. Despite having the qualifications to land any job right out of college, he chose to honor his commitment to his dad.

Liam was 23, and he stood out from the guys I had been hanging out with since starting community college. Most of the guys I spent time with were heavily involved in sports, particularly baseball and football. Liam was an active person, but his goals were more centered on his career goals rather than his athletic ability.

He was very smart and driven when it came to his career, which initially made me feel secure with him. Liam's commitment and loyalty were a refreshing change. However, as we reached the first year of our relationship, a troubling pattern began to emerge. I started to feel rejected and abandoned by him.

It started out with little things, like him spending more and more time with his friends or family and not setting aside quality time for us. I started to feel like he was taking me for granted. We rarely did anything just the two of us, and when we did it felt like we were disconnected from each other.

Looking back, I realize that some of the best times I had with Liam, especially in the beginning, were when we were both drinking. That is not to say that we didn't enjoy good times without alcohol, but I think he had a difficult time getting out of his head without it. At that age, most people I knew liked to drink socially. We got together during his college graduation weekend, and we partied that whole weekend, which included a fair amount of alcohol.

I didn't notice the role alcohol played in our relationship until around the one-year mark. It was then I realized I was the only one initiating any kind of intimacy when we were both sober. Liam always seemed to have an excuse as to why it couldn't happen, and I began to resent him for rejecting me. To make matters worse, the only time *he* ever initiated any type of physical intimacy was when he was drunk, and that hit *all* of my triggers.

As stable as Liam seemed when I first met him, there was also a pretty major red flag I chose to ignore. During his graduation weekend, I found out that he had a suspended license due to two DUI's. I liked him so much that I just chalked it up to him being in college, and making stupid choices—after all, I knew I had.

The longer we were together I could see that he didn't seem to be able to truly relax and have fun without alcohol acting as social lubrication. While it's not uncommon for people who lean towards introversion to rely on alcohol for social ease it became a problem for us. I started to feel like the only time he was attracted to me was when he was drunk, and that brought all of my insecurities screaming back to the surface. I tried to talk to him about it, but he would always revert back to his rational side and shut himself off to his emotions. The only time I saw him express deep emotion for me was when he was drinking, and whether we admitted it or not, the emotional divide between us was growing.

After our first year together, we lived with another couple for a few months. It turned out to be the first nail in the coffin of our relationship. As a full-time student living at home, I was at least five years younger than the other roommates and was not making enough money at my job to pay my part of everything at that house. Plus, living with another couple was not a good idea for any of us, so we started looking for another place to live.

What I didn't realize was that Liam had already decided he wanted to find a place just for him, rather than a place we could both afford. I found a little studio right downtown that was small but perfect. He didn't inform me until after he got the place that he would be living there without me.

That was a hard blow for me to take. I had never lived on my own before and made a lot of mistakes, but instead of discussing it, he just decided. Although the decision was probably for the best, I couldn't help but add it to the growing list of his crimes in the rejection and abandonment category.

My relationship with Liam continued, despite my feelings of rejection. I later realized that throughout our time together, I never felt like he put me first. I had been with Liam longer than I'd been with anyone and considered it to be the best relationship I'd ever had. However, at that time, my only experience with intimate relationships was a trail of men who had cheated on me, lied to me, and used me. Liam may not have put me first, but he was kind, and I don't believe he would've ever cheated on me.

During the time Liam and I were together, he was the one who actually helped me begin to see that I needed to set boundaries with my mom and sister. We talked a little about his family's issues with addiction, but not as much as mine. I don't think he wanted to talk about it, but I could see it weighed on him at times. He tried to compartmentalize it as much as possible, and he also encouraged me to set healthier boundaries with my mom and sister.

Liam's ability to seemingly close himself off to his emotions may have worked for him in some ways, but it continued to create distance between us. There were quite a few times when his tendency to suppress his emotions made it harder for him to empathize with mine. His way of problem-solving was much more analytical than emotional, and at that time in my life, I didn't have the emotional intelligence to not take that personally.

There was one issue that, for me, became the wound that slowly festered and infected our entire relationship. I had an abnormal Pap smear, and it was determined that I had HPV. This was *long* before it was widely talked about and over ten years before the vaccine was developed. I hadn't been intimate with many people, and Liam was the only person I had been with while on birth control and not using condoms. There wasn't much helpful information available back then, and I felt a lot of confusion and shame around the diagnosis.

My doctor had also told me there were pre-cancerous cells present they needed to biopsy. It was kind of a big deal, especially because I was also being told there was a risk that I might not be able to have kids. I was only 20 years old at the time, which was young enough that having that taken away from me before I even knew if I wanted to have kids was very scary.

I had to undergo a procedure near my hometown, so I had to travel the hour both ways on the day of the procedure. The doctor told me that it wasn't a terribly painful procedure, but it was still invasive. I didn't want to go alone, so my mom offered to go with me because Liam said he had to work.

My mom was good at that kind of thing—she could be very nurturing when I was hurt or sick. The procedure turned out to be much more painful than I had expected. As soon as it began, I was shocked at how painful it actually was, and when I looked at my mom tears immediately started streaming down my face.

As a woman, having someone rooting around your cervix is never fun, but this experience felt especially invasive. I was taken by surprise by how painful it was, especially since the doctor had downplayed it. Afterward, I felt a weird sense that I can only describe as feeling violated and depressed. I was cramping pretty badly afterwards, and I cried the entire hour-long drive home. My mom wanted me to stay with her, but I just wanted to get home and see Liam.

All I wanted was for Liam to rent some movies, pick up dinner and come over to hang out and snuggle with me for the night. But he had other plans. I had no idea he was planning to go to his friend's house to watch a pay-per-view fight and he didn't bother to mention it until after I got home.

I was so hurt, and actually pretty angry too, which translated to my go-to communication style at the time: passive-aggression. I couldn't believe that after knowing what I had been through, he didn't change his plans—or that he even planned to be anywhere else but with me in the first place. If the roles were reversed, he would have been my priority. My anger and passive aggression also stemmed from the possibility that he was likely where I got it. The doctor told me that people could be carriers without having any visible signs of the virus, which was also the case with me.

To make matters worse, he showed up at my house much later than he'd said he would, and he was drunk. There were many little things like this that made me feel I wasn't his priority, but this one really stuck with me. It eroded my trust in him, and as much as I tried to let it go, for me it was always there, lingering between us.

About a month shy of my 21st birthday, as we approached the two-year mark in our relationship, I earned the credits I needed for my A.A. degree. I planned to move back to my hometown and transfer to the local University. Liam had just started a job at the community college I just graduated from, so we decided to make our relationship work long distance. Despite our problems, I loved him and was committed to making it work.

I would only be an hour away from him, and I had made that trip many times when I would go home to visit my family and friends. I was trying to make the best out of the situation. I knew he was excited about his new job, but he just left a job working just seven miles away from where I was going to be living and going to school. He had known for close to a year where I would be transferring to continue the pursuit of my degree. He could have gotten a job anywhere if he wanted to be closer to me, but he made a different choice.

At that point, this was the longest relationship I ever had been in, and I envisioned us heading towards marriage once I finished school. But his actions were making me question if he felt the same. My abandonment issues were rearing their ugly head, but I just pushed them down and tried to stay focused on the excitement of what lay ahead for me.

I found a roommate and an apartment and planned to truly live on my own for the first time as a college student. I looked forward to seeing my friends and getting to see my adorable niece more often. At the end of June, I celebrated my 21st birthday with a road trip to Tahoe with Liam and some friends, which also ended up also being a good-bye party because I wouldn't be returning home with them.

I stood alone in the parking lot of my new apartment, watching Liam and my friends drive away. I felt deep sense of uncertainty about how this change would impact my relationship with Liam. I could not have imagined all that was to come.

CHAPTER 22

Liam vs. Brad

Before moving back to my hometown, I secured a job as a cocktail waitress in a Country and Western bar in a nearby town. It was a huge place with a large dance floor, a DJ during the week, live bands on the weekends, and even a mechanical bull. I worked there for a while, but I quickly realized I needed more money to cover rent and bills. I could practically hear my dad saying, *I told you; you weren't going to be making enough money at that job to pay all your bills.*

Eventually, I got another job at a café near where I lived, just down the street from my mom's favorite bar at the time. Between working two jobs and going to school full time, my time was limited, and it became difficult for me to find time to go up to see Liam. His days off were on the weekends, and that was when I had to work to make the good money cocktailing. We talked on the phone when we could, but again, this was before cell phones and video chats, so both of us had to be home and plan a time to talk.

Things were getting strained between us, and the lack of time together didn't help. The distance only intensified my feelings of not being a priority, and when I started getting attention from other guys, things only got worse.

As a cocktail server, there is definitely a level of flirting involved to boost your tips, but it was all pretty innocent—a smile with a flirty hair flip and a prompt drink refill could go a long way. I also really enjoyed meeting and talking with new people.

Being in that environment, whether I was working or just out having fun like any 21-year-old, made me realize how much I missed that feeling of being wanted. Not just wanted in a sexual way, but having someone who wanted to spend time with me and was willing to go to great lengths to do that.

It made me recognize how little of that I had been getting from Liam, and not just since I had moved back to my hometown.

As good as it felt to be getting all of this new attention, I still stayed true to Liam. That needy, insecure girl was still there, and even though I was back in my hometown, I could feel a shift. It had been three years since high school, and eighth grade felt like a distant memory. The time away had been good for me—I was starting to feel proud of the person I saw in the mirror. My confidence was slowly coming back, and it showed. People were suddenly drawn to me, and it felt really good.

By this time, my sister Shelly had married my niece, Kayla's dad, but after about two years of marriage, they filed for divorce. She and Kayla moved back in with my mom, while Kayla's dad moved back to the East Coast to be near his family. Since my apartment was just around the corner from my mom's condo, I was able to spend a lot of time with Kayla and Shelly during the day when I didn't have to work or be at school.

After I moved in with my dad, my mom met a man named Charlie, whom I'll admit I was skeptical about at first. My mom had dated a few strange guys, so when she told me Charlie had a hook for an arm, I thought, *here we go again*. I'll admit it: I judged. Charlie had grown up on a ranch and lost his arm—and a few of his fingers—in a machine accident.

My mom was so excited to have finally met "her cowboy," and once I met him, my concerns quickly melted away. He had led a fascinating life, including being a bull rider before losing his arm. He was quite the storyteller, and we would all gather around as he shared tales from his life. By then, he had moved in with my mom, and I could see how much he cared for her. He could also fix anything—he was more capable with that hook than most people are with both arms and hands. He just seemed to fit into our family and brought a sense of calm to the usual drama.

Charlie and Mom would often stay home with Kayla when Shelly wanted to go out. One night, my mom offered to watch Kayla so Shelly and I could go have a night out. Shelly came with me to the bar where I worked, but then she wanted to go back to the bar down the street from my second job. She wanted to see a guy, well actually two guys she had been seeing, Brad and Jordan, and she was sure they would both be there.

Brad and Jordan were friends, and while she was involved with both, nothing serious was happening with either of them. I didn't know much about her situation, but I knew she was spending more time with Jordan at that point. I was just having fun hanging out with my big sister and was once again happy that she actually wanted to hang out with me. That feeling I had as a little girl to have my sister want to hang out with me was still very present for me.

We arrived at the bar, and I walked in the door, completely oblivious to how much this one moment would impact my life. Brad and Jordan were there, hanging out together, and they were the first people I saw when we entered the bar. Both were good-looking, but I didn't think much of it at the time. I still had a boyfriend, and I didn't know what the deal was with them and my sister.

Brad looked familiar to me, but I couldn't place him and then I found out he was a year ahead of me in high school. When he told me his last name, I knew exactly who he was because I knew his younger sister. We weren't super close friends, but she was someone I really liked. I thought it was also a little weird when I realized that his older brother was someone my sister used to date before she got married.

Regardless of all that, they seemed fun, so we hung out with them, laughed, talked, and played pool until the bar closed. I had been drinking, so I left my car at the bar, and we all drove together to hang out at Jordan's house not far from the bar. It had been such a fun night we figured we would keep it going.

I didn't know Brad in high school, but I was aware of him. I thought he hung out with other guys in his class that were popular, but I kept saying that he looked so different from what I remembered. He swore he looked exactly the same but it just kept nagging at me.

I said, "Ooh, I just remembered I have my yearbooks from what would have been your senior year of high school in the trunk of my car from when I moved, we could go look! Oh crap, I forgot my car is back at the bar. Oh well, I will just have to look you up tomorrow when I get home."

Brad put down his beer and said, "Let's go right now and get it! I'll drive you to your car."

Feeling a little uncertain about hopping in the car alone with a guy I had just met—especially knowing I had a boyfriend, I said, "No, don't worry about it, it's no big deal. I'm probably just getting you confused with someone else. I can look tomorrow."

But Brad insisted, "Come on, it'll be fun to look at those old pictures." he pressed, and then he got closer and nudged my arm, winked and pointed at Shelly and Jordan and said quietly, "Besides, it will give these two the chance to have some alone time."

I really didn't want to hang around to find out whatever that meant, so I said, "Alright. Let's go. Are you sure you're okay to drive?"

He made a grimacing face and waved his hand at me and said, "I'm totally fine. Come on!"

Before we got out the door, Shelly called out, "Hey! Where are you guys going?" I replied, "He is taking me back to the bar to get something out of my car, we will be right back."

Brad drove a really nice truck. It was a full-sized black truck with a sleek looking monochromatic camper shell on the back that looked like it was custom-built for the truck. He opened the door for me, and I slid into the bench seat as he went around to the driver's side.

Once he got in, I reached for my seatbelt and he reached over and took it out of my hand and said, "Hold on a minute, we're in no rush. The bar isn't far away and they need some time. Let's talk for a minute."

He started up the truck and the engine roared with a seductive growl before settling into a soothing purr as we sat idle. He turned on the radio and the sounds of 90's country music poured over us. He reached over and lowered the music so it faded gently into the background and turned the heater on as we both shivered from the cold night air.

I was still a bit buzzed and feeling bold, so I asked, "Okay, so what is the deal with you, Jordan, and my sister? This whole situation seems a little weird to me."

Brad clicked the automatic door locks, settled into his seat, and turned his body so that he was leaning on his door facing me and said with absolution, "There is *nothing* going on between me and your sister. There has been some flirting and stuff, but she used to date my brother, and she and Jordan have already been hooking up. She might want something to happen with me, but it never will. I'm not interested in her that way."

The energy in the truck shifted suddenly and I felt a strong tension build between us. My heart started to beat faster as I tried to break the tension and said, "Oh okay. I mean, I think she is into you and she thinks you might be into her too."

He replied, "I have told her already it is not going to happen. She is fun to hang out with, but that's it for me. I wouldn't be here with *you* if I were into her."

I could feel my cheeks get warm and my stomach tightened up as I blurted out, "I have a boyfriend!"

He came back with, "I know, I know. You said he lives an hour away. All I know is that if I had a girlfriend that looked like you, I would never want to live that far away from her. He is crazy if you ask me."

Oh shit! My inner voice screamed inside my head. I had absolutely NO idea that he had ANY interest in me at all until that very moment.

Part of me wanted to jump out of the car and run back into the house and tell my sister we needed to go right now. But another part of me, the adolescent girl who never got noticed in high school, kept me from bolting. I wanted to bask in the glow of the fact that one of the guys I'd perceived as popular from high school—who probably never knew I existed before tonight— was hitting on me.

Only seconds passed as his words hung in the air. I shot him a look of disbelief and said, "That's nice, but—"

Before I could get the words out, he reached over, and softly grabbed the back of my neck, and said, "Come here…" as he leaned in and kissed me.

It happened so fast. The chemistry between us was so intense, and I got swept up in the moment. I felt a rush of adrenaline as my heart raced, my stomach fluttered with excitement, and the intoxicating feeling of being seen and desired by someone took over.

Liam and hadn't made me feel like that in a long time. I knew I should push Brad away, but it felt good to be wanted. And not just wanted by anyone, but by a popular guy from high school. The guy my sister wanted, but he wanted me instead.

From my vantage point growing up, my sister always got the guy she wanted. She went to every high school dance, she was among the most popular, and was rarely ever without a boyfriend. I on the other hand, rarely got the guy I wanted. And before Liam, every guy I had been with cheated on me.

SHIT! Liam!

Suddenly the reality of what I was doing and who I would be hurting hit me and I pushed him away, "NO, NO, NO, I can't do this! I've never cheated on anyone before, and I don't want to do that to Liam. We have to stop."

He backed away quickly, and put his hands up, "I'm sorry.

You're right. You have a boyfriend. I just couldn't help myself. I don't want to make you do anything you don't want to do."

I sat there, trying to process what just happened. Then came the tidal wave of shame and guilt, and I started beating myself up in my head:

Melinda! What were you thinking? What about Liam? Your relationship isn't perfect, but he doesn't deserve this. This is the worst thing you can do to someone, and you know that better than anyone. And what about Shelly? You know she is interested in him, even if she and Jordan hook up too, this is wrong. You are a terrible person!

I was drowning in what Brené Brown would call a "shame shitstorm," and slowly sinking into an abyss of self-loathing. Just when I thought I might implode from how awful I felt I heard Brad say, "Hey, so, do you still want to go get that yearbook? I'm kind of curious to see it after all these years."

His voice pulled me back to the present moment. We were still parked in front of Jordan's house, and from the outside, it looked like the lights were turned off. I didn't want to go back inside to see what was happening in there, and as much as I didn't want to admit it, I was enjoying being with Brad.

It felt good to have a guy be so attentive, and I felt a sense of power in being desired again. I hadn't felt that from Liam in so long, and that kiss had my head spinning! In this temporary bubble, away from everything I knew, it felt good, so I said, "Yeah, okay. Let's go."

He drove me back to my car at the bar, and I grabbed the yearbook from my trunk. I still wasn't quite sober enough to drive, so I hopped back in the truck with him. Instead of turning left toward Jordan's house, he turned right and said, "I know where we can go!"

His tone was excited, and for some reason, I didn't feel threatened, so I asked, "Where?"

He smiled, a Cheshire cat grin spreading across his face, and said, "You'll see…" With a twinkle in his eye, he reached over to turn up the radio, and off we went.

His energy was infectious, and I felt exhilarated. My rational brain told me I should just get my butt home and stop whatever this was before it went any further, but as wrong as it was, it also felt so good. I was caught up in that feeling, and I wasn't ready for it to end.

He was fun, and he had this way of lightening the mood that helped me escape my own thoughts—something I desperately needed in that moment. It was just a short drive down the road, and as we pulled in, I couldn't believe where he had taken me.

It was the pizza place where my best guy friend had worked in high school, and where we all hung out all the time. I hadn't been there in about three years, and it felt familiar, nostalgic, and disarming. As we got out of the truck, I grabbed the yearbook and walked up to the door, I said in disbelief, "I can't believe this of all places is where you took me. You work here?"

He touted proudly, with a hint of jest, "I'm the manager! You've been here before?"

I laughed, "Are you kidding me? One of my best friends in high school worked here, and we were here all the time. I haven't been here in years, though."

He motioned with his arm, "Well, come on in! You want a beer?"

Feeling myself finally sobering up, I shook my head, "No thanks, I'm not really a fan of beer, and I need to sober up a little more."

He smiled, reaching for a glass, "Okay, how about a soda then?"

Feeling relieved he didn't push me into drinking more, I smiled back, "Yeah, a soda would be good, thanks."

I pulled out the yearbook and said, "Okay, now let's find you in the yearbook to see why I keep picturing you looking different." I start flipping through to the senior pictures section, where he should be pictured, but he wasn't there. "Oh shoot! You're not here!"

I looked up at him, feeling a bit disappointed, and saw the guilty look on his face as he admitted, "I know. I knew I didn't have a yearbook picture that year. I just used it as an excuse to get you alone."

I should have been annoyed—after all, he knew I had a boyfriend, but he planned this whole ruse just so he could kiss me or whatever else might happen if I hadn't stopped it. In that moment, I was shocked, but also flattered that he would go to all this trouble just to be alone with me. He read me like a book.

I didn't see the manipulation; I just felt what I'd longed to feel since that night in eighth grade, when the boy ditched me as soon as Naomi and her cronies showed up. Or what I would've felt if my best guy friend had ditched all his other girls for me. I felt chosen. I felt seen. I felt enough.

We sat and talked there for a while, and then he drove me back to my car. I followed him back to Jordan's house, and as we walked in, Shelly said with a slightly annoyed tone, "Where have you guys been? You've been gone a long time."

"He took me to the pizza place! What a blast from the past. We just talked for a while, and I drank a soda so I could sober up a little more before I drive us home. We picked up my car on the way back."

I'm not sure if I was feeling guilty or if she seemed suspicious, but Shelly replied, "Oh, okay. Whatever. We need to get home now. Mom is going to be pissed at me if Kayla wakes up and I'm not there."

I was more than ready to end what had been a very eventful night, so we got in the car and left. The drive home, and the rest of the night, was a blur. I felt so conflicted. I had a really good time with Brad, and being with him felt good and exciting—but I still loved Liam.

The thought of hurting Liam made me feel sick to my stomach. I had always figured that Liam and I would end up getting married. We were just in different phases of our lives, but I believed that eventually, we would sync up and everything would be good again.

What I wasn't admitting to myself was that our relationship had probably ended when Liam chose not to come live with me when I went back home. Whatever valid reasons he had, in my heart he was once again choosing something or someone else over me.

I still wasn't ready to let go of Liam, so instead, I leaned in and held on tight. It worked at first, but it wouldn't be long before our relationship would be tested again. I had to decide whether I was staying with him out of love or out of fear.

I decided to come clean and tell Liam that I kissed someone, but that I stopped it before anything more happened. He was crushed. We had a long talk about it, and I think it woke him up a bit. He wanted to come down to visit me, and I was excited that he was finally willing to put in the effort again.

It had been a week or two since that night Brad and I kissed, but I hadn't seen or talked to him since. The night Liam was supposed to arrive, we hadn't made specific plans. I was excited that he seemed ready to fight for me, for us, but at the same time, I was also unknowingly resistant to spending time alone to work through our issues. He clearly wanted nothing more but to be alone with me—which made sense after what happened with me and Brad.

I told Shelly Liam was coming down and mentioned that we had been having issues. I wasn't exactly looking forward to being alone with him. We hadn't seen each other in a while, and I felt nervous about how I would feel when I saw him.

I still hadn't told Shelly what happened with Brad, and she was still hanging out with him and Jordan. She told me she was supposed to meet up with them and asked if it was okay to stop by later and bring them along. I don't know what I was thinking, but I said yes. That is a decision I will always regret.

When Liam arrived, I casually told him that Shelly was coming over with some friends. He was not thrilled about it, but I didn't really give him much of a choice. He also had no idea that Brad was the person I kissed.

Shelly, Brad, and Jordan showed up at my apartment, and at first, things started off okay. We all started drinking a little, just hanging out, listening to music, and joking around. But I noticed Liam was drinking heavily, and he just seemed off. His intuition must have been setting off alarm bells, because he started acting really arrogant and rude to Brad and Jordan.

Even though Brad and I weren't doing anything to hint that something had happened between us, Liam could sense it.

As the night went on, Liam got drunk, and I was buzzed, and the next thing I knew we were outside on the sidewalk, arguing. He was hurt—rightfully so—and everything finally exploded. He was both angry and hurt when he yelled out at me, "What the fuck is going on here? Why would you invite me here and then invite these guys over? Is one of them the guy you kissed?"

He was so angry. I had never seen him angry like that before, and it scared me. I didn't recognize the person standing in front of me. Liam had never shown this kind of anger or aggression toward me. I completely understood what he was feeling, but after months of feeling like he wasn't putting much energy or thought into our relationship, his reaction shocked me.

Letting Shelly bring Brad over was monumentally stupid on my part. I didn't consciously want to hurt Liam. I truly wanted to work things out with him, but I hadn't stopped thinking about Brad either. I think a part of me hoped that having them both in the same room would help me find clarity on what to do. Since I hadn't seen Brad since that night, I didn't know if that night was just a one-night thing. I was confused and conflicted.

I felt awful that Liam thought I was deliberately trying to hurt him by flaunting Brad right in front of him. In a panic, I lied, "I'm so sorry. I didn't know my sister was going to bring them here. Once they were here, I didn't know what to do."

I could see the hurt and betrayal in his eyes, "I was coming down here this weekend so we could be together and work through our issues. How could you do this to me? I didn't think you were capable of being this cruel."

Just then, I heard Shelly's voice, "Minna? Is everything okay out here?"

Liam and I were both crying at that point, but I yelled back, "Yes it's fine."

Shelly called out, "Okay, I think we're going to go. I'll call you later. Love you."

I turned back to Liam, but he was gone. He'd started walking away when Shelly and I were yelling back and forth, and now he was out of sight. I figured it was probably best to give him some space, so I went back inside and waited for him to return.

When Liam came back, we didn't say much to each other. We just went to bed, though I doubt either of us got much sleep. In the morning, with the alcohol wearing off and no one there but the two of us, we finally had a calmer conversation.

I started by saying, "I really am sorry about last night. I hope you know I would never do anything purposely to hurt you."

He replied, "Well you did…hurt me. The whole night just went from bad to worse really quick. I'm not proud of how I responded to everything, but I just felt blindsided. It just felt like you invited me here, but you didn't want to be with me."

My voice was hoarse from the night before, breaking as I started to talk, "I don't know what I was feeling. When the kiss happened, it was confusing. I didn't want to hurt or betray you, but I also liked how it felt. When we talked about it on the phone, I thought I was clear about wanting to stay with you and work through everything, but then once I knew you were coming here, I started to feel anxious. I have felt so disconnected from you, even before I moved down here. Without you here with me, I guess I just got used to living my life that way. It is not something I planned or wanted, it just happened."

Liam began to get a little defensive, "What was I supposed to do? Leave my job to come down here to be with you?"

I threw my head back in frustration, "No…I mean I don't know. It's just that I feel like I am in the middle of college life and being 21 and on my own, and all that comes with that, and you are settling down. But even when I lived up there, Liam, you seemed to always choose something or someone over me. Whether it was your friends or your family, I never felt like I came first. And when you didn't want to move down here with me, it felt like once again you weren't choosing me."

He threw his hands up, "So all of this is my fault? I just got a job at the college, and I actually considered finding work down here to be closer to you, but I figured it would be good for you to have the experience of learning how to be on your own."

I leaned in, "It is good for me to do that…I just didn't think that in doing that, it would change things between us. But, if we are honest, things between us have been different for a while."

He put his hand up and cupped his mouth the way he always did when he was anxious, then he took a deep breath and said, "So what do you want to do?"

I put my head in my hands and said, "I really don't know. I'm scared. I don't want to lose you, but we obviously need to figure some things out."

We decided to take a break and give each other some space. We planned to meet up in a week to talk and make the final decision. I was relieved we had that time to talk after the train wreck of the night before.

I was still so confused about everything. I just needed some time and space to figure out what I truly wanted without any pressure. Time alone was what I thought I needed, which would have happened if Brad hadn't been just the right amount of charming, persistent and eager for my time and attention.

The day Liam left, Brad called to check on me. I don't remember how he even got my phone number, but I was happy to hear his voice.

"Hey. I don't want to bug you, and I know your boyfriend is

there. I just wanted to check in on you after last night. It sounded like things got pretty bad between you two when you were outside."

Suddenly, all the hard stuff and the bad feelings that had come up between Liam and me just melted away. I felt embarrassed wondering how much he heard of our fight. My voice still hoarse, I replied softly, "Liam already left to go back home, but thanks for checking on me. Last night was really bad. He figured out that you were the guy that kissed me, and that sent him over the edge. It was pretty stupid of me to think it was okay for you and Jordan to come over."

"Yikes! Yeah, I could see how that would piss him off. I sensed that he was getting into a weird competitive thing with me, but I didn't know you told him about the kiss for sure. It all makes a lot more sense now. I can tell by your voice it was a pretty rough night."

I dropped back into my shame pit, "Yeah, I'm an asshole and an awful person."

He quipped back, "Stop it. No, you're not. You stopped things before they went too far. If anything, I'm the asshole. I knew you had a boyfriend."

I started to come back around a bit, "Yeah, I guess. But…I don't know. I'm just exhausted and drained from everything that happened last night."

He agreed, "Yeah, you should try and get some sleep. I will let you go, I just wanted to make sure you were okay. Maybe I'll check in on you again later."

Part of me was excited to hear that, but another part of me felt guilty. Liam had just left not long before Brad called and it was just all too much to process at that moment. I needed to crash, hoping that after some rest, things would feel clearer.

MELINDA VELASQUEZ

That was not the last time I heard from Brad. In fact, during the week Liam and I were taking a break, we ended up spending time together almost every day of the week. Brad had the home field advantage, while Liam was an hour away. I kept running into Brad out at the bar where we met when Shelly and I went out, and some nights he would come over after work, which was usually around 10p.m. Looking back, I should have heeded my dad's warning about a man's intentions if he calls after 10p.m.

By this time, Brad had admitted to me that he and Shelly *did* have sex once before the night he kissed me. That felt really weird to me, so I kept my guard up about it. It was a complete red flag that he was talking kind of negatively about my own sister to me, but I always found a reason to excuse it.

One day early in the week, he invited me over to his house to hang out and made me lunch. We had a little picnic on the floor in his living room. He must have sensed my hesitation about him and Shelly because he made sure to tell me that Shelly had never been over to his house. He seemed to be doing everything he could to make me think I was special; that he *chose* me.

He was smart enough in finding out just enough about the cracks in my relationship with Liam so he would know exactly how to win me over. He told me, "That first night you walked into the bar, I turned to Jordan and said, you can have Shelly, she's *mine*."

My eyes widened, and I felt my face flush as I looked down, trying not to show how flattered I was by what he had just said. He took his hand and lifted up my chin with his finger and leaned in to kiss me. My whole body tingled. Mission accomplished. In that moment, I was his. He knew it, and so did I. That was it— the turning point where I became so lost in him that I lost sight of who I was altogether.

I kept what was going on with Brad a secret from everyone, especially Shelly. I didn't know how things would turn out with him or Liam, and I just didn't want to talk about it until I had answers. At least, that's what I told myself.

The truth was, I knew it was wrong. Wrong because of Shelly, and definitely wrong because of Liam. I wasn't being fair to him. How could I give my relationship with Liam a real chance when I was too busy being distracted by Brad's attention?

Brad and I were mostly hanging out and talking, but there was kissing, touching, and teasing as well. I was adamant about not having sex with him until I knew for certain that Liam and I were done. Looking back now, that week seemed like so much longer than a week. I was having fun with Brad, and it felt good to be wanted the way he wanted me. The chemistry between us was so intense, almost impossible to resist, and spending time with him only led to even more bad choices.

I started missing school a lot. He would get off work, go out, and then call me once the bar closed, coming over to "snuggle" with me. It would be so nice laying around with him in the morning that I would just not go to class. I was also lying to my sister, not telling her about Brad. Liam and I weren't technically broken up yet, and I was seeing Brad while I was supposed to be sorting out my feelings for Liam. I rarely went to any of my classes that week, and was getting caught up in a very bad pattern.

I talked to Liam a couple of times during the week and we made a plan to meet on a Sunday at a park halfway between where we both lived. By this point I had pretty much made up my mind that I was going to end things with Liam and continue them with Brad. Unfortunately, that decision was not made after giving myself the time and space to figure out if it was truly what I wanted.

Then, I made a fateful decision that would shape my path before I even talked to Liam and heard him out…the night before my meeting with Liam I had sex with Brad. In my mind, he had been so patient all week, never pushing me into it. It never occurred to me at that time that this might be his plan all along. He probably figured that having sex with him was the one thing that would solidify my breakup with Liam. Part of me always felt manipulated by him that final night into having sex.

I was a willing participant, but things between us had already started to progress emotionally. I felt I needed to prove my loyalty to Brad before meeting Liam the next day. I always felt that Brad knew once I crossed that line, there was no going back for me. Kissing was one thing, but sex was a whole different level of betrayal. I couldn't look Liam in the eye and try to mend our relationship without being honest about having sex with Brad. Brad knew that.

After we had sex, I felt as if I had given a part of myself away that night that I could never get back. That part of me that said, I could never do that to someone else after it had been done to me over and over. I lost respect for myself that night, and it would be a long time before I would get it back.

But what was done was done. I left Brad's house and went home to get ready to meet Liam. My stomach was in knots. I was nervous to see him, especially after what I had been doing with Brad. I was so sure that there was nothing he could say that would change my mind. It was over. We would say what we needed to say to each other, and then I would go back and be with Brad.

I drove to the park and, when I got there, Liam was already there. He looked nervous, but when our eyes met, we both smiled. I was surprised at how good it felt to see him. There was always something steady and safe about him that grounded me. In that moment, I realized it was trust. I had been in that newness phase, having fun with Brad all week and I forgot how good it felt to be with someone who knew me so well, and who I knew I could trust.

I got out of the car and slowly walked over to him. I could feel in every cell of my body the weight of what was about to happen. We hugged for a long time before sitting down on a large log that was there to be used as a bench. We held hands as we looked at each other and he said, "You look good. How are you?"

I smiled and looked down at the log. Being face-to-face with Liam again brought a wave of shame and regret crashing down on me, particularly for what I had done with Brad that week, and especially the night before. I pulled myself together and replied, with sadness in my voice, "I'm okay. It is good to see you."

He was holding an envelope, and looked down at it as he said, "I have been trying to think about what I wanted to say to you all week, and I didn't want to mess it up or forget anything, so I wrote you a letter. Before we say anything else, can you just please read it first?"

He wrote *me* a letter? That had always been my move when I felt I was losing someone. It was usually a bad idea, but from him it was a pretty grand gesture. But what kind of gesture was it? I was convinced that it was nothing but pages of horrible things about me—more of the kinds of things he'd said during our last fight, which I knew I deserved.

I took the letter from him, my hands shaking as I opened it up and started to read. Almost immediately, I realized it wasn't at all what I thought. It wasn't filled with words of anger or hurt at all.

Instead, it was this beautiful surprise, filled with all the things I ever wished he would say to me and things I never imagined he felt. He told me how much he loved and respected me, and how proud he was to be my boyfriend. He told me I was smart, beautiful, and a good person. He said things like, "I love the way your hair looks when you just get out of the shower" and all of the sweet little things he never came close to saying to me before.

As I continued to read, tears began to flow uncontrollably. I couldn't believe what I was reading. I can't remember everything that he said in the letter, but it was everything I ever wanted him to say to me—things I never knew he felt. I knew, after reading that letter, that if I hadn't had sex with Brad the night before, I would have gotten back together with Liam that day.

I felt sick to my stomach. He had done what I asked him to do, but it was too late. I went from being so happy to read his letter to feeling like I had been punched in the gut. *What did I do? How could I be so stupid?*

Liam could see that I was happy reading the letter, and then I looked up at him, crying and with desperation in my voice I said, "Why did you wait until now to say all of this to me?"

He was now crying too, "I don't know why it took me so long, I guess I took things for granted. I'm so mad at myself for not realizing that sooner. But it's true. It's how I feel."

I could barely get the words I had to say out of my mouth, but I forced out the words, "But now it's too late."

I kept replaying it in my head—if I had only waited to have sex with Brad until after I met with Liam, then maybe we could've worked things out. I had thought I was going to marry Liam, and now our relationship was ending.

His voice cracked as he said, "It's not too late! We can still fix this!"

I felt devastated and defeated, and above all I felt awful for not giving Liam, not giving *us,* a fair chance. Seeing the pain in his eyes was one of the most painful moments of my life. I said, "Who knows what the future holds, but right now I think we just need to break up."

I wasn't trying to give him false hope: I genuinely believed there was a chance we would get back together, but I just knew it couldn't be right then. As painful as it was, we were both at very different points in our lives, and it was becoming too difficult to make it work.

The distance and our conflicting schedules didn't help either. Too much had happened, and most of all, I knew that if I told him I had sex with Brad before that day, he would never be able to forgive me. Maybe, some deep part of me knew that breaking up with Liam was a choice I didn't have the strength to make on my own, so I found a way to sabotage things to make sure it happened.

We hugged one last time, cried, and kissed each other good-bye. We then got in our cars and drove our separate ways. I cried the entire drive home. I cried so hard that day that puffy pink crusty patches formed at the corners of my eyes and stayed there for another full day. I had planned to meet up with Brad once I got back home, but at that moment, I just wanted to crawl up in a ball and not talk to anyone.

When I got home, I took a little time before calling Brad. I just needed to take a beat. I had just ended the longest relationship of my life, and I felt awful. Not only was I emotionally drained, but I also wasn't physically well either. As karma would have it, my decision to have sex with Brad the night before left me with the wonderful gift of a painful UTI. Not at all surprising, considering the choices I had been making.

Brad picked me up, and we went to a bar to have a drink. I guess it was supposed to be celebratory, but I really didn't feel like celebrating. I was sad and should have just stayed home alone. Not to mention I was super uncomfortable siting on a barstool with a UTI.

MELINDA VELASQUEZ

We decided we needed to come clean and tell Shelly that we were dating now that Liam and I were officially broken up. She was mad at first, but then seemed to be okay about it because she was still sort of seeing Jordan.

In the less than four months since I turned 21, I ended things with Liam and started openly dating Brad—a decision I continued to question, but at least I was no longer keeping it a secret from the people I cared about. I felt a sense of relief that all the recent drama in my life was finally coming to an end. I had no idea that the worst was yet to come.

CHAPTER 23

Brad

Reaching the age of 21 had been something I looked forward to for years. Ever since I got my driver's license, I'd seen the words *AGE 21 IN 1996* stamped across it in big, bold red letters. To me, those words symbolized all the things I wasn't allowed to do until I reached that age. Now, here I was, 21 years old, and things like legally drinking, going into a bar, or getting into a club were finally possible. But they had quickly become part of the problems that seemed ever-present in my life.

I was preparing to finish my first semester at the university after transferring from community college, but things at school had taken a sharp turn for the worse. I'd missed so many classes and fallen so far behind that I seriously considered dropping the entire semester. The past few months had been incredibly stressful and emotionally draining. On top of all the boy drama, my student loan had arrived super late, leaving me struggling to make ends meet.

I was still working the cocktailing job and at the café, but I still wasn't making enough. Brad was working at the pizza place, and I occasionally helped out a little when I visited him and it was fun. It also helped him out too, so I started working there regularly. I made more money there than I did at the café, so I quit that job and kept the cocktailing job and the pizza place.

At first, working with Brad was fun, but within a couple of weeks after breaking up with Liam, the dynamic between us began to shift. He became more distant and closed off. I was determined to try to make it work, especially since I had ended things with Liam because of what happened with Brad. We saw less of Jordan, and we spent less time alone. Instead, we were out at the bars more often, and spending more time with Shelly.

Sometimes it was nice because I got to see my niece more. During this time, we spent a good amount of time at the bars, but during the day we would hang out and do things together. At first, it felt good, but then I started noticing little things that were concerning.

When all of us first starting to hang out—back when I was still with Liam and things with Brad and I were still a secret—Brad would always take Shelly home first and me last. That was often the only chance we had to be alone, and many times he would stay longer with me or we would go for a drive. But as time went on, I started noticing subtle looks between Shelly and Brad. Then, suddenly, he started taking *me* home first.

Things began to deteriorate when Brad started getting easily annoyed with me and made rude comments about things I said or did. It started out pretty benign by just poking fun at me, but the jokes started to get more personal. He was always careful to disguise it as a joke with little jabs about how loud I was, or comments about my body he knew I was insecure about.

It got even worse when Shelly was around. She had been doing things like that to me my whole life, and she knew even more about my insecurities. She too framed it as humor, but it wasn't funny to me. I began to feel like I was the only person in the room *not* in on the joke.

When I tried to talk to Brad about it, he just brushed it off and told me I was being too sensitive. I asked him point blank, "Should I be worried about you and my sister? I know you two were together before we were, and things just suddenly feel different. You have been really distant with me lately, and suddenly you and Shelly seem closer than before."

Brad would roll his eyes and act as if I was crazy for even suggesting it, "Shelly and I are just friends, you know that. I already told you that you have nothing to worry about with her."

At first, his assurance made me feel better, but whenever I was around them my intuition raised red flags. There were a couple of times when I was at school, and Shelly, Brad, and Kayla would hang out without me. Shelly hadn't worked since moving back in with my mom, and Brad only worked at night. Instead of listening to my intuition, I just shut it down since I didn't have any concrete proof.

Things continued to be awkward between all of us, and as the holidays approached at the end of the year, Shelly, Kayla, and I decided to take a trip to visit Dad for a couple of days. I hadn't seen Liam since the breakup, though we had spoken on the phone once or twice. After being together for over two years, we still had belongings to exchange, and it felt good that things were still amicable between us.

I told him we were coming up to visit Dad for the holidays, and he told me that he moved into a new apartment. He invited us over to check out his new place. I didn't tell Brad about it, and I didn't even tell Shelly until we were on our way up there.

Things just felt off with Brad, and I didn't want Shelly telling him. I hadn't seen Liam since the day we broke up, and things with him never really felt resolved for me. I was also feeling insecure with Brad and at that point I wondered how much Brad even cared about me now that I wasn't a prize to be won. All of those feelings combined only reinforced my concerns that I had made a mistake letting Liam go.

The conversations Liam and I had before our trip up to see Dad reminded me of how much I still cared about him. Being in such a vulnerable, uncertain place with Brad, it also made me realize how much I missed the sense of safety and trust I had with Liam.

When Shelly found out we were going to Liam's before heading to my dad's, she was pissed. She turned to me and said with a condescending tone, "Does *Brad* know we were coming here?"

I snapped back, "No. It's not a big deal. We both have each other's things to give back to each other, and he just moved into a new place and wanted us to come and check it out. He hasn't seen Kayla in a while either, so I thought we would just stop by for a visit."

Something told me not to be entirely honest with her. For all I knew, Brad might be saying things to her, turning her against me the same way he had turned me against her in the beginning. I was being cautious and didn't want Brad to find out from her that I saw Liam during our visit.

When we arrived at Liam's and knocked on the door I was overwhelmed with happiness when I saw his face. His apartment was so nice. It was a far cry from the tiny studio he lived in before I left. He showed us around while Kayla bounced around on the couches, and I felt that familiar sense of calm wash over me in Liam's presence. I missed that feeling, and I took it for granted when I had it.

He took us on a quick tour, and it felt so strange seeing familiar things from his old studio in this new place I had never been. He still had the comforter set I bought for him for Christmas when he was living in his studio. I smiled when I saw it, but I felt sad at the same time. I began looking around and thinking about all the plans I had for our life together and I felt such a strong sense of regret. In that moment I just wanted to come back and live there with him.

Everything in my life had just gotten so bad since that first night I kissed Brad and then finally broke up with Liam. I had been feeling so lost lately, and being in Liam's presence just felt like home. We had been through so much together, and suddenly, it all hit me hard.

Liam must have seen it in the look on my face because he reached over to touch my arm, as if to snap me out of it and said, "Are you okay?"

My eyes had started to well up with tears. Then I got caught up in my feelings and said something I never should have said. I was filled with so many emotions being there with Liam in that safe place, and feeling so insecure with Brad, but the words just flowed out, "This is so nice, I wish I could just move back and live here with you."

A mix of happiness and shock spread across his face, "Really? You would want to do that?"

I was starting to pull myself back to reality, but still not considering his feelings and the mixed signals I was giving, "I don't know, I mean this is what I always wanted for us. To be living together. It's only an hour to commute and it would only be when I had classes. It's not like it is impossible. Is that crazy?"

He looked at me with a look of hope, but still keeping his guard up, "No, it's not crazy. But are you sure that is what you want to do?"

Suddenly, I looked around and realized Shelly wasn't in the living room and Kayla wasn't there either. I looked at Liam concerned and asked, "Where did they go?"

Liam in a reassuring tone said, "They just went in the other room to use the phone."

I figured they just went to call my dad to check in to let him know we were in town, but when I opened the door and saw Shelly with the phone in her hand it looked like she just got caught committing a crime. Not understanding what was going on I asked, "Who are you talking to?"

She held the phone out to hand to me and said, "It's Brad."

You could have knocked me over with a feather in that moment. My stomach jumped into my throat and my inner voice slowly leaked out the word, *SHIT*... Then my brain launched into rapid-fire question mode. *How much of what I said to Liam did she hear? What did she tell Brad? Why the hell would she call him?*

I knew that technically she was with Brad first and I didn't have the right to feel betrayed, but he chose to be with me, and she was with Jordan when it all happened. Now, it felt like she was inserting herself not only into my relationship with Brad but also with Liam. That moment was a turning point in how I felt about my sister. I knew in that moment I could no longer trust her.

As I held the phone to my ear, my cheeks felt hot, not knowing what to expect on the other end of the line, "Hello?" I said, my voice coming out shaky and uncertain.

His voice was calm, but filled with contempt, "So...you're staying at Liam's house?"

Suddenly, I forgot about all the things I had said to Liam and desperately tried to make Brad believe that my intentions were not to cheat on him with Liam, "No! Liam and I talked and we both had some each other's things to give back. I knew I would be coming up to see my dad so I told him we would come by to see his new place and give back each other's things. We are staying at my dad's house."

I could hear the hurt and anger in his voice, "So that was your first stop, and you didn't even tell me? I had to hear it from Shelly."

I felt awful and realized what a huge mistake all of this was, "I'm so sorry. I was going to tell you when we got back. It is not a big deal, I promise." I neglected to mention all that I just said to Liam in the other room. Hearing the hurt in Brad's voice made me realize he did care about me. I just created another big mess and now I had no idea what was going to happen next.

I don't know how much of that Liam heard, but he was sweet and gave me a hug good-bye as we left to go to my dad's house. He looked me in the eyes and said, "Call me later." I shook my head yes as I turned to leave. A few minutes before that I was so happy being there with Liam, but now I was more confused than ever.

I knew I would always have love for Liam, but at that moment, Brad was the one I wanted. At least, Brad was the one I wanted to want me. Hearing his voice on the phone pulled me right back to focusing on him. The fact that he had been pulling away from me only made me want him more. Once again, Liam was pushed to the side without even realizing what my indecision might be doing to him.

Instead, I fell right back into my pattern. I was now desperately focused on Brad. I tried to call him while we were at my dad's but never got a hold of him. I couldn't wait to get back to talk to him in person to work it all out, but that didn't happen.

When I finally saw Brad, he seemed cold and indifferent. I

apologized again, but it was too late; the damage was done. He said, "We're done. Maybe it's for the best. You clearly have some things you need to sort out about Liam. You went straight from a long-term serious relationship with him into a relationship with me without a break. Maybe that was a mistake."

I was crushed. "No! I want to be with you! I was just feeling like you weren't into me anymore, and I still think there is something going on with my sister…even more now after she called you from Liam's."

His eyes flashed with anger, "She was just being a good friend by telling me what was going on, and I told you we are *just* friends!"

He might have been done with me, but I was not done with him. I was determined to prove to him that he was the one I wanted to be with, not Liam. Since we still worked together, I saw him quite a bit. He had become so cold toward me. He would only talk to me when he had to, and he started rushing out of work before I could leave, eager to get down to the bars before I did.

When I wasn't working my cocktailing job, I did everything I could do to put myself in Brad's path. I still talked to Liam sometimes, but my focus wasn't on him. When Brad wasn't at the bars I would drive by and, sure enough, his truck would be parked at my mom's house where Shelly lived, often late into the night.

Things between Shelly and I were not good, and I knew they were having sex. I felt like I couldn't even go to my mom's house anymore because Shelly was always there. When I did visit, Brad would sometimes show up, and being with the both of them became unbearable for me. Spending time with my niece was the only reason I continued to go there.

THE WEIGHT OF SILENCE

This continued through the rest of the year, with them insisting they were just friends. I had to work my cocktailing job on New Year's Eve, and after the bar closed, I went to an after-party. That's when I found out that Shelly and Brad had been together all night, and it wasn't just as friends. I was devastated and furious.

The next day, I went to brunch with Laura. She was now married and pregnant with her first child, and getting close to her due date. I enjoyed our time together. I was putting my mouth on her belly talking to the baby. I wanted to make sure she would know my voice when she was born. We laughed and talked through breakfast, and I felt better after spending time with her. I always did.

After brunch, I headed home to get ready for my shift at the pizza place. I was on a mission to win Brad back and hoped that working together all night would give us a chance to talk. I was running late to work and stupidly was so focused on getting Brad's attention that night that I was rushing and putting my make-up on while driving.

I approached the stop sign right across the street from the pizza place. It was a one-way stop that crossed a street that led right into a freeway on-ramp. The people getting on the freeway had the right of way. There was a line of cars as I pulled up to the stop sign and as I looked in my rearview mirror to put on my lipstick on, I lightly tapped the car in front of me.

"Shit!" I yelled. The driver in front of me signaled to pull over, and I was relieved when I saw that there didn't seem to be any damage to their car. Distracted again, I tried to see where the driver of the car would pull in to the parking lot at my work. Visibility was compromised because it had been raining pretty hard all day. I was already late, and now I would have to face the embarrassment of telling Brad I'd hit someone. He would surely have something to say that would add to how stupid I already felt.

I pulled up to the stop sign and made a quick look in both directions before pulling out toward the pizza place parking lot. I barely reached the middle of the intersection when suddenly I collided with a large sedan going upwards of 45 miles per hour as it was accelerating on the approach to the freeway on-ramp.

It was the first day of 1997, and I had just gotten into my first major car accident. The Universe was screaming at me to change course and shift my focus, but I just kept heading down the same toxic path. I was so desperate to have Brad want me in the way he did when we first met that I was causing destruction all around me—first with Liam, then school, and now this.

The car accident happened in a matter of seconds, but time seemed to slow down as the front of my compact car slammed into the sedan, easily twice the size of my car. My car spun, nearly missing a second collision with the sedan. I heard the horrible sound of crunching metal, along with the squealing of the tires as they tried to grip the wet ground on that rainy day.

The centrifugal force thrust my body back into my seat as my car spun and my seatbelt dug into my skin. My hair flew in front of my face, and a strange smell filled the air as my windshield shattered, sending glass flying around me before the car finally came to a stop.

As soon as my car stopped, I heard a woman scream and a child cry. Terrified and disoriented, I tried to figure out what had just happened. In the moments during the crash when time slowed down, I experienced the phenomenon of my life flashing before my eyes. I saw my family, and my life growing up before things got bad and my family fell apart.

As soon as I comprehended what was happening, the screams from the other car echoed in my mind, and I was worried if everyone was okay. The next thought in my head was: *My dad is going to kill me.*

THE WEIGHT OF SILENCE

I just knew my dad would be disappointed. That was always one of my first thoughts when I made questionable decisions—it stemmed back to my constant need for his approval. And with all the bad decisions I had been making lately, wrecking my car was pretty high on the list of fuck ups.

Once I began to orient myself again, I looked up to see Brad running towards my car with a terrified look on his face. When he reached my car, he anxiously said, "Are you okay? Can you move?"

I opened my mouth to speak, only to realize there was glass from my windshield in it. I spat it out, tried to assess my injuries, and then I just started to cry. Not long after, I heard sirens. The police and a couple ambulances arrived quickly. My car was inoperable, and there was a urgent effort to get me out of the car as quickly and safely as possible.

I asked if the person in the other car was okay, and that is when someone told me that it was a pregnant woman driving with her young child in the car. My heart sank. I got even more upset, and that was when I realized how much pain I was in. They reassured me that she was doing okay but was being taken to the hospital to be checked out, just to be safe. I was so relieved.

They loaded me up on a gurney and into an ambulance to take me to the hospital. I was terrified—I had never been in an ambulance before. When we arrived at the hospital emergency room, they assessed me and determined I didn't have any life-threatening injuries, but still I needed x-rays. So, they rolled me into a hallway and left me there to wait until they could get to me.

I'm not sure how long I lay there by myself, but it felt like an eternity. I was cold, scared and had never felt so alone in my life. I figured Brad would have to call my family to tell them what happened, and eventually my mom showed up.

I finally got my x-ray, and while nothing was broken, I had bruised ribs, a bruised sternum and I was extremely sore and stiff. They didn't mention whiplash, but my neck was never the same after that accident.

My mom took me back to her house since I could barely move with the pain in my ribs and sternum. It hurt so bad to laugh or cough, or even speak or breathe deeply. When we got to my mom's house, my sister told me that Brad had called to check if I was okay and said he had my purse, which he would bring by after work.

Even after all that had just happened, I was still focused on him. I got my hopes up that maybe him witnessing the accident from the pizza place would wake him up and make him realize he wanted to get back together.

Just then, I looked up to see Dad walk in to Mom's living room and he said, "I brought someone with me who was really worried about you." Right behind him was Liam. I guess my dad had called to tell him about the accident, and they sat together waiting to hear if I was okay. Liam asked my dad if he could drive down with him to see me.

It had been pouring rain all day and night, and Liam and my dad made the hour-long trip down to make sure I was okay. It was such a sweet gesture, and a sign of just how much he cared about me. But all I could think about in that moment was that if Brad came over and Liam was there, it would ruin everything.

I don't remember exactly what I said to Liam, but the energy I gave off was anything but warm and welcoming. In fact, I made it painfully clear that I didn't want him there, and he picked up on it pretty quickly. That is another moment I will regret forever.

Liam didn't deserve that. I just gave him hope about us before Christmas, and now I was giving him a completely different vibe. It was not my finest moment. I was just too focused on getting Brad back to see the damage I was doing to Liam.

After the accident, I quit my cocktailing job. I had been ready to leave for a while, and the accident seemed like a good time to make a clean break. I stayed at my mom's as long as I could stand it, but things between Shelly and me were still tense. As soon as I was able, I went back to my apartment. Just five days after my car accident, Laura gave birth to a beautiful baby girl. My car was totaled in the accident, and I was still trying to get back with Brad, so I asked him for a ride to the hospital.

In true Melinda form, I wrote Brad a poem and a letter and I gave it to him. He and my sister still hadn't admitted to me that they were having sex, but I knew. It had been confirmed by reliable sources the night before my accident. Still, I convinced myself that what *we* had was different than whatever was going on with him and Shelly. I told myself that he turned to her to hurt me after I had hurt him with Liam.

Brad picked me up from the hospital after it looked like Laura was going to be in labor for quite some time. He said, "I read your poem and your letter. Thank you." He said in a sincere tone and then he paused before saying, "Do you have to go home right now?"

A sudden rush of hope washed over me, as I said, "No, I just need to check in with Laura in a bit to see how it is going."

"You want to go for a drive with me?" he asked, with a confidence that made it seem like he was granting my greatest wish in that moment.

I answered quietly, still not trying to get my hopes up too much, "Yes."

MELINDA VELASQUEZ

He took me for a drive up to the spot in the mountains where we used to go when we first got together. He put on one of his favorite country singers, someone I had come to love as well, and who we would always listen to together. My heart fluttered—I could sense something had shifted in his energy.

He parked the truck, turned off the engine, and faced me. Suddenly, I was right back in that truck with him that first night in front of Jordan's house. Butterflies in my stomach, feeling nervous and excited about what was about to happen. I asked in hopeful anticipation that I would hear the answer I wanted, "What are we doing here?"

He turned toward me, just like he had that first night, and said, "I just thought it was a good idea to have some time alone together. I don't want things to be weird between us anymore. I miss being with you, but I just don't know if, after all that has happened, we can go back to the way it was."

I felt my face turn red as I tried to fight back the tears, but I couldn't contain them. He scooted closer to me and said, "Don't cry. There's no crying in baseball." It was a line from the movie, *A League of Their Own* he liked to quote to break the tension. It made me laugh a little.

Then he looked at me and grabbed my chin and kissed me. Just like that first night, the intense chemistry between us was still there. We ended up having sex that night, but nothing between us was solved, leaving me feeling more confused and more insecure than ever.

We weren't back together, but we weren't apart either. Somehow, he convinced me that keeping it between us would relieve some of the pressure on us. I would soon realize this was code for, if no one knows we are still together then I can still be with you and do whatever I want with whomever else I want.

THE WEIGHT OF SILENCE

The last year of my life was incredibly stressful. I had moved out on my own and struggled to pay my bills while managing a full college load. Since transferring to the University, my grades had dropped, and I was at risk of having to repeat an entire semester of classes. I had been back in my hometown for less than a year, and it felt like I was sucked back into the cycle of chaos that I felt when I was 12 years old.

But I wasn't that 12-year-old girl anymore; I was a 21-year-old adult woman. In record time, my life went from calm and safe while living with my dad to a drama-filled mess. I didn't realize that I had transferred my need for love and acceptance from my dad to Brad. I was so distracted by Brad, that I couldn't see just how bad things had become.

After the car accident, I was down to just one job working at the pizza place. While I made decent money there, it wasn't enough. I had to borrow money two months in a row to pay all my bills, and that was all it took. I hated asking people for help, especially my family. I had always figured out a way to take care of myself, so I did it again. I needed to find something more affordable.

As luck would have it, Jenny's mom had a vacant room in her home and was willing to rent to me. The rent was far less than what I was paying at my apartment, so I jumped at the chance. It was a very small room, but I didn't need much and I needed to make it work.

By this time, Brad and I were still in a weird place. We weren't together, but we continued to spend time together and have sex, usually when it worked for him. I knew that living at the new place I wouldn't have the same kind of privacy with my personal life that I enjoyed living in my apartment. It had been easy for me to hide what was or wasn't happening with Brad from close friends and family when I was living in my apartment.

MELINDA VELASQUEZ

I knew what we were wasn't good for me, at all, but I just couldn't seem to walk away from him. The small amount of self-esteem I had managed to rebuild after high school was being chipped away with each day I remained involved with him. I knew my family and my closest friends like Laura and Leisa, knew how toxic Brad was for me, so I started keeping my time with him secret from everyone. I hoped that moving to a new place would bring a fresh start, but all it brought was more drama and an avalanche of pain.

After I had been living at Jenny's mom's house for a couple of months, I noticed that Shelly started spending a lot of time with her. Shelly even began working for her at her home business, and they quickly became inseparable. Now Shelly was always at the house where I was living, and after work, she would go hang out with everyone at the bar. During this period, Brad got really good at playing Shelly and me against each other, and we both fell for it. He found ways to manipulate the situation so it best suited him.

Now that my living situation had changed, keeping what he was doing with me a secret seemed to serve him well. I no longer had my own apartment with ample privacy, and he knew he could be hung-over and hang out all day with my sister when my mom and Charlie were at work.

He had a habit of having one or more women on the side, always under the guise that they were just hanging out as friends. It was even better if the girl had a boyfriend because then he could make it look even more like he was just her friend. It may have started out that way, but always progressed to a sexual relationship.

He did it with me, and I fell for it. I didn't know much of this for sure at the time, but I always knew he wasn't honest with me. Regardless of what I knew deep down, he still had this weird hold on me. Each time I thought I was ready to move on, it was like he had radar on my emotions. He would suddenly pop up, saying and doing all the right things, and I would be back under his spell again.

Brad became my addiction. When it came to him, I was reduced to a desperate pile of pathetic mush. He was a master manipulator, and I fell for his game every time. Each time I did, I lost more and more of my self-respect and sank deeper into the belief that I was not good enough. It was a really demoralizing and painful time in my life, and though I tried so hard to get away from him, he was just always there.

During this period, I went through a particularly desperate phase. I met Brad just a couple of months after I turned 21, and by the time I turned 22 my life had become a tragic and toxic mess. I often refer to age 22 as my "dumbest age". I was trapped in this cycle with Brad, spending every night wondering who he would go home with—my sister or me. I drank a lot during this time, sometimes to numb the pain, but mostly because I knew that if I was drunk, he would feel like he had to take care of me.

He didn't want to be my boyfriend in public, yet he also didn't want me to be with anyone else either. He had this covert way of saying things to me that were a way of putting me down and making me feel small. He got really good at disguising it in the form of a joke.

Anytime I was getting positive attention from people or making people laugh, he found a way to shut it down. He would usually say something like, "You're being too loud. You are making a fool of yourself." If I was making people laugh, he would cut me down, jokingly of course and when people responded poorly to it he would just say, "What? It was a joke!"

Sometimes, he'd even find ways to compare me to my sister in our conversations. I remember one time he pointed out that the hair on my legs seemed to grow back faster after shaving than it did on hers. I knew this about my sister, she had told me of the multitude of ways her body changed after she had given birth to my niece. But, hearing it from him like that hit differently.

I started imagining them sitting around, talking about how my sister was prettier, sexier, and just overall better than me. It was mostly little comparisons, but always framed in a way that highlighted me as the lesser one. It was just one of the ways he found to gaslight me, making me question my worth even more than I already did.

I knew it felt bad when he did these things, but he was really good at maintaining the balance of breaking me down and building me back up. By that point, I was so broken down that I couldn't even recognize what was happening. It was a confusing, disorienting experience that wreaked havoc on my emotional state.

My sister and Brad had both become regular fixtures at Jenny's mom's house, where I was living, and at the bar where we all hung out. Even if I tried to avoid them by not going to the bar, the whole gang would often show up at the house after the bar closed for the after party.

Brad was still stringing me along, and he was having sex with my sister, sometimes under the roof of the home where I was now living while I was there! Both of them were lying to me about it, and all of the people who were supposed to be my friends knew about it, yet no one told me. Instead, I felt like they had all turned against me.

Jenny and her mom seemed to turn cold toward me during that time, Brad had suddenly become everyone's buddy, and my sister seemed to have taken over *my* life. I became depressed and spent a lot of time hold up in my room, only coming out to get ready for work. I was no longer fun to be around, so I felt discarded by people who were supposed to be my friends, and even by my own family. I sank right back into victim mode, settled in, and got comfortable.

The life I was living then was not a healthy life, but I didn't know how to pull myself out of it. I was so deeply entrenched in this toxic, dysfunctional world because it mirrored what I had come to know as normal. People were drinking, partying, and staying up all night all weekend long, and sometimes during the week. There was partner swapping, bringing the whole bar home after closing, and then waking up and going to work the next day like it was no big deal.

I slipped back into feeling abandoned, alone, and isolated. I had good friends like Laura and Leisa I could reach out to, but I was too afraid of what they would think of me. I was drowning in shame. I found myself at the lowest point I had been since my eighth-grade nightmare, and then came the final blow to knock me even deeper into my destructive spiral of shame…a call from Liam.

It was well after midnight during the week, which only added to my surprise when I heard his voice on the other end of the line. At first, I was happy to hear his voice, but I quickly realized he had been drinking. He almost never drank during the workweek when we were together, especially not to the extent that I could hear in his voice that night. Then it got worse. His tone was laced with pain and anger, one I will never forget.

"Do *you* have any idea how much *you* hurt me? I wouldn't wish what you did to me on my worst enemy."

He paused, and I thought I heard him crying. I asked, with great concern, "Liam, are you okay? What is going on?" Then I remembered that the last time I saw him was the night of the car accident, and how I had acted toward him came screaming back to my mind. It had been months since we'd spoken, so it was a shock to hear from him.

"You ruined my life!" he yelled, his voice filled with agony.

I felt my face and chest grow hot, my stomach tightening as I started to cry, "Liam, I'm so sorry. I feel like a horrible person for what happened with us. I never meant to hurt you."

"Well, you did. More than anyone ever has. FUCK! Why did I even call you?" He said this almost as an aside to himself, but loud enough for me to hear it. "Why can't I just forget about you and move on? Fuck this!" Then before I could say anything else, he hung up on me.

I was dumfounded. This was not the Liam I knew. I was genuinely shocked that our breakup had this much of an impact on him. I had never seen him express this kind of emotion when we were together. In fact, I always felt like he tried to maintain control or keep me, and his emotions at arm's length…except when he was drinking.

Then it all came rushing back to me—the times we had our biggest fights were always when he'd had too much to drink. That was also when he would be the most amorous with me and when he would exhibit deep emotion. Soon after the call, I learned he'd started drinking quite a bit since we broke up and had gotten a third DUI. He already had the two from college, and once you get a third, the penalties are far more severe.

Even though he had the two DUIs when I met him, I always saw him as so responsible. He would drink and have fun on the weekends but never during the week. He was always so focused on his goals—much more than he ever seemed to focus on me. Even though we had been together for over two years, I could have never imagined our break up would have had such an impact on him. I already felt bad, but now I felt monumentally worse.

Hearing the words from his mouth that I was the cause of his pain was like being hit by an emotional wrecking ball. If I had never gotten into that truck with Brad, so much would be so different. I started believing that everything that had happened since I moved back home was my fault. As a result, I felt I deserved all the bad karma that came along with it.

During this time, I was also diagnosed with hyperthyroidism, an overactive thyroid, and I was scheduled to have surgery to remove most of it just over a month after my 22nd birthday. I would be in the hospital for a few days and then I would need a place to recover. I planned to stay with my mom during that time. Shelly still lived there, but she was hardly ever home since she was always at hanging out where I was living.

I was miserable living at Jenny's mom's house, and it was pretty clear no one wanted me there either. I planned to find a new place to live after my surgery, but things got so bad that I left early to stay with my mom. One night, I was alone at my mom's house, feeling sorry for myself, so I went to lay down in her bed and watch television, like I used to when I was a little girl. But I never turned on the TV. Instead, I just sat there and cried.

I was replaying everything in my mind— feeling guilty about Liam, betrayed by Brad, and a mix of guilt and betrayal when I thought of Shelly. Even though by now I had received my karma in spades, I still couldn't let myself off the hook for starting anything with Brad in the first place. I had clearly underestimated the depth of Shelly's feelings for him.

I was at an all-time low. Through my tears, I looked up and focused on a bunch of pill bottles on my mom's nightstand—some were her prescriptions, others just pain relievers. In that moment, I considered reaching over and swallowing a bunch of pills, and ending all of my pain.

MELINDA VELASQUEZ

This was the second time in my life I'd thought about ending my life. The first time was in eighth grade when I was being bullied. I never thought I would feel that way again, but there I was. I'm grateful that both times, I was not so far down the pit of shame, depression, self-loathing, and emotional pain that I couldn't stop myself.

Instead, my thoughts in both situations were more about how bad *they* would all feel if I just wasn't here anymore. I wanted to show them. But then I wondered, would they even care? I was so hurt and angry, and I just wanted the pain to stop. Maybe then, everything would get better. But once again, I thought of all the people I loved—how devastated they would be if I took my own life—and I couldn't bear to put them through that pain.

I also thought about Liam and our last phone conversation. I didn't want to inflict any more pain on him than I clearly already had. After the drunken phone call and everything he said to me, there was a good chance me taking my life and having those be the last words he said to me would haunt him forever. I didn't want that for him.

I was stuck in this needy, depressed, dark hole, and all I wanted was to find my way out. Thankfully, I was not completely devoid of hope. I had a moment of clarity where I realized that I needed to regain some control over my life.

After recovering from surgery, I decided I needed to make a clean break from Brad, so I quit working at the pizza place and got a job at a retail store in a nearby mall. I also found a place to live with a roommate in the next city over from my hometown. My new home and job were only about seven miles away from all the drama that had consumed my life, but that little bit of distance was exactly what I needed.

It had been about a year since that fateful night when I first met Brad, and this was the first time I had physically distanced myself from him. I was settled in my new place, working a new job I really enjoyed and had become fast friends with my new boss, who was close to my age. Most importantly, I was steering clear of Brad, Shelly, and all the drama that came with them.

For the first time in a long time, I started to enjoy my life again. I wish I could say that I was done with Brad and barely thought about him, but that was not the case. The time and space helped, but he still had a hold on me, and for some reason I wasn't ready to let him go.

The pattern continued with us. Just when I was starting to feel a twinge of happiness and independence, he would show up again. He always had a way of coming clean about something to earn my trust again. This time, he was finally honest with me about him continuing to have sex with Shelly. Not only did he admit to having sex with her, but he had also gotten her pregnant.

The pregnancy didn't result in a birth, but he wanted to make sure I heard it from him first. You'd think that would have been enough to deter me, but it didn't. I guess finally knowing the truth helped me believe maybe he *had* changed. I figured he must love me—why else would he keep coming back to me? So, I fell for it…again, and eventually I took him back.

Things were good at first. But within a month or so, he fell right back into his pattern. He got a job at the restaurant down the street from my house, and he started spending more time at my house. He worked nights and would stay after to drink with the rest of the staff, then come crash at my house. It was all very convenient for him.

MELINDA VELASQUEZ

My house was just a straight shot about a mile down the road from his work. It was a back road that was not well-traveled at night, so he could drive home drunk without worrying about being pulled over. I would leave for work in the morning, and he would still be sleeping in my bed. When I got back, he would have made himself a bed in the middle of the living room floor, where he sat, watched television, and talked on the phone all day.

I didn't have a television in my room, so he just made himself comfortable in the common space. And if that wasn't an arrogant enough move, most days I came home, he would be laughing and flirting on the phone with his "friend" from work, who also happened to be a female. He would spend hours on the phone with her, but of course, they were "just friends".

Eventually my roommate had enough and she asked me to move out. At the beginning of 1998, I moved *again,* this time to a town west of where I grew up. It was about a 15-20 minute drive from the University I was attending in my hometown. Brad and I broke up again, and once again I tried to make a clean start without him.

My new place was a one-bedroom duplex that my roommate had converted into a two-bedroom. She made the living room into her bedroom, While I took the original bedroom. We shared a single bathroom and a kitchen, where there was a small table up against the wall with two chairs. There was also a large outdoor deck, where we spent a lot of time. It was a short walk from the cute downtown area and felt like yet another chance at a fresh start.

Things were going well. I got promoted to assistant manager at my retail job and transferred to a bigger store in a nearby city. I was also finally doing better in school again. My roommate was also attending the University, so it was nice to have someone who had a similar focus.

I hadn't been hanging around the usual bars as much, and the distance seemed to help, as the weirdness between Jenny and me had subsided. My sister also seemed to be staying away from Brad as well. Unfortunately, it wasn't long before Brad wormed his way back into *my* life again.

This time, I was more skeptical of his intentions, and I kept it very quiet. Despite everything that had happened between us, I just kept hoping that he could be that man I wanted him to be. He would pretend to be that guy when he wanted me back, but that guy didn't hang around for too long after that.

Part of me also thought, I'd suffered so much with him, if he *had* truly changed, why should another woman benefit from it? It started out really good, which it always did, and once again I thought maybe he really had changed.

He seemed more attentive. We weren't going to the bars all the time like we used to, and we were spending quality time together. He even cooked for me pretty regularly. But like always, the honeymoon period came to an end.

He wasn't working at the restaurant near my old house anymore, so he started working a bar he used to go to a lot when we first met. He was a good friend of the main bartender there. She was older than him, by at least 25-30 years, and I never felt threatened by their friendship. In fact, I became friends with her too. She was always very sweet and protective of me whenever I would come into her bar.

I was still working full-time and going to school full-time, so I was often home studying or writing papers while he was at the bar. Since meeting him, I had neglected school so much. I had gone from being on the President's List at my community college to being close to academic probation at the University. I had finally gotten back to a good place in school, and didn't want to mess that up.

Brad once again started closing down the bar, whether he was working or not, and would eventually end up back at my house, usually drunk. One night, I was in bed and I could've sworn that I heard his truck pull up in the driveway. I waited for him to come in, but he never came in, and I could still hear the truck running.

I walked out to check on him and found the truck still running, parked in my spot. I opened up the driver's side door and initially thought he was passed out. He was so drunk that his eyes were mostly closed, and he was weaving back and forth in his seat. I'm sure if he tried to walk at that moment, he would have fallen down. He had just driven 20 minutes from the bar to my house in that condition.

As I looked closer, I noticed he was also drooling. He chewed Copenhagen, which I hated. He had a routine of putting in a fresh dip before getting in the car to drive home from the bar, partly to mask the smell of the alcohol on his breath, but it never did. It just became a disgusting mix of both smells. The smell of Copenhagen is unmistakable to me, and that smell became an unwelcome trigger to my central nervous system.

He had obviously put a fresh dip in his lip that night, but before he could get out of the truck, he started passing out, drooling chew in his lap. He used to spit in an empty soda bottle, which was in his hand, but clearly, he wasn't able to manage that in his condition. I still don't know how he made it to my house that night without killing himself or someone else.

The caretaker in me kicked right in, and I reached in to help him, but he just sneered and slurred angrily, "I'm fine! I got it!"

THE WEIGHT OF SILENCE

At that point, I was pissed and didn't want my roommate to wake up and decide that she didn't want to deal with him anymore either and kick me out. I reached in, turned off the truck and grabbed his keys so he didn't try to drive again.

I knew he drank a lot, but we were in our early 20s, and I had grown accustomed to hanging out in bars and being around a lot of people who drank heavily. Many of these people were like my mom; they drank a lot but still managed to function in their lives. This, however, felt different.

Growing up in a family of addicts, witnessing this behavior set off alarm bells, but it also had a way of desensitizing me at the same time. I knew his drinking was problematic, but dealing with it had become something I was used to avoiding and not talking about.

There were plenty of red flags regarding his alcohol use, but I always found ways to excuse them. Given that my mom and sister were using meth, their issues with alcohol seemed less pronounced. But what I witnessed that night was something I couldn't ignore. It stuck with me, but I had no idea what to do about it.

After that night, things with Brad and I continued downhill from there. Seeing him drunk and drooling in my driveway changed things for me. It was the first time I could not ignore that he was an addict. I had always been waiting for him to be the man I wanted him to be, but that moment made it glaringly obvious that would never happen.

I felt myself slipping back into that familiar unhappy pattern with him. Once again, he started acting indifferent towards me while he focused on another woman. Just like before, I would come home from work or school to find him still lying around in MY bed, in a room I paid the rent on, talking to a girl on the phone. Then, conveniently, once I was home, he had to take a shower and get ready to go work at the bar, or be anywhere else but with me.

He tried to convince me once again that it was completely innocent, and became defensive and mean when I pushed back. "She is my brother's wife's sister. Don't be stupid, we are like sort of related. And besides, she's a big girl." He tried to say that because she was overweight, in his opinion, it made it even more irrational that I thought anything was going on between them. "Nothing would ever happen between us. We are just good friends. You're being too sensitive and insecure."

This time, I wasn't buying it. I was fed up with him freeloading at my house only to come home to find him hung-over and laying in my bed, talking to another girl. The tension between us mounted, and he started spending less time at my house. Eventually, we decided to take some time apart, which was the beginning of the end for us for real this time.

After about a week apart, I was surprised by how happy and relieved I felt. I didn't have to worry about what he was doing or who he was with, or who else he might be having sex with when I wasn't around. Something felt different this time; I was ready to be done trying to be his girlfriend.

By late October 1998, we decided to fully end things between us. Even though I knew it was the right decision, it was still hard. Not hard in the way it had been before, but just a difficult time. I wasn't pining for him anymore the way I would every other time. It had been two years of ups and downs, gaslighting, and manipulation. He was so good at finding a way to suck me back in, and I would always focus on the good times and forget that the bad far outweighed the good.

It was around this time that I found out some news about Liam. He had been dating a woman for a while, and through the friend grapevine, I heard some not-so-positive things about her. I learned that he was going to marry her, and suddenly, the reality that Liam and I would never find our way back together hit me hard.

I felt sick to my stomach and, in a panic, made a huge mistake by calling him. I somehow thought it was a good idea to speak negatively about the woman he was planning to marry and even questioned his decision to marry her. Who the hell did I think I was?

As if I hadn't made enough mistakes with Liam, this time I went way too far. He sounded hurt, angry, and so done with me. After all he had been through with me, the drinking, the DUI—and now it seemed like he was finally in a good place and I just come along and shit all over it. I tried to apologize, but I couldn't undo what I had done. After that day, Liam never spoke to me again, and I can't blame him.

Not long after Brad and I broke up for the last time, I started a new job at a clothing store in my hometown. Even though I knew ending things with Brad was the right decision, I was still in a funk, grappling with all my feelings surrounding the situation. I felt raw and unsure of myself.

Emotionally abusive relationships are tricky. There are no visible scars, no moments of terrifying violence where you fear for your life. My experience with emotional abuse was something I didn't even realize I had endured until I was finally free of the person doing it. And the really confusing part was that, despite knowing I was happier and far better off without him, he still had this strange hold on me.

I was primed for this kind of abuse, growing up in a family that struggled with addiction. All the small things said or done to me—or to each other—systematically chipped away at my self-esteem and sense of self-worth. It set me up to seek out the familiarity of dysfunction without even realizing it.

MELINDA VELASQUEZ

I was grateful that this time, after Brad and I broke up, he was not always in my face. He stopped coming to the bar and wasn't everywhere I went. Getting him out of my system was going to be a process, but the difference now was that I really wanted to be free of the hold he had on me. I was ready to reclaim my life and stop living in the shadows of shame and self-loathing. I couldn't have imagined that another loss in my life would provide a much-needed salve for my wounded soul.

Around Thanksgiving of 1998, I got the call from my dad that my grandma passed away. She'd suffered a sudden stroke, which caused her to fall, and she never recovered. My dad thought I wouldn't want to make the trip to Oregon for the funeral, but I felt strongly that I needed to go.

I was grateful to be there, to feel connected to family again, and to be there for my dad. Watching him mourn the loss of his mother was profound, bringing out a vulnerable side of him I had rarely ever seen. My grandma had lived a long life, but it didn't matter; in that moment he was just a little boy who had lost his mom. I was so grateful I could be there to support him through that and to understand the impact that had on him.

My dad always tried to put on a brave face, but there were multiple times that day, I caught his eye, and I could tell he was glad I was there. I saw the pride in his eyes as he introduced me to people after the service.

At the end of the day, he gave me a big hug and let me know how much he appreciated having me there as well. I was once again so grateful that I had chosen to live with him those few years. That time together created a bond we didn't have before that.

Another beautiful surprise that day was seeing a picture of my grandma that I had never seen before. My grandparents on my dad's side were the only grandparents I had ever known, but I always thought of them as older. My grandma was not able to go down to the creek and play with me when I was little the way my mom did with my niece. There was so much about my grandparents and their life together that I didn't fully understand or appreciate until I grew older.

When I saw this picture of my grandma, I suddenly felt connected to my family in a way I never had before. I always knew I had my grandmother's natural curls, but seeing this picture of her, I could clearly see myself in her face. As I looked closer, I realized I could see my sister too.

It is hard to describe how I felt in that moment. Staring at the picture and seeing myself reflected back, I felt my existence and my connection to my family validated in a way I had never experienced. I think it helped me find a piece of myself that I had been missing for a long time. I asked my grandpa for a copy of the picture, and he gave it to me. It quickly became one of my most prized possessions.

That short time with my family brought some much-needed healing. Afterwards, I felt like I got a little part of myself back as well and continued to move further away from Brad.

After I returned home some time passed, and Brad and I eventually talked. He finally confessed everything to me about continuously cheating on me with my sister, but also a lot of other people too, including the older bartender friend of ours. After more than two years of being gaslighted into thinking I was irrational and making me feel like I was this crazy jealous person, I finally knew the truth.

I felt so conflicted once I knew everything. I had long sought the truth, but discovering that it was far worse than I imagined left me feeling both disgusted and foolish. I couldn't believe I had allowed him to control me and lead me on for so long, especially when, deep down, I already knew the truth. I had chosen to believe his lies over trusting my own intuition.

The final confirmation that my intuition had been right all along came when I found out one last piece of information: the last woman he talked to for hours while lying around in *my* bed all day—his brother's wife's sister—was now in a relationship with him, and he had moved in with her.

After Brad moved in with her, he kept calling me, inviting me over to *their* house to have sex. It was a sort of karma that I admit felt a little like vindication. After him asking me many times I finally gave in once and did it. But that day, I realized the intense chemistry I once felt with him was gone.

That was the moment I knew the hold he had over me was no longer there. He also told me he was seeing a counselor, but I never believed that was true; and if it was, I no longer cared. After that, I realized I no longer wanted anything from him. I was finally done.

Little by little, I was reclaiming my power back, and it felt so good!

CHAPTER 24

Corey

The time had come for me to find a new place to live *again*. I found a great house right around the corner from the University, with three female roommates who also went to school there. It was a four-bedroom house, and while I had the smallest room, it fit my budget and felt right.

I was so ready for a new beginning, eager to leave behind all the bad things that had happened over the last two-plus years. It felt like the Liam and Brad chapters of my life were finally closed, and I was getting a fresh start. For the first time in a long while, I was genuinely happy and excited about what was ahead.

My new home was at the top of the list of positive changes. I loved the new living situation. My room was pretty small, but the house wasn't. It was a two-story, four-bedroom, three-bathroom house with plenty of common space, a two-car garage, and a backyard with a deck and a lawn. But the best part of my new living arrangement was definitely my new roommates.

There were four of us living in the house, and I got along great with everyone. My life and family culture were very different from theirs, but none of that seemed to matter. Before long, we became friends as well as roommates. Having moved six times in two years, this house and these people were quickly becoming my favorite part of college. As a transfer student who had never lived on campus, it was the first time I truly felt like I was getting to have that fun college experience.

For the last few years, I had watched myself slowly disappear, turning myself inside out, trying to make Brad want to be with me. Those years with him led me into the darkest parts of my shadow self, and the decisions I made from that place were some of the worst in my life. The fact that it took me so long to admit to myself just how bad things had become, only added to my shame.

I had a lot of practice pretending things were not as bad as they actually were. Growing up in a family struggling with addiction made it easier for me to normalize toxic relationships and the emotional abuse I endured. As a child, downplaying the severity of situations became a means of survival. It also taught me how to silence my own voice, not ask for what I needed or wanted, and accept abusive behaviors. Even though things did not start out that way in my family, they evolved as a result of the drugs, alcohol, and divorce.

That year continued to be full of big changes in my life and in the lives of my friends. In 1999, not long after my 24th birthday, my close friend Leisa got married to her longtime boyfriend Ricky, and I was in the wedding. I was so excited for them both. I had spent a lot of time with them and just knew they were going to be married forever and become wonderful parents. It was a fun, memorable day, and I felt honored to be a part of it.

Around the same time, I was promoted to store manager at the clothing store I had been working at for about a year. But it started to become too much. I was already going to school full-time, and with the required 48-hour workweek as a store manager, I was completely burnt out.

I needed a job that wouldn't stress me out while I was going to school, but would still pay enough money to cover my bills. I had cocktailed part-time at the bar we all hung out at when I was living with Jenny's mom, before I got promoted to store manager. As luck would have it, they were looking for a bartender. I would work four shifts a week, and none of them interfered with my school schedule. I was also working nights so I had my days off to focus on my schoolwork.

One slow Thursday night in October of 2000, a younger guy came up to the bar and said, "Hey, my buddy Corey over there thinks you're really hot. Can I get your number for him?"

He pointed to another young-looking guy standing across the room at the jukebox, his back to me. I had seen this group of guys in there a few times before—they stood out because they looked younger than the normal crowd. I had never really given this particular guy a second look as someone I would be interested in dating.

For a moment, I felt like I was back in junior high and reacted, slightly annoyed, and said, "He sent *you* to ask me instead of him coming to ask me for it?"

His tone was quiet, "Nah, it's not like that. He doesn't even know I'm telling you all of this. I just know he has been interested in you for a while, so I thought I'd see if he had a chance."

I replied, "That's sweet, but I don't think so. Thanks for asking." I handed him the beers he ordered and walked away to help other customers.

A few minutes later, Corey walked over to the bar and got my attention, "I'm sorry about my stupid friend bothering you. I didn't ask him to do that." He had a sweet shyness about him and kept looking down as he talked to me.

I said, "It's fine. It was kind of sweet. I'm flattered. He told me it was all him and that you didn't know he was coming to talk to me for you."

He said, half-jokingly and half angrily as he talked to me loud enough so his friend could hear, "Yeah, and now you probably think I'm an IDIOT for not talking to you myself!" He let out a nervous laugh, then looked down and said, "I saw you on the night of my 21st birthday and thought you were beautiful and wanted to meet you. You're the reason I came back to this bar."

His honesty and his energy were refreshing, flattering, and charming. It was sweet to hear that I had made such an impression on someone without even realizing it. He didn't look like most guys I dated—he was a little frumpy and shorter than I preferred, especially since I am pretty tall for a girl at 5'10". But he had sweet eyes with long eyelashes that he batted at me as he looked up at me with a hopeful smile.

I could feel my cheeks warming as I blushed at his sweet comment. I was 25 at this time, and I had always dated older guys. He seemed so young to me so I asked, "How old *are* you?"

He seemed a little offended by my question and proudly touted, "I'm 22," as he puffed up his chest and tilted his head back like he was a *big* man. Then, just as he was starting to win me over, he set a pack of cigarettes down on the bar, and I shut it down.

I asked accusingly, "Do you smoke?"

He quickly grabbed the pack, as if ashamed and sheepishly said, "Yes."

I threw my hands up and said, "Sorry, I don't date guys who smoke." Smoking was a deal breaker for me. Growing up in a home full of smokers, I always felt like a bad person for not wanting to breathe in that awful smell or have it seep into my hair or my clothes. I vowed never to date a smoker.

Many of my friends who hung out at the bars smoked, but I absolutely despised it. By then, smoking had been banned in bars in California, but people still did it at this bar. We'd just fill an empty beer bottle with water for them to use as an ashtray, so if a cop walked in, it wouldn't be obvious. Most nights, I went home with my clothes and hair reeking of cigarette smoke.

I had to deal with the smell of cigarette smoke at my job, but it also irritated my sinuses and triggered my asthma. I was not about to go down that road, especially with a 22-year-old guy who barely showed up on my radar before that night. Nope!

He leaned back, looking disappointed, but with a tinge of hope in his voice he said, "Well, I have been wanting to quit, but I haven't yet. Maybe we can at least be friends then?"

He extended his hand as if requesting to shake on it. I smiled and shook his hand. He asked for my number as friends, and I gave it to him. He seemed harmless enough, and sweet. He never did call me, but he kept coming into the bar while I was working. I started paying attention to how he acted, watching him drink and have a good time with friends.

He was still flirty with me but was never pushy about dating me or even hanging out as friends. He was always sweet and polite, never rowdy or acting foolish like some of his friends did. One night, I saw him chewing a bunch of gum and I said, "What's up with the gum?"

He smiled and said, "I told you, I'm trying to quit smoking."

I smiled and gave him an approving nod as I said, "Good for you!" He smiled back at me, rubbed his hands nervously over his head, then went back to his friends. I appreciated his effort but hoped he was actually doing it because he wanted to and not because he was trying to prove something to me. If that were the case, it probably wasn't going to last long.

At the time, I was casually dating around but nothing serious. I kept seeing Corey and his friends in the bar but didn't engage with them other than small talk while serving drinks. One night, a guy I had been seeing came in to see me, but I was getting tired of the games he played. I was growing tired of just seeing people and finally starting to want to try something more serious again. This guy was there to see if I wanted to meet up with him after I got off work, which was usually like 3:00 a.m., but I was over it. So, I told him no and sent him away.

Corey's friend saw me talking to the other guy and came up to me right after, asking, "Was that guy your boyfriend?"

I looked up and noticed Corey was standing a few feet behind his friend. Suddenly I saw him differently. There was also a feeling of safety because he definitely seemed to be more interested in me than I was in him. Other than Liam, it seemed every guy I dated, seriously or not, was two-timing me with another girl. But here was this sweet guy, putting himself out there and being upfront about how he felt. I thought, maybe I should give him a chance.

I looked over his friend's head right at Corey, smiled, and said, "Nope. I'm single. You have my number—you should use it."

THE WEIGHT OF SILENCE

He stood there with his hands in his pockets, his eyes widening as he took out one hand and pointed to himself in surprise and asked, "Me?"

"No, the guy behind you," I said sarcastically, "Yes, you!"

I bought him and his friend a beer, and he stayed until closing, sitting on a barstool in my station. Before leaving, he gave me a hug and told me he would call me tomorrow…and this time, he did call.

After that night, we talked for hours on the phone for the first three weeks. He told me more about the huge crush he had on me, mentioning that all of his friends knew about it and he had even talked to his mom about me.

He told me again that when he saw me that first time on his 21st birthday he knew he had to meet me, making it his goal. Now, I really understood why his friend kept intervening on his behalf. He was sweet and romantic, and the more I got to know him, the more attractive he became to me.

There were a few red flags, like the smoking, but he was trying to quit. I also made it clear that I didn't date anyone who did drugs. He got worried because he smoked pot sometimes, but pot was not something I was ever concerned about. I often said I would rather smell pot than cigarette smoke.

He still lived at home with his mom and stepdad, but he insisted they were really close and actually worked together. By then, I had been living on my own for so long I found it hard to relate, but I thought that if my family wasn't so full of drama, I might have lived at home too at 22.

The last red flag was the one that had my intuition kind of screaming at me. He told me that he had just broken up with someone not long before he talked to me that first night. I thought at first maybe they hadn't been dating that long, but then he told me they dated for three years. My stomach dropped when I heard that. Three years with someone is a long time, and they hadn't been apart for very long.

It felt very similar to my situation with Liam and Brad. He was even around same age I was when I made a whole string of really bad decisions regarding my relationships—age 22, my self-titled "dumbest age". But I wanted so much to stay in the happy place of thinking, well, he saw me and knew he had to meet me. Maybe we were just meant to be together.

I completely avoided thinking about the fact that after he saw me and couldn't stop talking about me and wanted to meet me, it would be almost a year before he would break up with his long-term girlfriend. He was with her while thinking about me and making it his goal to meet me. After years of feeling like I was always the one pursuing guys, instead of focusing on that as a red flag, I saw it as flattering and a welcome change.

During those first three weeks, we really delved deep, talking for hours on the phone and sharing stories about our lives, families, and past relationships. I felt safe opening up to him because, for once, I wasn't trying to be someone I wasn't to make a guy like me. In fact, I think I was testing him by being so honest, seeing if he would still feel strongly for me. After everything I had been through, I was afraid of trusting someone again.

In the beginning, I felt like I had the upper hand and wasn't overly invested in where this might go, so it seemed like I didn't have much to lose. At first, it was just nice to have the attention of someone who was putting in the effort and seemed to genuinely want to be with me. But as we talked more, that began to change.

THE WEIGHT OF SILENCE

He told me about the long-term girlfriend he had recently ended things with. I told him all about my relationships with Liam and Brad, sharing all the drama that had plagued my life as a result. I also told him about my family's issues with addiction, and he shared similar stories about his family with me.

He understood what it felt like to have addicts in the family. I could talk about it with him in a way I never had before with others in my life. It was something that deepened our connection. Instead of feeling pitied or judged, our shared pain made it feel as if we were kindred spirits.

He was sweet, vulnerable, and persistent in all the right ways. He was just about everything I said I had always wanted in a guy. He gained my trust, which allowed me to open up and let myself be vulnerable again. I was still terrified of being hurt, but his kindness and consistent attention helped me lower my guard down.

As I got to know him better, I found myself increasingly attracted to him. He was always telling me how smart, sexy and, beautiful I was, and he would express how hard it was to be around me without acting on those feelings. A part of me felt safe falling for him, specifically because he not only told me but he constantly showed me how deeply he had fallen for me.

After we had been dating for about three weeks, he invited me over for dinner to meet his family. I got along great with his mom, and it was obvious that they had a close bond. Things were going well at dinner until they took an unexpected turn.

His mom had been drinking since she got home from work, and by the middle of dinner, she was pretty intoxicated. I think Corey was embarrassed and they ended up getting into an argument. It became clear to me pretty quickly that this was a regular occurrence.

Corey ended up drinking a lot that night, and I saw a side of him I hadn't seen before. He became really loud, obnoxious, and really angry with his mom, and then it overflowed into his attitude with me. He didn't say much that night, but he had this angry energy about him and he just seemed to shut down.

It felt like he decided to get drunk too so he didn't have to deal with what happened with his mom. That pattern of avoiding problems was very familiar to me, especially around issues related to addiction in my own family.

He ended up staying with me that night, but I didn't get much sleep. The dynamic I witnessed with his mom was very triggering to me. I couldn't stop thinking about it, spending most of the night trying to sort out how I felt about him and everything that had just happened.

I felt very conflicted about Corey. On one hand, I felt like we were kindred spirits, both having mothers who were functioning addicts. On the other hand, his behavior after dinner was concerning and made me wonder if anger and shutting down was how he coped with things. It reminded me *a lot* of my sister, and not in a good way.

I got up and got ready to go to work, while he ended up sleeping all day. He didn't come down to the bar to see me at work that night, but I was glad he didn't. I needed some time and space to figure out my feelings. I knew I needed to talk to him about how I was feeling, but I wanted him to be clear-headed before that conversation.

The next morning, he called me really early. I was still tired from my shift the night before. His voice was sullen and quiet, and I could tell he wasn't in a good place. "I'm sorry about what happened at dinner with my mom. She gets like that sometimes, and I hate it. Sorry I got so drunk too; I just didn't want to deal with it, and it made me so mad."

I felt bad for him; I knew that feeling all too well with my own mom. My mom usually didn't cause a scene or fly off the handle in front of people she didn't know well. I had only been asleep for a few hours when he called, and I did want to talk more about it with him, but not on the phone, so I said, "It's okay. I get it. I'm sorry, I do want to talk to you, but I need to get a little more sleep. I need to do some research today for a paper I have to write for one of my classes. Can we talk later?"

He replied sweetly, "Yeah, I'm sorry I woke you up. I just wanted to hear your voice."

I got off the phone feeling more confused than ever. I wished he hadn't been so sweet to me. I decided to go about my day and focus on other things. I was busy all day and ended up spending a lot of time online. Back then, there was only dial up Internet, so it kept my phone line busy most of the day. I had no idea that Corey had been trying to reach me all day.

It was late when I finally finished my research and got off the Internet. Around 11 p.m., my phone rang, and I saw Corey's number on the caller ID. I answered, and he sounded anxious at first, "Hey! I have been trying to get a hold of you all day but your phone line was busy."

I replied, "I'm sorry; I was doing research all day for that paper I have to write. Is everything okay?"

He fell silent again, "Something happened today after I got off the phone with you…my ex showed up at my house and wanted to talk."

Not being sure where this was heading, I hesitantly asked, "Oh…what did she want?"

He said, "She came over to tell me that she thought we owed it to each other to give our relationship one more chance. She wanted to get back together. We talked about a lot of stuff and then decided together that we would give it one more chance."

I just sat there letting his words echo through my head. After all he had done to pursue me, and how much his friends and he told me he was so into me, just like that, he got back together with his ex? I thought I would have had a stronger reaction, but in that moment, I felt strangely numb.

Maybe it was because I was already trying to sort out my feelings for him after what had happened at dinner with his mom. Even though I was shocked to hear that he had gotten back together with her before even talking to me about it, I wasn't surprised it happened. I had been there before myself.

I knew from my own experience with Brad and Liam how that can go. He had a level of comfort with her that we didn't have yet. It was that safe and easy feeling that pulled me back to Liam at times. Especially when things with Brad got complicated. I remembered how confused I felt at age 22, and the age difference between Corey and I was close to the same as Liam and me.

I was quietly processing what he just told me when he asked, "Aren't you going to say something?"

I said in a calm voice, "Well, I'm not surprised this is happening. I told you that I thought you two weren't done with each other yet."

He said, "I just feel like I owe it to her to give us another chance. I don't think it is going to last. I know that you and I will be together again someday. I still want to stay friends with you,"

I'd heard this all before from guys; it was usually their way of letting me down easy by saying they wanted to remain friends. It was their way of keeping their options open and keeping me close. It translated to, they don't want to be with me right now, but they don't want anyone else sniffing around me either.

I was getting annoyed. I didn't want to give him the satisfaction of seeing any reaction, so I said, "That's fine, but I probably will never call you or reach out to you. And if we do talk again as friends, it will not be the way it was when we were together." In my head I thought, *you don't get to have it both ways.*

I followed up with, "Out of respect for me, please give me at least a week before you reach out or come into the bar. I have to be there to work, and I don't want to deal with being forced to see you right now. I need some space."

He replied, "I already have plans to go out with my friends on Tuesday night because it is Halloween, but I don't know if we planned on going to the bar."

I said, "Thanks for the warning. You know I don't work Tuesday nights, and I don't know what my plans are yet, so do whatever you want that night. I won't be working."

He said, "I figured you weren't working, but I just thought I would let you know in case you saw me downtown."

I didn't want to drag this on any longer, so I said, "Okay, well I'm gonna go."

He sounded a little disappointed and regretful and said, "Okay. I'm sorry about how all of this happened. But just know you WILL be hearing from me again."

I rolled my eyes and said sarcastically, "Remember, I asked you for at least a week before I heard from you. I gotta go. Bye."

It was late, so I went to bed after we got off the phone. I didn't want to tell anyone what happened because I didn't want to see that sad look on all my friend's faces. Even though I felt conflicted about Corey, I had really started to fall for him. I wasn't ready to ditch the whole thing yet. I still felt numb, but everything changed the next morning.

I woke up that Monday morning feeling really sad about Corey dumping me for his ex, and all the feelings I had for him before we hit that bump after the dinner with his mom came rushing back. I still didn't know if I should trust my feelings. Did I really want him, or was I just feeling the sting of wanting something I suddenly couldn't have?

By Tuesday, I was still really sad and really wanted to call him, but I stopped myself. Then, he called me. He told me that after our conversation, he couldn't stop thinking about me and had ended things with his ex-girlfriend again before they even really got started. My heart felt like it could leap out of my chest, but I stayed cautious, I said, "Wow! That was a quick turnaround."

He said, "Not really. It never felt right to me. I knew after I talked to you that night that I made the wrong decision. I didn't want to hurt her, but I didn't want to hurt you either."

I said, "Well, I think it's a little late for that..."

We ended up talking more in person, and when I told him I was still nervous about his feelings for his ex, he said emphatically, "That is over! We are still friends, and we will always care about each other, but we realized there was a reason we broke up in the first place. Also, I couldn't stop thinking about you, and I knew I made a mistake letting you go."

We sat and talked for the rest of the night. It felt good to be with him again, and he seemed to be in a good place mentally. We discussed our families, their addiction issues, and I told him how I was feeling about how he acted after our dinner with his mom. By the end of the night, he had won me over and I decided to give him another chance. He came home with me that night.

Things were really good between us after we got back together, and I was so happy. About two weeks later, Corey told me he loved me for the first time, and I told him the same. It was the happiest I had felt in a relationship in a long time. I was excited about spending our first Christmas together. He even bought me the Claddagh ring I told him I loved that had my birthstone as the heart.

Some refer to those rings as an Irish wedding band, but it is also known to symbolize friendship, love, and loyalty. He gave it to me on Christmas day, hidden inside a large jewelry box he had also bought for me. I was ready to move towards marriage at that point in my life. I knew Corey loved me, but I could tell wasn't quite ready to take that step. Still, to me, the ring symbolized that he wanted to get there eventually.

Christmas was great, and then we rang in the New Year together. I was working on New Year's Eve, but we managed to steal a midnight kiss amidst all the chaos. By that time, I was getting tired of always having to go to work at a bar and be working in the middle of the fun everyone else was having. All I wanted for years was to have a boyfriend to stay home with, cozied up together, ringing in the New Year together. Now that I had a boyfriend I loved, I wanted that even more.

Since I had to work on New Year's Eve, I decided to make it up to Corey with a romantic dinner at my place a couple of weeks into January 2001. I made dinner for the two of us, and we had the house all to ourselves because my roommates were still at their family homes for winter break. We had one of the best nights I thought we ever had together. Corey stayed the night, and in the morning, he got up early to head to work.

It had been such a good night that I told him I thought he might be the one for me. I was surprised how fast and hard I fell for him, especially after not even wanting to date him at first. Things had been so good since we got past that first hiccup with his ex, and for the first time in a long while, I felt like I was happy in a relationship again.

That morning, not long after he got to work, he called me. I was so happy to see his work number come up on my caller ID. I couldn't wait to hear his voice and smiled as I answered thinking he was calling me because the night before had been so great for him too. But something in his voice sounded weird. I felt my cheeks get hot, and my stomach felt like it jumped into my throat.

Fearing that something bad had happened, I asked, "You sound weird, are you okay?"

His voice sounded choppy, like he was trying not to cry. He said, "Last night with you was so amazing. I had such a great time with you that it scared me."

Suddenly I was relieved for a minute as I said, "I know, it scared me too. I haven't been that vulnerable with someone in a long time."

There was silence on the other end. Just as I was about to check if he was still there, he let out a guttural sound that sounded like a mix of frustration and anguish as he said, "Ugh…when you say things like that, it makes what I need to say so much harder."

He let out another frustrated growl as he seemed to force out the words, "I think we need to take some time apart. I realized that I went straight from my last girlfriend of three years to you, and things got so serious so fast with us. I think I just need some time to myself."

I felt like I had been hit by a truck and launched 100 yards into a pile of quicksand. Was he really doing this to me again? I trusted him, opened myself up to him, and now he was tearing my heart into a million pieces—again. And the worst part was that he chose to do this after the wonderful night we'd just shared. I was completely blindsided.

  I felt sick to my stomach and tried desperately to understand what had caused this quick turnaround. With feelings of confusion and despair clinging to my voice as I fought to hold back my tears. The only words I could force out in that moment were, "What do you mean? Last night, I felt closer to you and more connected to you than I ever had before! What the hell happened?"

  He responded quickly, "I still care about you, I just need some time to sort some things out. I didn't see this coming either. I just woke up today, and after I talked about it with my mom, I knew I needed to call you and tell you how I was feeling."

  My head was spinning. Just a few months ago, I didn't even know this guy existed, and when he asked me out, I turned him down. How did I go from not even liking him to falling so hard, so fast, only to have my heart shattered into a million pieces without warning? But there were so many warnings…I just chose to ignore all of them.

  The girlfriend of three years whom he barely broke up with before he started pursuing me. Him dumping me to go with her after being with me for only three weeks, and days after he introduced me to his mom. And there was also the age difference and the gap in maturity.

  He was three years younger than me. I had learned the hard way with Liam that in your early 20's, that age difference can matter *a lot*. This time, I was the older person in the relationship, with a college degree. I was ready to meet someone I wanted to marry and start a life with. I was looking forward to not spending my life working in, and hanging out at a bar. But he loved being at the bar and always wanted to go there, even when I wasn't working. That's where we spent most of our time together.

Once again, we were broken up—or in his words, "taking time apart"—and suddenly, I went from being the one being pursued to feeling completely broken-hearted. That first week we were apart, I felt so raw and vulnerable that I didn't even want to be around anyone.

I couldn't stop crying, and the worst part was how confused I was by how he went from one extreme to the next. Yes, there were red flags, but they fell off my radar because he made me believe he loved me. What made it so much worse was that I truly didn't see any of it coming.

I sequestered myself in my room as much as possible until I finally had to go to work later in the week. It was too painful to see people or to talk about what happened. I felt like such a fool. I had been dumped by the younger guy who pursued me, who had somehow conned me into falling for him, even though I had no interest in him when I first met him.

Once I was back at work, it felt good to be busy and not be so focused on him, but that relief didn't last long. My job as a bartender in the place we met—and where he still liked to hang out—left me feeling so vulnerable. Most people go to work being pretty certain they won't run into their ex in the middle of their day; my situation was the opposite.

This time, I hadn't even thought to tell him to keep his distance. Part of me *still* wanted to see him, but I didn't want to lose control over when that happened. Knowing that Corey could walk in at any moment, without warning, while I was working was torture. And by the weekend after our break up, he finally showed his face.

That Saturday night, the bar was packed. Jenny worked there too, and we were both bartending that night. We worked really well together, and things were just humming along as we found our busy groove behind the bar. For a little while, I stopped thinking about Corey, and it felt good. I was making the cocktail waitresses drink orders, and I had just finished a big order for her. As she walked away, the space in front of my station cleared, so I looked down to assess whether or not I needed an ice refill.

When I looked up, suddenly, there he was.

He smiled at me, but there was hesitation in his expression, unsure of how I would respond to him. He knew that if he was going to be there, he'd better check in with me and make sure I was okay with him being there. One word from me, and the bouncers would have shown him the door.

It was a shock to my system to see him out of the blue in the midst of the chaos at work, especially after all that had happened. I took a deep breath, raised my eyebrows, and looked at him, not really sure of what to say when he blurted out, "Hey."

I responded with a half-annoyed, half-sad, "Hey."

He sensed that it was safe to engage, he asked, "How are you?"

His question echoed in my head, how was I? I thought in my head that what I wanted to say was, *I've been miserable and sad and missing you like crazy, and I'm mad at you for putting me through this <u>again,</u> and how dare you show up at my job and ask me how I am after you just smashed my heart into a million pieces.* But what came out was, "I'm fine. How are you?"

He responded with, "I'm alright. It is good to see you."

I felt a swirl of emotions. Part of me was glad to hear that he was happy to see me, but the other part of me was just mad and hurt.

Keeping my guard up, I said, "Did you want to order a drink? We are slammed, so I don't really have time to talk right now."

He gave me a look, as if he snapped back into reality, and said, "Yeah, I'll take a beer."

I handed him the beer and then told him the price, making sure he knew there would be no free beer for him now that he was no longer my boyfriend. He paid me and then handed me the tip like he was doing me some big favor. Just before he walked away, he held my hand as I grabbed the tip and said, "You look *really* good."

UGH! The nerve!! I was so irritated. I pulled my hand away with the tip, rolled my eyes, and said, "Thanks." Then I turned away from him as fast as I could and started helping other customers.

I didn't hear from him for the next week after that night at the bar, and then he started showing up again. He kept saying he still wanted to be friends, but what he really wanted was to have me—and his freedom too. This felt all too familiar to me, and not in a good way. The next few months were really frustrating and difficult for me.

At some point, we started going past friendship again, but we were not back together. I was trying to give him the space he needed to figure things out, but it wasn't long before a familiar unhealthy pattern started again for me. I fell right back into losing myself and doing everything to please him or not push him too much. I was so focused on giving him what *he* wanted and needed, and I ignored my own wants and needs.

It was around this time that he started voicing his opinion on what he liked me to wear or how I wore my hair. He preferred when I wore low cut tops that showed off my cleavage, and liked when I wore blue because it brought out my eyes, or red because he thought I looked sexy in red. He also only liked it when I wore my hair down.

THE WEIGHT OF SILENCE

It was a subtle shift that began when we were dating and continued on in this weird in-between situation we were in at the time. It wasn't like he demanded I dress a certain way or where my hair a certain way, but he made sure to express his dislike when I didn't.

A few times he came up to me while I was working and reacted to a shirt I was wearing that didn't show cleavage and he made a face like he was disgusted or disappointed. Once, while I was working behind the bar with customers all around, he actually put his finger on the neck of my shirt and pulled it down in an effort to expose my cleavage. After disrespecting and humiliating me in public at my job, he then he made a scowling face and walked away making it clear he disapproved.

Like Brad, he would always do it in a joking way, but it was still completely demeaning to me. He would do the same type of thing if I dared to wear my hair up in a ponytail or anything other than down. I found myself thinking about what he would want me to wear whenever I got dressed and waiting for him to show up and compliment me. My pattern of seeking the approval and acceptance of the man in my life was, once again, ever-present.

I found myself right back in the same kind of situation I had with Brad. I lost myself in trying to please Corey and get him to want to get back together with me. We were still having sex and spending time together, but it was all on *his* terms. It didn't start out that way, but the longer it went on, the worse it became. My insecurities were at an all-time high again, and I felt like I was once again walking on eggshells, fearing that one wrong move and I would lose him for good.

I put up with a lot during the time we were broken up, but I finally reached my limit one night. I was off work, and we made plans to meet up downtown and hang out. He showed up with some of his friends and was acting standoffish with me.

MELINDA VELASQUEZ

I tried to have a good time and not let him upset me, and I ended up getting drunk. I was falling back into yet another unhealthy pattern of making myself seem vulnerable so that the object of my affection would feel the need to take care of me. At that time in my life, drinking also had a way of giving me the courage to speak my truth. It often didn't go well, and this night was no exception.

He told me earlier that he would take me home that night. So, when I was ready to leave, I went to find him, only to have my good friend Jack tell me that he left. I tried paging him a number of times, but he never responded. Once again, I felt like such a fool. After everything he had put me through, to ditch me so disrespectfully was the last straw. Something inside me just snapped. I was pissed, and I was on a mission to let him know.

My friend Jack was very protective of me and he offered to drive me home, but I told him I wanted him to take me to Corey's first. Jack tried to get me to change my mind, but there was no stopping that train. I really wish I had listened to Jack.

We got to Corey's house and his truck wasn't there but I decided it was a good idea to pound on his window while yelling his name and swearing. It was after midnight at this point, and I felt like a woman possessed. I had been disrespected by him so many times and did everything to be patient with him. I had reached my limit and I was tired of him treating me like this.

He wasn't home, but his mom was. When she heard the sounds of a crazy woman banging on the window, she came to his room. Jack tried to stop me from doing that too, but you know, hell hath no fury like a woman scorned. Then I heard his mom's voice yelling back at me, "MELINDA! MELINDA! STOP! He's not here!"

She was talking to me from inside his room, and was trying to calm me down through the window. Seeing her thrust me back into reality, and I went from angry and frustrated to humiliated and embarrassed. I regained my composure and pulled myself together and said, "I'm so sorry. I don't know what I was thinking. I'm so sorry I woke you up."

Jack got me back into the car and drove me home. I sat there silent, trying to hold back my tears as Jack attempted to make me feel better. But unfortunately, there was nothing he could say or do to ease my pain. I just sat there and let the shame eat me alive for the ride home and the rest of the night.

I tried to page Corey when I got home to warn him about my encounter with his mom, but he never returned my call. After almost three months of mixed signals and emotional rollercoasters, I finally reached my breaking point. I was in that place again, that pathetic insecure pile of mush. What I didn't realize then was that I had never left that place; it was always there lurking, waiting for the right emotional trigger to release it once again.

He never explained where he went that night or why he didn't call me back. He brushed it off as a misunderstanding, claiming he didn't even remember telling me he would drive me home. All that did was make me feel even more pathetic. Not long after that night, I decided to tell him that either we were going to be together exclusively or not at all.

I was exhausted from wondering when or if we would get back together. I was scared at first, but by the next day, I felt relieved. I was tired of being in limbo, and at least this way a decision would be made. I thought I had taken back my power, but all I really did was once again hand my power over to him. If I wasn't happy, I should've just ended it, but I had that familiar feeling of all the time I invested in him, in us, I wasn't ready to give up yet. Besides, it seemed that anytime he was not able to be with me or talk to me, he never could stay away for longer than a day or two.

This time was no different. He came around quickly and said he wanted us to officially be boyfriend and girlfriend again. He said, "I know it's been hard with me not being sure about us. I do have love for you, but I'm still not sure that I feel as strongly as you do."

I wasn't sure how to take that at first. It stung a little, but then he clarified, "I'm still figuring out who I am and what I have to offer someone before I can say whether any one person is the one for me."

I appreciated his honesty. I understood he was three years younger than me and had just came out of long relationship with his high school sweetheart before dating me. It made sense that he wouldn't want to jump too quickly into a life-long commitment. Not everyone was as ready and open to love as I was. I fall hard and fast; once I give my heart to someone, I give it completely. It didn't occur to me then that I deserved more than what he was offering.

We got back together that night and once again, I felt hopeful. However, after having my heart broken twice already, I was moving forward with my guard up. We both agreed that some things needed to change if we were going to make this work. I was cautiously optimistic that things really would be better this time around.

We had never actually dated; we just ended up spending a lot of time at the bar since I worked there and he loved coming there. We made an effort to do things outside of the bar and to spend less time there in general.

By then, I had become pretty unhappy working at the bar. There was always some kind of drama, and my world had gotten really small and revolved around the bar life for far too long. The worst part was that one of the owners—the one with the controlling share of the business—was a raging alcoholic.

We all walked on eggshells around him. He was either the sweetest guy, or he was a straight up mean drunk. I often came in for my night shift to find him stumbling around behind the bar, drunk while he was working. I would have to call his wife to come get him, or call a cab to take him home. He would always rant about the other owner, urging us not to listen to him, but would often forget what he said because he was blackout drunk.

The two owners were on the outs pretty regularly, but this time turned out to be different. The owner with the controlling share told us not to allow the other owner in the bar, but none of us took him seriously. I had always pushed back when he told me to do something I didn't think was right. He always told me how mad it made him, but also how much he respected me for it. This time I felt what he told me to do wasn't right, but when I pushed back, he actually fired me. I was shocked and a bit angry at first, but after I got over the initial shock, I realized I felt relieved.

I found a new job pretty quickly at a beautiful restaurant nestled in the turning basin of the river in the next city over from where I lived. It was considered fine dining, and instead of cover bands on the weekend, we had live jazz on Friday nights. I was still bartending, but now I was working in a tiny little bar all to myself. I still worked the same days, Thursday-Sunday, but most nights I was off work by 10 p.m., and the latest I worked on the weekends was midnight. No more working until 2 a.m. and arriving home at 4 a.m.

I was making as much, sometimes more than I made at the bar, and the environment was a really nice change. I graduated with my bachelor's degree before leaving the bar and had been thinking about my next steps. The vibe at the bar had become pretty toxic, and I was more than ready for a change.

MELINDA VELASQUEZ

I realized how tired I had become of being just "the tall blonde with big boobs behind the bar". Playing up the sexy image and flirting was fun for a while, but it got really old. I was growing tired of being looked at as just an object—especially now that Corey seemed to be treating me that way, too.

At my new job, I felt seen and respected for what I brought to the table. My new boss, Kevin, was always willing to listen and implement my ideas, and he was constantly boasting about me to customers and the owners. As hard as it was to be fired, it didn't take me long to realize that it was a blessing in disguise.

I was thriving at my new job, and having something so positive to focus on started to highlight the areas in my life that weren't as fulfilling. The happier I became in other parts of my life, the clearer it became that my relationship with Corey was not heading in the same direction.

Being in a new work environment shined a light on the fact that Corey and I were in very different places. He wasn't a bad guy, but we were both just at different phases of our lives. I also started noticing how much he relied on alcohol and weed as coping mechanisms.

He'd get excited about things like having a day off during the week because it meant he could "wake and bake"—get stoned the minute he woke up, something he couldn't do on workdays. He was smoking weed a lot more than I remembered, and when he was stoned, he acted like a totally different person.

When he drank, he tended to lean more towards anger and aggression. But when he smoked pot, he would go to the opposite end of the spectrum, laughing at the smallest things and acting really silly. That familiar feeling of not knowing which version of him I'd get—the angry, brooding guy or the laughing goofball—was wearing on me.

There I was again, walking on eggshells. I didn't see the pattern at the time, but I knew that being around that kind of energy was toxic for me. The connection we had over addiction running in our family was what bonded us so quickly; but I came to realize that it was also the thing that started to pull us apart.

I struggled with my own issues with food, and in my early 20's, with alcohol. While working at the bar, I encountered casual drinkers, alcoholics, and even drug addicts. But just as I felt with my family at one point, part of me always felt like I didn't belong. The only time I could ignore that feeling was when I was drinking. With addiction running strong in my family, it was a dangerous place for me to be.

Eventually, I reached a point in my life that I felt a strong need to distance myself from that world and the people in it. For me, the hardest part was the people. I fought against myself for a long time, trying to hold on to people who were not good for me. Unfortunately, Corey had become one of them.

It got to the point where he was stoned more than he wasn't. I never had an issue with people smoking pot before, and I still didn't, but with him, it became a turn-off and a point of contention. I became fixated on "helping" him by trying to get him to quit smoking or at least cut back on the pot smoking. Once again, I was so focused on "fixing" the man in my life that I lost sight of myself and what truly made me happy.

So much had happened between us, and me being removed from the environment he wanted to still be entrenched in was pushing us further apart. By the end of July 2001, we mutually decided to break up. I was 26 years old by then, and was ready to move into a different phase of my life, and I knew that phase didn't include him. I knew it was the right decision, but I still needed time to process my feelings. There were very few people in my life I felt like I could trust implicitly, and after all the drama, I needed to get the hell out of town and go see my best friend, Laura.

CHAPTER

25

I hadn't visited Laura since she moved to Oregon, and by then she had another baby—a boy. It was a six-hour drive, and I had never driven that far by myself before, but I was really looking forward to the time alone to process everything. I had saved up enough money in tips to buy my very first cell phone, a Motorola flip phone, just to have it with me on the trip in case of emergency.

The drive to Laura's was very therapeutic. The weather was warm but not too hot, so I had my windows down, the sunroof open, and my music turned up loud. It was the perfect combination to help cleanse my soul from all the heartache I had been through. The timing was perfect, and I was ready for a real, lasting change.

I was looking forward to spending some quality time with my best friend and her kids—my "niece" and new "nephew". Once I arrived at Laura's house, we spent the day hanging out and catching up while Laura's daughter modeled different princess dresses as we all loved on and tended to the new baby. Laura's husband was working as a seasonal fire fighter, and since he was on duty that week, he was staying at the firehouse.

We had the house to ourselves, with few distractions, and it was exactly what I needed. I was only six hours away from home, but there is nothing like a change of location to shift your energy. Being with Laura, no matter where we were, always felt like home. It was pure bliss.

That night, as I got ready for bed, Laura came in to make sure I had everything I needed to be comfortable. She had a book in her hand and said, "I know you have been going through a lot, and I thought you might want to check this book out."

Laura was not the type to push something on anyone or even offer unsolicited advice, so I was intrigued. She continued, "I'm not a fast reader, and I don't read a lot, but this book I couldn't seem to put down. It helped me figure out some stuff for myself, so I thought maybe it could help you too."

The book was "Are You the One for Me?" by Barbara DeAngelis, Ph.D. The title hit home right away. I had always been pretty open to anything that could help me grow, learn, and heal, so I said, "Okay, I'll check it out."

She said in an excited tone, "Oh yeah and I'll get you a pen and some paper too. The book includes these exercises that are really helpful."

I smiled and said, "Great! I'll take all the help I can get right now!"

Once I was settled in bed, I dove right into the book. Laura was right—it sucked me in right away. After reading for a bit, I reached the first exercise:

MELINDA VELASQUEZ

Exercise 1: Write down the names of your last three intimate relationships, and underneath their name, write down three to five of their negative traits. After completing this first step then continue reading for further instructions.

This was not a difficult task for me, particularly with the last two relationships. I wrote down all three names across the top of the paper: first Liam, then Brad, and finally Corey. It didn't take me long to come up with a list of negative traits for each of them. Liam was the hardest, but even with him, I didn't struggle as much as I thought I would.

I completed each list under the corresponding names and moved on to the next step of the exercise:

Now that you have your three lists, go back and circle which traits they each have in common.

And that is when my "A-ha!" moment happened. All three of them had some form of addiction they weren't willing or ready to seek help for. It was something that both drew me to them and, in the end, pushed me away.

I realized I had been on a rescue mission, trying to save each of them from their addictions or their families' struggles with addictions because I hadn't been able to save my own mother and family. This pattern was strongest with Brad and Corey, but even with Liam, it was there—especially the guilt I felt when Liam's life seemed to fall apart for a while after we broke up. I put that all of that on myself.

I also realized that with all three relationships, I fell in love—or stayed in love— for their potential, rather than who they actually were in the present. I had heard the term *codependent* before, especially in relation to people with addicts in their life, but this time, I was smacked in the face with the reality that I was deeply codependent. Growing up in a family of addicts had set the stage for the types of relationships I found myself in, particularly with these three relationships.

A textbook explanation, provided by Dr. Nicole LePera, The Holistic Psychologist, of what codependency looks like in a relationship is the following:

1. Obsessive focus on your partner's behavior.
2. Trying to control, change, or fix someone.
3. Enabling harmful behavior and lack of boundaries.
4. Separation brings anxiety and fear of abandonment.
5. Betraying yourself and your own needs in order to be chosen.
6. Feeling responsible for the wellbeing, emotions or actions of others.
7. Feeling loved and needed through finding and fixing the problems of others.
8. Saying 'yes' when you actually want to say 'no'.
9. Consistently feeling like you have been taken for granted and resentful for giving more than you receive.
10. Obsessively (unconsciously) attempting to control the behavior of others.

All ten of those traits on that list showed up in some way in all three of my last relationships. And not only did they affect my intimate relationships—they bled into my friendships and nearly every aspect of my life.

Unfortunately, it would take me far longer than one night with an insightful book to fully figure that out. But for now, that book had shone a light on the harmful pattern of how I had been showing up in the world, especially in my relationships.

MELINDA VELASQUEZ

It was like walking around with a pain in my foot every time I wore a certain pair of shoes, but never figuring out why—until one day I discovered there was a rock in the shoe. Dealing with this discovery wasn't going to be as quick a fix as removing the rock from the shoe, but at least I knew what the problem was and why I kept repeating the pattern.

I could now see how often I'd been doing this, but I had never connected the dots until that moment. The thing about codependency is it's a lot like addiction; as much as you want to change and not do the thing that you know is bad for you, and everyone you love, recovering from it is a process.

To truly make a lasting change requires determination, an unwavering focus on self-awareness, patience with yourself and others, and a deep sense of self-love and acceptance. Along the way, there will most likely be a few relapses or close calls, and that is okay. It is also something that will always be there, lying in wait, ready for you to fall back into your pattern—sometimes when you least expect it.

This was certainly true for me on my journey as a recovering codependent woman. When I first discovered this about myself, I had no idea what my process of recovery would look like, but I was grateful just to have the awareness of the problem, which was the first important step.

I couldn't wait to tell Laura about my revelation and thank her for the book that led me to it. We spent the day together, and the next day, I headed back home. I read a bit more of the book that night, but I never finished it. I had always planned to, but never did. It gave me exactly what I needed at that time. The rest, I would figure out along the way.

The drive home was another welcome time for reflection. I let the music wash over me as I made my way back home and contemplated what all of this meant. One thing that became clear pretty quickly was how focused I had been on helping and fixing Corey, rather than allowing him his own process of self-discovery.

Instead of choosing to let him go when I realized our values and beliefs weren't lining up, I held on even tighter, trying to force something that wasn't meant to be. I had done the same with Brad, and even with Liam. Even when I knew I wasn't happy with either of them, the anxiety of being abandoned whenever I felt them pulling away only made me cling harder.

It was all about control—something I felt I didn't have when it came to my family. I couldn't help my mom with her addiction, or even my sister, so I tried to control whatever I could in my life. Unfortunately, that included people in my life as well.

SECTION FIVE

Full Blown Adulting: Buckle Up!

"Learn from yesterday, live for today, hope for tomorrow."
~Anonymous

CHAPTER

26

I was 26 when I had my big epiphany about codependency. In hindsight, I probably should have seen a therapist to start working through everything, but once again, I just pushed forward. I figured that simply knowing I was codependent would be enough to avoid falling back into those patterns. "White knuckling" is a term used in addiction recovery when you try to quit your addiction without doing the work to get to the root of the problem, and that is what I did with my codependency.

Being the capable person I was, I assumed that having this newfound awareness would be enough to keep me from getting caught up in it again. And to some extent, it did help—especially when it came to the kind of men I chose to date. Even without therapy, I did have some new tools in my toolkit to help me not get sucked into old relationship patterns.

After my last breakup, I took a brief break to recalibrate. I dated a few guys, but by then, my relationship intuition was sharper.

MELINDA VELASQUEZ

I could tell pretty quickly if I wasn't feeling it with someone. At that point in my life, if I didn't feel like this person was someone I could marry, I was out. I was no longer willing to waste years with someone who didn't treat me with love, dignity, and respect.

By that time, I had decided not to pursue a teaching credential, so I figured I would just work for a while and see what came my way. Things were still going really well at my job at the restaurant. Kevin and I worked really well together, and it wasn't long before he started training me to take over for him as Event Coordinator. Not long after, I was promoted to Event Coordinator and Front of the House Manager.

We hosted a lot of weddings, but the first one was memorable to me for a number of reasons. As the guests arrived, I recognized a few people, one being my eighth-grade school counselor. I had spent so much time with her during that horrific year, and now, here I was over a decade later, serving her drinks at a wedding.

She recognized me right away and asked how I was. She apologized for not doing more to help me back then, but she admitted she didn't really know what the right thing to do was. I felt validated, and it was a little bit of closure that felt better than I realized it would.

At the end of the wedding, the bride and groom somehow ended up stranded. There was a mishap with their car, and all the other guests had already left. They ended up sitting at my bar, having a drink while they waited for someone to pick them up. We chatted for a bit, and I asked them how they met. They both broke into big smiles, looked at each other, and said simultaneously, "We met online!"

An online dating site, to be exact. This was 2002, long before online dating had become the norm. Before this, people met in chat rooms and similar platforms, but it was still considered taboo by many. I was intrigued.

I peppered them with questions and learned the name of the site where they met. I had grown so tired of meeting people in bars and was excited about the possibility of connecting with someone new—someone I hadn't met before or known through others. I had casually dated a lot of guys, and even beyond my codependent tendency, it felt like I kept meeting the same guy over and over again, just in different bodies.

By the time the newlyweds left, they convinced me to set up my account on the dating site where they had met. They gave me tips on what to do and what not to do, and I was eager to get started. That night, when I got home, I dove right into setting up my profile.

I realized I needed to upload a picture and I wanted something recent, so I enlisted my good friend Kate to help with a photo shoot. Kate and I had met when I worked at the bar. She was the general manager at a nearby busy steakhouse. Both owners of the bar came into her restaurant regularly, so that was how she ended up coming to the bar. We clicked immediately, and I knew she was one person I was meant to know—a friendship soulmate.

Kate and I started spending more time together during all the Corey drama outside of our occasional chats at the bar. She became my new dancing buddy, a mentor in my job, and a trusted confidant. Since she was single too, after taking my pictures for my dating profile, she decided to set up a profile for herself as well. I was so happy to have someone else in this new adventure with me.

I started on one dating site but eventually ended up joining two others that offered a larger pool of potential people to meet. I started receiving hits right away and began talking with a few different men. I would spend a little time chatting with them first before I met up with them for a date. It was an interesting process, and I had more than a few interesting interactions.

MELINDA VELASQUEZ

My online dating adventures kept me busy and provided me a refreshing break from the bar scene, but they could be just as weird and frustrating as meeting someone in a bar. Often, things would start off really well, but as I got to know them a little more, the other shoe would drop. This was how I learned to talk with them for a bit first before agreeing to meet in person.

One guy revealed that he was engaged and temporarily living far away from his fiancé. He was just looking for someone to have sex with until he could be reunited with her. No thanks! There were more than a few who were looking to have a regular hook-up.

Kate and I often sat on her patio, sipping wine and sharing our funny and horrific online dating stories. We started spending a lot more time together. We both worked the same schedule, so we liked to go out to a nice dinner and sometimes wine tasting on our days off. Sometimes we would go to a few other bars in the area if we didn't get off work too late and wanted to dance on a Saturday night.

We both had an interest in astrology—she a Capricorn, and I a Cancer. We often joked with each other saying if only you were a man, we would make a perfect fit! While astrology might not agree, we believed otherwise.

I turned 27 at the end of June in 2002, and by then I was growing weary of the dating scene. By the 4th of July, I began to feel a deep longing for something more meaningful. That day, my sister and my niece, now age nine, came over, and even my dad drove down to spend the day with us at my house. It brought back memories of the joyful 4th of July celebrations from my childhood.

A couple of years before, I had managed to reunite the whole family for Thanksgiving at my house. Both my parents and their new partners, along with my sister and her boyfriend, came together. It created a positive shift in what had been a tumultuous family dynamic for years. Using *my* home as neutral territory, after that we got used to spending many of the holidays together as a whole family. For the first time since the divorce, both Shelly and I liked mom and dad's new partners, and it felt like a little piece of our family had been healed.

My roommates went home for summer, so I had the house to myself on the 4th of July. Dad came without his girlfriend, and mom was doing something else that day. My dad, my sister, and my niece hung out for the day. I was enjoying the day, and then, before it even got dark everyone left. Before I knew it, I was sitting home alone.

One of the girls I knew from work told me she would be at a party just down the street from my house, so I decided to walk over and meet up with her to check it out. When I arrived, everyone was drunk, and I just felt completely out of place. In that moment I realized how much I had outgrown that crazy party life. I still drank sometimes, but I had stopped doing it for attention, and rarely ever got truly drunk anymore…at least, not on purpose!

I thanked her for the invite and got out of there as fast as I could. That night, when I got home, I felt the loneliest I had in a long time. Sitting on my bed, I let the tears flow as I thought about everything I had been through and how much I just wanted to be happy. I was ready to meet the person I wanted to spend my life with, but I was so exhausted from constantly searching for him.

I decided to quit two out of the three dating sites I was on, and I was seriously considering taking down my profile from the last one as well. Since my subscription had already been paid through the end of July, I figured I'd wait until then to make a final decision. Something told me not to cancel while I was feeling so funky about everything.

MELINDA VELASQUEZ

About two weeks after the 4th of July, while I was online, I received an instant message from someone on the dating site. The message read, "Wow! You're beautiful!"

Intrigued, I clicked on his profile to check him out. He was good looking, tall, non-smoker, no kids, had never been married—hitting several of the preferences I had at the time. This guy had come out of the blue and piqued my interest. I was still skeptical, but I was also keeping an open mind.

I didn't recognize the name of the city where he lived, and by that point, I had already told myself that my future husband probably didn't live in Northern California where I lived. I wanted someone with a different energy than the guys I had been dating, who all seemed to be very similar. I took a chance and replied back.

I said, "You must live in Southern California…"

He came right back and said, "How'd you know?"

I said, "I had never heard of your city before, but something just told me it was in Southern California."

We chatted for quite a while back and forth, and he was very sweet and charming. I told him I needed to get ready to go to work so I had to sign off, but we made plans to chat again later. Just before he signed off, he said one thing that had me spinning in a good way, he said, "Oh yeah, I'm a Capricorn, if that matters to you."

Did that matter to me? I recalled the many conversations my Capricorn friend Kate and I had about the compatibility of our signs for each other. I tried to contain my giddiness in response to him telling me he was a Capricorn and simply said, "Interesting. It does matter to me. I'm a Cancer, if that matters to you."

After the chat ended, I felt butterflies in my stomach, and my chest felt warm. I tried not to get my hopes up too high, but something about this guy felt different. The second I got off the chat, I picked up the phone and called Kate and told her all about it. She was just as excited—and cautious—as I was. But honestly, both of us were more excited than anything.

His name was Louie, and he was 33, which, at my age of 27 felt like a good age difference. He was 6'1", he had this beautiful dark hair that was sun-kissed with natural highlights, tan skin, and he had these beautiful light eyes—mostly green but sometimes appearing blue depending on what color he wore. He worked as a Landscaper for his dad's company, and also did work for himself on the side.

Over the next couple of days, we chatted a few more times, and then I said to him, "I need to hear your voice. Let's plan a phone call."

He agreed, and once we started talking on the phone, we never went back to the chat. His voice was nice, and I could hear the faintest accent when he spoke so I asked, "What ethnicity are you? I can hear a little bit of an accent in your voice."

He said, "You can? I'm Mexican, but I was born here."

I asked, "Do you speak Spanish?"

He said, "Yes. I have since I was a kid. My parents can speak English too, but I mostly speak to them in Spanish because it is easier for them."

I loved the fact that he spoke Spanish; it only made him more interesting to me. We spent hours talking on the phone. Back then, video chat wasn't as accessible, so getting to know someone by phone was interesting. I had a picture of him, but I'd learned the hard way that pictures can be deceiving. The only way to truly see if there was the right kind of connection was to meet them in person.

MELINDA VELASQUEZ

I'd thought I had a connection with someone after talking to them for a while, but then when we met in person, the connection just wasn't there. It made for quite a few really awkward first dates!

It had been almost two weeks since he first messaged me, and I said, "Okay, this is starting to feel like it could get serious. We need to meet in person to see if this is going to go anywhere before we get too attached."

He agreed we should meet, and we started figuring out a good halfway point. I looked at a map of California and tried to find the halfway point between the two of us. I loved the ocean, so I focused on the coastal areas. I found a cute little town on the Central Coast where we would meet in person for the first time and have our first date.

It was about a four-hour drive for him and five hours for me. We were set to meet the very next Sunday. I found a cute little spot with a restaurant, bar and hotel online that looked like a perfect place for a romantic rendezvous.

I had set up a plan with Kate to call when I got there, just to let her know everything was okay. Louie and I talked all the way up until the time we left that day, and called each other from the road along the way to update our locations. He ended up arriving about an hour before me and decided to drive around and check out the area.

I called him to let him know I was finally getting close, and he said he was parked in the parking lot at our meeting spot, waiting for me. By the time I got there, I was so ready to get out of my car. But it wasn't until I actually pulled into the parking lot that my nerves really kicked in.

I parked, turned off my car, and took a quick look in the mirror to make sure I looked okay after the long drive. Stepping out, I stretched a bit to shake off the stiffness from the drive. I spotted his car a few spots away from mine. Just then, I saw him exit the car, and we both started walking toward each other.

He was gorgeous—and tall! That was one of the things I had been fooled by on a few occasions with other dates before him. My heart started racing as we got closer, and he said in the sweetest tone, "Hi Baby!"

He started calling me "Baby" during our phone calls and I liked it coming from him. As we reached each other, he smiled and said, "You're even more beautiful in person!" Then, without hesitation, he opened his arms out and went right in for a kiss.

I was so overwhelmed by all my feelings and his. I could immediately feel there was a really strong energy between us, and after the long drive, I wasn't quite ready to dive into it all just yet. I pulled back, letting out a nervous giggle, and said, "Hold on, I just need a minute. That was a really long drive, and I really need to go to the restroom."

He said, "Oh yeah, there is one right inside. I'll show you."

I stepped into the bathroom and freshened up a little, and was grateful there was no one else in there. After splashing some water on my face, I looked in the mirror, trying to take it all in and center myself. "I said out loud to myself, "Woah!" I was trying to take in the moment and how I was feeling about seeing him in person for the first time. I took a deep breath and whispered out loud, trying to contain my excitement in case he could hear me outside the restroom, "He has really gorgeous eyes!"

The spark was definitely there, and it was powerful. He obviously felt it too. I came out of the restroom and felt much better. Sensing the need to break the ice a bit, he said, "There is a bar right over here, you want to get a drink?"

My eyes got big, I smiled and sighed with a sense of relief and said, "Yes, that sounds like a good idea."

There was a lot of pressure, having driven all that way, hoping that the connection we had on the phone would translate in person. I think the anticipation had me more on edge than I realized. But after we had a drink and talked a bit, I started to feel a little more relaxed.

The place we met was very cute. After finishing our drinks, we went back outside to walk through the gardens they had on the property. It was beautifully landscaped, with a winding pathway that made it feel like we were walking through an enchanted garden. We both loved the wishing well, and there were a bunch of romantic little nooks.

By then, I was feeling much more like myself. We found a little private spot in the garden and tried again with a kiss. I was *not* disappointed. In fact, once we started kissing, we had a hard time stopping. Chemistry was not a problem with this guy.

We went back inside and sat on a couch in the lounge next to a huge fireplace and kissed a little bit more. Then Louie said, "Are you hungry? We could go check out the town and find a place to get something to eat."

I wanted to keep kissing him, but after that long drive, I needed food, "Yes, I'm starving! Let's go find somewhere to eat."

We drove down to a cute restaurant in the center of town. We talked, laughed, and were having a really good time. At one point, I noticed the song "Feels So Good" by Chuck Mangione playing in the background. It brought back memories of my dad playing it all the time when I was a kid. I hadn't heard in years, and it felt like a positive sign from the Universe.

After lunch, we decided to take a drive to a place with a view of the ocean. We found a secluded bench overlooking the ocean and sat there, kissing for about two hours. There was a little bit of talking in between and looking at the ocean, but mostly we were kissing.

Since it was such a long drive, we had talked about possibly staying overnight when we first planned the date. We didn't want to add any more pressure, so we agreed to wait and see how we felt once we got there. Sitting together on that bench, I knew I wasn't ready to leave, and he felt the same. We decided to get a room and stay the night.

We decided to head back to our meeting spot and pick up my car. We were on our way back to pick up my car, and suddenly I remembered, "Oh shit! I was supposed to call my friend, Kate, to let her know you aren't an axe murderer!"

I looked down at my cell phone and realized I had no service. I had been so caught up that I completely forgot to check in with Kate. His phone didn't have service either, so when we got back to pick up my car, we found a payphone in the hotel lobby. I called Kate and let her know I wasn't dead on the side of the road and that things were going really well.

The hotel where we met was a little expensive for a one-night stay, and it wasn't even close to the ocean. So, during our drive, we found a cute little hotel by the ocean and decided to rent a room there for the night. When we went to check out the room, the décor was pretty outdated—wall to wall *intense* floral wallpaper—but it was clean, reasonably priced and we could hear the ocean.

We picked up where we left off on the bench for a while in the room. Then, out of nowhere, he sat up and said, "Let's go out. That bartender told us they were going to have live music at that place tonight, and I want to take you out."

Here we were, getting pretty hot and heavy on the bed in a hotel room, and he wanted to take me out. He had no idea at the time, but he scored major points for that! I said, "Okay, yeah that sounds fun. I love live music."

Louie was a musician. He was in a band playing bass at the time, and he could also play drums and acoustic guitar. The more I learned about him, the more I liked him. So we freshened up a little and headed out for the night.

The live music was great, and we had such a fun night. The cozy lounge where we sat had the large fireplace lit. It was really romantic. Honestly, it felt like a dream first date—the best one I had ever had.

We stayed for a while, listening to the live music, but eventually, we started to get tired and realized we hadn't eaten dinner. By now, it was around 9 p.m., and the restaurant at the venue had already closed, so we decided to head downtown to find a place to eat. It was just a short drive downtown, but when we got there, everything had closed up for the night. This place was very touristy and had no fast-food restaurants or any restaurants that were open at that time on a Sunday night.

We were starving, so we ended up at the only place open with food that time of night—a gas station. Our first romantic dinner together was frozen burritos, sodas, and vanilla Zingers for dessert. But it didn't matter; we were having so much fun it only added to the charm of the evening.

As powerful as the attraction was between us, I was worried that once we got back to the hotel, the pressure would be on to have sex. We *did* rent a hotel room, but I wanted to wait until the time felt right, and I didn't want to be put in a bad position. Thankfully, I didn't need to worry he didn't put any pressure on me and we both decided it would be better if we waited.

I couldn't have pictured a better first date. We kissed a little more, talked, and fell asleep next to each other, listening to the ocean. But when I woke up the next morning, suddenly a feeling of panic came over me.

THE WEIGHT OF SILENCE

I was freaking out. I sat there before he woke up just staring at him and for some bizarre reason, I was trying to find something wrong with him. Things had been so perfect, and that's exactly what scared me. I had a history of things going bad for me when they seemed like they were good.

When Louie woke up, he was still being as sweet as ever, but by that point, I had already started to put up my walls. I didn't know at the time what was happening for me, but I was starting to sabotage whatever was happening with us before it even got started.

As we got ready to leave, suddenly I couldn't get to my car fast enough. My anxiety was in full control of my body. We kissed goodbye and planned to follow each other until we got to Highway 5 and had to go our separate directions.

It was about an hour drive to the 5 Freeway, and as soon as we had cell service again, he called me. I was still in panic mode so I didn't pick up at first. He kept calling me, and he wasn't giving up. Suddenly it was like I snapped out of my little freak out and said to myself out loud, "What the hell are you doing? This guy is great. He is everything you said you have always wanted. You had a great time. Get over your fear and pick up the damn phone!"

I hadn't realized until that moment that I was scared. I had been through the wringer with guys and was terrified of being hurt again. But something told me this time could be different, so I got out of my head, and out of my own way, and picked up the phone.

When I answered, Louie sounded concerned. "Hey! I was getting worried when you weren't picking up. Is everything okay?"

I smiled as soon as I heard his voice, "I'm sorry. To be honest, I was freaking out a little bit. I have never had a first date like that before and I think it scared me a little."

MELINDA VELASQUEZ

He said, "I know, I had a really great time too. You don't have anything to be scared of with me, Baby."

We stayed on the phone until we reached a gas station at the 5 Freeway where he would head south and I would head north. By the time we got out of our cars, I couldn't wait to see him again. I realized that my fear was only there because I sensed how real and different this connection with Louie was—and that's exactly what scared me.

Louie and I hugged, kissed, and made plans to talk again on our way home and once we got home. Later that day, when we both were back home, we talked on the phone and decided we were going to be exclusive. Even though we lived seven hours away from each other, we were both willing to make it work.

Louie and I started a long-distance relationship, and even though I had not been with any men I could trust in a long time, I never worried about him. For the first time in my life, I was not living in constant fear of my boyfriend cheating on me. He was nearly 300 miles away, and I trusted him completely.

For the first time in a long while, my love life was going great. I knew this was *the* man I wanted to introduce to my dad. Louie and I had been dating for about three months when I got a call from my dad asking for my sister and me to come up and visit him. He sounded strange and said that he wanted Shelly and me to come up because he had something he wanted to tell us—something he wanted to tell us in person. It felt weird and cryptic, and something told me it wasn't going to be good news.

CHAPTER 27

My sister and I tried to get my dad to tell us what was going on over the phone, but he wouldn't, so we made the hour-long drive to see him. We talked in the car about what it could be. I told her I thought either he and his girlfriend had gotten married without telling us, or he was sick.

When we arrived at his house and walked up to the front door, both he and his girlfriend, Susan, came to the door and opened it. The minute I saw him, I knew he was sick. He looked thinner than usual, and his skin looked yellowish.

Before they could even say hello, I blurted out, "You're sick, aren't you?"

He looked at Susan with a look of disappointment and said, "Dammit, I thought I was looking pretty good today."

It was cancer. Secondary liver cancer, to be specific. And just like that, all that was good in my life vanished, and my heart crumbled. They kept talking to us, but I was in shock. It felt like I left my body for a moment.

We sat down in their living room, the same place that was my home for a few years, as they gave us more information. I couldn't focus on their words, so I stared out into the backyard and noticed two crepe paper bells hanging from the covered patio. It turned out I was right about both things—they had gotten married while waiting for the doctor's results. They didn't want to take any chances that she couldn't be involved in every step if it turned out he did have cancer.

They told us that it was early and he was going to go through chemotherapy. They were trying to give us all the hopeful talk, but something told me this wasn't good. He explained that he was jaundiced because it was in his liver, but I knew in my heart when I saw him, it was bad.

We didn't stay long. It felt like we had just arrived, and soon we were back in the car heading home. As we drove home, we tried to process what we had just heard and what it meant for all of us. Shelly wondered how much she should tell my niece—who was only around nine years old at the time—about her Papa's condition.

The drive home took us right alongside the Russian River, where we had shared so many fun river-rafting trips with dad. I flashed to a memory of us floating in the inner tubes he had tied together and anchored to the boat, so we wouldn't get separated. Everything was fine until we hit some rough rapids, and the inner tubes—with us in them—got tangled in the ropes and caught in the trees. It was a little scary at first because the current was strong and the water was deep. Dad had to swim over and cut the ropes to free us. Once we were safely out, we all joked and gave dad a hard time about his "grand idea", laughing about it for the rest of the trip.

I loved those river-rafting trips, and when something went wrong, it just gave us another great story. There were so many times we floated down the river for hours, wondering how close we were to the spot where we had left our car. Dad always pretended to have full confidence in his planning, so he just kept saying, "It's just around this bend" over and over.

As the memories continued to flow during the drive home, so did the tears I had been holding back. When we got back, Shelly and I went in to talk to my mom. Dad had already told her but had asked her not to tell us, as he wanted to tell us in person. Despite the bitter divorce and the 15 years they had been apart, both having found other loves in their lives, I could see how much it affected my mom. I wasn't happy that she was sad, but it brought me comfort to know that she clearly still had love for him in that moment.

When I got back to my house, I realized I had forgotten that I'd told my friend, who lived across the street, what I thought might happen before I left. She saw my car pull in and called me, so I gave her the news. She happened to have a good friend over who actually worked at a nearby renowned cancer research hospital, and told me if I had questions to come over and she could maybe answer some questions for me.

I headed over, and the first thing she asked me was, "Do you know what stage the cancer is?"

Back then, I didn't know much about cancer and could only repeat what Dad and his wife had told me, "They said it was stage 4, liver cancer, but it's early and he's going to do chemotherapy, so hopefully he has at least a couple of years…"

I will never forget the look on her face in that moment. She turned to my neighbor with a look of dread and shook her head, and then looked back at me and said, "No, honey. I'm so sorry…" she paused and sighed and said, "he's got three, maybe four months max."

MELINDA VELASQUEZ

If I had been standing, I think I would have collapsed. I just sat there, not knowing what to think or feel. My face got hot, and the tears started flowing again.

My neighbor sat next to me, held me, and said, "I'm so sorry honey."

At first, I felt a wave of anger that she decided to drop that bomb on me, but later, I was grateful for her honesty. I told them I needed to leave and ran back across the street to my house. I rushed upstairs to my bedroom and grabbed the phone to call Louie, desperate to tell him everything that had happened.

One of my first thoughts was how much I wanted Dad to get to know Louie. He was *the* guy I wanted to introduce to my father, and now I had just been told that my dad had a terminal illness that would likely kill him in three or four months. I was devastated, confused, and overwhelmed. I wished Louie wasn't so far away — I just wanted him to hold me while I cried.

CHAPTER 28

My dad started chemotherapy right away, and I visited him whenever I could. One time, I saw him just after a chemo treatment, and I was surprised by how good he felt and how much energy he had. Susan told me that they pumped him full of vitamins and nutrients to try to counteract some of the toxic effects of the chemo, so right after his treatment he always felt pretty good.

However, by later that night or the next day, the sickness would set in. He'd start feeling terrible becoming physically ill. They gave him some medical marijuana, and Susan made him pot brownies to help try and boost his appetite. The treatments also left him extremely tired, so he had to rest a lot during the day.

While all of this was going on with my dad, I was also trying to maintain my long-distance relationship with Louie. We visited each other as much as possible. And we planned for him to come up and spend five days with me during the Thanksgiving holiday. I really wanted him to meet my dad, so we arranged a day while he was here to make the drive up and see my dad.

I was nervous to introduce Louie to my dad, but I knew I wanted them to meet. Louie had already met my mom before we headed up to see my dad, and after we left, she called me and said in a sing-song voice, "You're gonna marry him." My mom had never said that about any guy I had dated before. Not even close.

We arrived at my dad's and right away I could see he had lost weight since the last time I saw him. He wasn't jaundiced anymore, but he looked paler than usual. I introduced Louie to my dad, and we sat down to chat. Unfortunately, after what felt like no more than 20 minutes, my dad said, "I'm really sorry, I'm getting really tired. I'm going to have to go and rest."

We knew Dad wasn't coming back out, so we said our goodbyes to him before he retired to his room for a nap. It definitely wasn't the meeting I had hoped for, but I was grateful that Louie had been willing to drive all that way with me to meet my dad. We stayed and talked with Susan for a bit, but we could tell she probably needed a little downtime too, so we got ready to head out.

I think we were in the house for less than an hour from start to finish. Louie and I got back in the car and headed back to my house. I said, "I wish we could have had more time with him. I wish you could have met him before he had cancer. You're not really getting to know him at all when he is like that."

Louie replied, "It's okay, baby. I'm so sorry you are going through all of this. I just want you to know I am here for you."

I tried to enjoy the time I had with Louie while he was there. It was hard not to think about my dad, or worry about him, but there was nothing I could do for him. Susan was taking really good care of him, and I did the best I could to stay positive.

While Louie was there, I made my first ever Thanksgiving meal, just for the two of us. One perk of having college-aged roommates was that during school breaks, I usually had the house all to myself. I did pretty well with dinner—until it came to making the gravy. Then I had to call my mom for help!

That weekend, I decided to take us on a drive up Highway 1 along the coast. We drove all the way up to one of my favorite spots on the Mendocino coastline. Louie was so shocked at the fact that there were hardly any cars on the road the entire drive. He said, "In SoCal when you get close to the beach, there are cars and people everywhere!"

He loved how peaceful, quiet, and slow-paced things were where I lived; I loved seeing a place I had lived my whole life through fresh eyes. I loved how he looked at things with such wonder—things I had either never even noticed or taken for granted. It made our time together feel even more meaningful, and it made leaving each other at the airport that much harder.

Meanwhile, my dad had reached a point in his treatment where he could venture out a little more. He still got tired easily, but he was able to do more things than he could in the beginning. He wanted to come down to visit the Christmas tree farm and the apple farm that was a beloved holiday tradition in our family. We weren't sure if he had the energy to cut down a tree, but we were excited he wanted to go. I decided to invite my good friend Jack to join us as well.

Jack and my dad really had really hit off the last time we went to the Christmas tree farm. Jack and I remained really good friends, and he knew everything that had been going on with my dad. Jack and Kevin, my boss at the restaurant, were two men I counted on a lot when I was single and needed a male perspective. They were always there to help me with my car or other things I didn't know how to handle.

Jack brought his girlfriend, who was also a friend of mine, and Shelly and Kayla came too. Shelly brought her boyfriend as well. It was a fun day, but like with so many things during that time, we couldn't help but wonder if this would be the last time we would do this with Dad. We were nearing the three to four-month mark my neighbor's friend had warned me about. Though Dad wasn't healed, it seemed like he was having more good days than bad ones.

I tried to focus on the positive, and having that day together was a really good thing. We got our tree, our free bag of apples, spicy apple bread, and enjoyed our usual hot dog, nachos, and Hawaiian Punch in the can by the fire. It was a tradition we had with Dad since we were little, and I was so grateful for that time together. The rest of December flew by, and I had plans to spend Christmas with Louie in SoCal.

I hadn't really met any of Louie's family yet, so I was both nervous and excited when he introduced me to his parents. I was looking forward to seeing that part of his world. We went to his parents' house, sat with them, and talked for a bit.

When I saw his dad for the first time, I thought to myself, *Wow! Louie looked like a younger, taller version of his dad!* His father was outgoing, welcoming, sweet, and very charming. He greeted us with a big smile and he was clearly really happy to see Louie. His mom, on the other hand, was a little tougher to read.

She was quiet and more reserved. She was very soft-spoken and spoke mostly in Spanish. When she did speak in English, she spoke so quietly that I struggled to hear her. She was giving me a look like she was sizing me up the whole time I was there. She let her guard down a little bit when she pulled out some cute pictures of Louie when he was younger. Louie had warned me she might take a while to warm up to me.

By the time we were ready to leave, Louie's dad gave me a big hug. I walked over to Louie's mom and went to hug her, but I could tell she was not feeling it! She just sort of kept her arms out, but never seemed to complete the hug. She mostly just patted my shoulders. I didn't take it personally, and I was happy I got to finally meet them.

We enjoyed our first Christmas together, but I had to head back home before New Year's Eve. We made plans to watch a movie together while on the phone on New Year's Eve. We both rented the same movie and ordered our own takeout and snacks. We got on the phone and started the movie at the same time so we could watch it together.

I was so happy to not be in some bar, working and dealing with loud, drunk people. Even though we weren't in the same place that night, I was happier watching a movie on the phone with him than being anywhere else. I had wished for so long to have a boyfriend and a quiet night on New Year's Eve, and I finally had both.

CHAPTER 29

My dad was doing okay, but I didn't get to see him much. He and Susan had taken a trip to Hawaii and decided to go first class all the way. By that time, he had officially left his job. They visited me at work once on their way back from somewhere, and when he walked in, I was shocked at how skinny he'd become.

He was still putting up a brave front, trying to stay positive, but he had to travel with a pillow everywhere because he had lost so much weight that sitting for long periods hurt him. Dad had a really hard time accepting what was happening to him. I hadn't realized how much until one day, I got a call from Susan and she sounded panicked.

"Melinda, is there any chance you can drive up to the house today to see your dad? He is having a really rough day, and I'm stuck at work until 5 p.m. and I can't leave." Susan had been dad's main caretaker and had already taken a lot of time off work.

Without hesitation I replied, "Yeah! I don't have to work until later tonight. I will get ready for work and head up there, and I will stay there until I have to leave for work."

She sounded grateful and relieved, "Thank you! Oh, that is so great. I'm not even going to tell him you are coming up; it will be a nice surprise for him."

In that moment, I realized how much she had taken on and how little I had actually been able to see him since he got sick. I said, "Of course. Thanks for reaching out and asking me. I wanted to go see him anyway."

I got ready and headed up to his house. When I got there, I used my key to get in. As I opened the door, Dad popped his head up from the couch, saw me, smiled, and said, "What are *you* doing here?"

I said, "I just missed you and wanted to come hang out for a bit."

He gave me a sheepish smile and said, "Did Susan call you?"

I said, "Maybe…but I'm glad she did. It has been too long since I got to spend quality time with you."

It felt good to see his energy shift. I could tell he was really happy I was there. We had a really good talk that day. He opened up a little bit about how he was feeling about everything, and for the first time, he admitted to me that he was scared. I think everything was finally hitting him all at once.

I just sat with him and listened. He got me caught up on what had been going on, and he asked me how things were with Louie. I realized in that moment that I needed that time with him just as much as he needed me that day. By then, we both knew he wasn't going to get better, but we hadn't come out and said it until that day.

MELINDA VELASQUEZ

I looked right at him and asked, "When you go, you're going to come back and visit me, right?"

He looked at me, a little surprised at first, and then his faced softened into acceptance. He smiled and said, "Yes."

Our family had a history of having spiritual connections. My dad had been visited by my maternal grandmother after she passed and my mom told me about a few things that happened to her. My sister had experienced it as well, but I was the only one who hadn't tapped into that part of myself. It wasn't that I didn't believe in it—I just hadn't experienced anything significant enough to remember.

I wanted to make sure he knew that I believed that, even when he was no longer here on Earth, I knew he would always be with me. I couldn't imagine what he was feeling with all he was dealing with, but I hoped that brought him a little bit of peace and comfort. Being with him that day was the best gift I could have ever asked for, and I was so grateful Susan had called me and asked me to come.

I cried most of the way on my long drive to work that night. On the drive, I called Louie and told him about the day. I was struck by how fast everything had advanced with my dad's cancer, and how quickly life can change. It was around that time that Louie and I started talking about our next steps.

The last time he visited, as we walked to the car at the airport, I opened the trunk to put his bag in and I said to him, "I'm not in a place right now where I can pick up and move."

I already didn't see my dad as much as I wanted to, and I knew that moving to SoCal would make that even harder. As much as I loved Louie, I had no desire to move to SoCal, and emotionally, I wasn't ready to leave the area I lived at that time.

He just calmly smiled, looked at me, and said, "I know."

I didn't want him to think that meant I wasn't ready to have us be together in the same place, so I said, "I mean, I know it is a lot to ask of you right now, but I want us to be together."

He smiled again and said, "It's okay. I think I'm in a place where I am ready to make a move."

I smiled, grabbed him, and hugged him. I was so happy. I had never felt such a strong connection to anyone before, and with every step, he kept reassuring me that he was right there with me. From that point on, we started planning for him to move to NorCal, and we decided to move in together when he did. Some people thought we were crazy or moving too fast, but we knew better.

We worked pretty quickly to get the plan in place for Louie to move up to NorCal. Everything seemed to fall into place so easily for us to start living together by the end of April 2003. I connected him with a local Landscaping company, and he had a job interview there. He had been working hard on a side job and had saved up enough money to hold him over until he found something more permanent.

I gave my notice at the place I was working and planned to start a new job as Floor Manager of the restaurant in a nearby high-end hotel. I was looking forward to the new opportunity and ready for a change—I was getting burnt out on the bartender life. The restaurant by the river had closed, and I had been recruited to work at a new bar and grill nearby. The new place was open later, so instead of being off by 10p.m., I was working until midnight or later most shifts.

I worked my last bartending shift and headed straight to the airport to get my man! The plan was for me to fly down, help Louie pack, load everything into the moving truck, and drive back together—towing his vehicle behind the truck. My roommates had found someone to sublet my room, and I'd secured a cute little place for us out in the country. Everything lined up perfectly, and I was so excited to finally have Louie with me full-time.

As we drove up the hill to our new home, I could tell Louie was a little nervous. He turned to me and asked, "Where are you taking me?"

I said, "Trust me, you'll love it."

Once Louie got a look at the whole place, he was actually impressed and very happy. I had already moved most of my stuff in, with my sister's help, and now it was just a matter of getting Louie's stuff in too. We began the process of blending our belongings and settling into our new home. It felt so good to finally be together in the same space.

We were so busy during those first few weeks, getting settled into our new life together. I had started my new job, and Louie got a job with a landscape company. We were so caught up in setting up our lives that I hadn't talked to my dad or Susan in a while. Then, a few weeks into May, we got a call from Susan's sister that launched us out of our happy bubble and back to reality.

Susan's sister and I got along really well, but she had never called me before. When I heard her voice on the phone I was surprised, and then it hit me that this wasn't a *good* call. She said, "I think you girls need to get up here as soon as possible to see your dad."

She didn't have to say more—I knew exactly what she meant. Suddenly I felt so much guilt for not being up there or seeing my dad. It had been almost a month, but there was so much going on that I just lost track of time.

I called my sister, and she quickly arranged for someone to

take care of my niece. I told her I would pick her up as soon as I got things ready. After saying goodbye to Louie, I left to get Shelly for the drive to Dad's house. I thought the time we drove up for him to tell us he had cancer was a difficult drive, but this time, it was far worse.

I'd always loved that drive, often heading up to visit Dad when I needed an escape and some respite. Now, though, we were pretty sure we were going up to say our final goodbyes. Neither of us knew exactly what to expect, but we knew it wasn't good.

I had seen my dad just before going to pick up Louie, but in just a month, the cancer and the chemo had taken its toll on him. He had lost so much weight, and he looked like he had aged 20 years in seven months. It literally sucked the life right out of him, and it was heartbreaking to see him like that. I had already lost plenty of people in my life, but it doesn't matter how old you are, losing a parent is a loss like no other.

Shelly and I tried to mentally prepare ourselves as best we could, but we really had no idea what to expect. When we arrived, Dad was in the living room in a wheelchair, looking very frail. He tried to fake it, but it was clear things were really bad.

Susan told us that she was struggling to get him to eat, and that was a bad sign. She told us that they had called Hospice and that they were going to have someone come out and answer questions. Susan said she needed a few things from the pharmacy and I offered to go get them.

Shelly came with me but she stayed in the car while I ran inside. One of the things Susan asked us to pick up was something to help with my Dad's chapped lips. Even though it was a small pharmacy, I started to feel extremely anxious when I couldn't find anything to help with Dad's chapped lips. Suddenly, everything hit me all at once, and I just lost it, breaking down in the middle of the pharmacy.

Thankfully I was the only customer there. Someone came out from behind the counter and tried to comfort me, asking, "Are you okay?"

I turned to them and blurted out, "My dad is dying, and I need something to help with his chapped lips."

The staff was very kind and helpful, showing me the product I was looking for. I turned to the person helping me and said, "Thank you so much. I'm so sorry—I just felt suddenly so sad and overwhelmed."

I fought to hold back the tears again as they said, "No need to apologize. It is completely understandable."

I pulled myself together before heading back out to the car. I told Shelly what happened and took a moment to pull myself together. We had one more stop: the grocery store. Susan had asked us to buy some cans of a nutritional drink called Ensure, which the doctor recommended for when Dad did not want to eat.

We found the Ensure and, while we were there, decided to grab some of Dad's favorites to see if we could get him to eat something. We picked up canned fruit cocktail, chocolate pudding, and a few other things that might be easy to feed him. Susan was skeptical when we brought home the food, but when he took a few bites, she exclaimed with a sense of relief, "Good job, girls!"

Unfortunately, it was a short-lived victory. He was no longer able to sit in the wheelchair and needed to lie down in the bedroom. The lady from Hospice showed up and talked to us a bit about what to expect as he moved closer to his final moments of life.

She told us, "The fact that he isn't eating was a sign that he was nearing the end of life. You may notice his toenails might turn a different color, and his skin might change color as well. He may start making sounds like he is trying to talk, but you can't make out what he is saying. He may even appear to be in some kind of trance, talking to people who aren't there."

It was a lot to take in, and as unsettling as it was, it was also helpful being able to ask questions and get clear answers. It was sad, scary, awful, and comforting all at the same time. Once the woman from Hospice left, we had no choice but to wait.

He eventually reached a point where he was not really cognizant of anything going on around him. I wanted to just lie on the bed and be near him, but as we got closer to the end, he seemed to grow more agitated whenever Shelly or I were in the room. I don't think he wanted us to see him like that. We said our goodbyes to him and stepped out of the room.

We knew the end was near, and Susan was the only one he wanted by his side. She was talking to him and trying to keep him calm. It was too painful for Shelly and me to hear him suffering, so we went out to the garage and sat in his shop area to try to escape it. I thought to myself, *I don't want him to suffer or to be in anymore pain...*

Just then, we heard Susan let out a loud, anguished scream. We knew he was gone. He was only 56 years old. I had just been wishing for his pain to end, but the moment he was gone, I wasn't ready. I immediately felt the pain of the loss of him surge through my body like a lightning bolt, and I wanted him back. I couldn't stand to see them wheel him out of the house, so we stayed in the garage until Susan's sister let us know it was safe to come back inside.

We knew Susan needed her privacy. She had been through so much, not just as his wife, but also as his caretaker. We wanted to give her some space. I called Louie to let him know Dad had passed, and that Shelly and I were going to head home. The whole way home I think I was still in shock and I just felt kind of numb. I dropped Shelly off and drove home to Louie.

It was the middle of the night by the time I got home, and Louie was already in bed. I lay beside him for a few minutes as he held me. Then I said, "There is no way I'm going to be able to sleep tonight. I'm going to go in the living room and start making phone calls." He had to work in the morning, so I knew if I stayed in there, I would just keep him up too.

I took out my address book and started making phone calls, starting with family and moving on to my dad's good friends. I was shocked to find out that some of my dad's friends didn't even know he was sick. It had only been about eight months since he told us about the cancer, and his decline had been so rapid. He only made it about four months longer than my neighbor's friend had predicted.

We started working with Susan on the plans for the memorial service, and that's when things started to get a little bumpy with Susan. I had been pretty close with Susan and always got along well with her. Shelly liked her too, but spent less time with her and dad than I did.

I was so appreciative of Susan; she had been there for my dad in every way possible. She invited Shelly, Kayla, Louie, and me to the house to put together pictures and things for his memorial service program. It started out good, but then things got really weird.

Susan had some friends over, and they started drinking wine. Before we knew it, the energy shifted. She got *really* drunk and started talking loudly, saying negative and private things about my dad—things his kids and granddaughter didn't need to hear, especially at that moment. She seemed angry and was clearly struggling. I can't imagine what she must have been feeling, but he was our dad, and Kayla's grandpa.

THE WEIGHT OF SILENCE

Louie had only met her once before and he began feeling extremely uncomfortable, as did the rest of us. I can't quite describe it, but suddenly it felt like we weren't welcome in our dad's home. We knew it was her home too, but in a moment when we hoped to come together and work on something important, it just felt like it everything had become about her. She had invited us to work together on the program, but everything just went sideways.

We held the service at one of my dad's favorite wineries, outside near the bocce ball court. It was a beautiful day, and we told everyone to wear Hawaiian shirts and dresses instead of wearing sad, dark clothing. My dad loved traveling to Hawaii, and he was always the life of the party. We wanted the celebration of his life to reflect that spirit.

I had been keeping myself busy helping with all the planning and worrying about how Susan was handling everything—I just wanted it all to go perfectly. It wasn't until I saw the look on my cousin's faces as they walked up to greet me that the immensity of my dad dying truly hit me.

I had been so concerned about Susan, getting things ready, including everyone who loved my dad while not hurting anyone's feelings, and even managing my sister's meltdown in the parking lot right before the service. But when I saw the empathy for *me* on my cousins' faces, the magnitude of losing my dad finally hit me. As usual, I had been so worried about everyone else that I had completely forgotten about my own loss.

It was so comforting to see my cousins. I knew how much they loved my dad, and they reminded me of those happy times from my childhood. Leisa and Laura were there too, of course, and Leisa wrote me a wonderful letter to read later. I was so grateful for all the love surrounding me that day.

MELINDA VELASQUEZ

A family member, who was a pastor, performed the service. He had known my dad as a kid and talked about my dad's life beautifully, in a way that reflected all phases of his journey and including all the people who loved him. We had a bunch of round tables set up with umbrellas, and Susan was sitting with a group of friends and co-workers. When the pastor reached the part of his story about Susan, her table let out a loud cheer, and someone yelled, "Finally!"

Everyone else looked around in disbelief, and to me, it was extremely rude and disrespectful. Susan was not the *only* person who lost my dad. Every person who he encountered before he met her made him the person she fell in love with, and I just couldn't understand why she or they didn't seem to respect that.

My sister and I prepared a joint speech, filled full of meaningful moments and funny stories. We arranged it so that we could take turns reading each section of it. I was glad we worked on it together and stood together to read it. It felt like the perfect send-off for our dad.

We ended the day gathering again at Dad and Susan's, and by the time we got there, I was completely exhausted. Thankfully, things were not weird at the house the way they had been before, but it was clear they would never quite be the same again.

At one point, I told Susan that I believed the Universe had other plans for her, and that when she was ready, I hoped she would find someone to love again. I knew how deeply she loved my dad and how devastated she was by his loss. We ended up having one last Christmas at Dad's house, with Susan and our whole family. I told her that she was part of the family and that I hoped she would continue to be in our lives.

Susan told me that my dad wanted me to have my grandmother's wedding rings and gave them to Louie, so he could give them to me when he was ready to propose. My grandparents had been married 52 years, only separated by death, so I figured the rings had some pretty good juju. It meant a lot that my dad, who had only met Louie once when he was pretty sick, saw something special in him too.

What I really wanted was to be able to go through my dad's things and look through old photos and things, the way you do when someone dies. But I also wanted to be respectful of Susan and her grieving process. With everything that happened, I didn't want to ask for too much. I trusted that when she was ready—before she got rid of his things—she would reach out to us, let us sit with everything, and take what mattered to us.

The night of the service, I did ask her for my favorite sweatshirt of his, and I waited forever to wash it because it still smelled like him. One of the things I would've liked to have had was a letter opener I always remembered him having on his desk in his den. The bottom part, which opened the letter, was shaped liked a crescent moon, and the top was a figure of an ethereal-looking woman. It was just something I could have on my desk so that whenever I saw it, I would think of him.

My dad was cremated, and in his will, he wanted his ashes be scattered on the Russian River. To me, it was a much-needed nod to Shelly and me, letting us know how much he too cherished those memories of river rafting with us. Unfortunately, we never did get the chance to go through Dad's things. Susan slowly began disappearing from our lives and eventually cut off all communication. We later found out that she had scattered Dad's ashes without us—and had actually done it before the Celebration of Life even happened. Not only did she do it without us, but she also spread the ashes in a place that was about her and Dad, not the Russian River as he had requested. I was pretty devastated when I found out.

MELINDA VELASQUEZ

Having her exit from our lives without a word, and feeling deprived of being able to go through Dad's things and scatter his ashes only added to the immensity of his loss. It wasn't at all how I had imagined things ending, and it made an already painful time in my life even harder to bear.

In the end, Mom, Shelly, Kayla, and I decided to have our own little ceremony for closure. My mom was actually very supportive throughout all of this, and I could see how much she still did love my dad. He was the father of her children, and *she* understood what it was like to lose a parent.

CHAPTER

30

Not long after we laid my dad to rest, Louie proposed to me on my birthday. It wasn't a huge surprise since he had been given the ring after my dad passed, but I had been dropping hints and wasn't sure when he would actually do it. There was no elaborate event—just the two of us in our first little home together—and I was over the moon happy.

We decided to get married in early November 2004. Fall was my favorite time of year, and where we lived, in early November we usually still had just enough sunshine and warmth. Living in wine country, we were surrounded by the breathtaking colors of the changing leaves, not just on the trees but in the vineyards too—stunning shades of red, orange, purple, and yellow.

We found a cute little place near our house we could afford to have both the ceremony and the reception in the same space. Kevin signed on as our caterer and gave us a phenomenal deal, which was great because we shopped around and had no idea how we would afford the food otherwise. A good friend who owned a bakery even offered to make our wedding cake for free! We were so grateful to both him and Kevin for their amazing gifts.

Everything was falling into place perfectly. I even found my dream wedding dress. It was a white, high-waisted, A-line dress style with a train, straps, and a sweetheart neckline. But my favorite part was that it wasn't plain white—it had little touches of my favorite shade of red, the color I loved most at the time. At the center of the chest, the white overlapped a beautiful deep red insert with sparkles, and a matching red ribbon crossed the waist and flowed down both sides of the back of the dress. My mom even made the perfect veil to match.

Mom and Charlie were still going strong; they had been together for about nine years, and he continued to be a welcomed part of our family. Charlie and my mom just seemed to fit, in ways that Mom and Dad never did. My mom and I had been happily wrapped up in the wedding plans, and then something happened that sent shockwaves through our family.

The phone rang, and I heard Shelly's panicked voice: "Something happened to Charlie, and he has been taken to the hospital in an ambulance. It's really bad, Minna. He might not make it."

I felt my chest tighten, my face grew hot, and the tears start flowing down my face as I tried to take in what she just said, "What? What happened?"

She said, "They think he suffered a heart attack and then after the heart attack, a blood clot went to his brain and caused a stroke."

I was in shock. He was only in his fifties and seemed pretty healthy. He was thin, so weight wasn't an issue that would cause a heart attack. What I didn't know at the time was that he was also doing meth—right alongside my mom. I don't know for sure if that caused the heart attack, but I'm sure the meth didn't help.

Louie and I rushed over to the hospital as soon as we could. My mom was really stressed out but was trying to hold it together. The doctors told us that Charlie might not make it, and that they would let us know as soon as they had any news.

Charlie was in the Intensive Care Unit (ICU), so only my mom was allowed to stay with him. I couldn't even begin to imagine our family without him. Even Louie had grown really fond of him. He was a good man, and my mom was so happy with him. The thought that he might not make it was devastating.

It had been just about a year since my dad passed away. Although Mom and Charlie weren't married yet, I thought of him as my stepdad. The idea of losing both my dad and stepdad within a year of each other, and knowing neither of them would be at my wedding, hit me really hard.

The next day or so was touch and go with Charlie. He had to undergo surgery to repair the damage from the heart attack and to assess the damage from the stroke. We had no idea if he would even wake up after the surgery.

It was an incredibly stressful time, but when we learned that Charlie had woken up and was going to make it, we were all thrilled and relieved. However, the next update we received was that, because they weren't sure how long he had been unconscious after the stroke, he would most likely experience cognitive and physical impairments.

Charlie had been alone, resting upstairs in their bedroom after coming home from work when the heart attack and stroke happened.

Mom came home after work and found him, but she didn't know how long after he got home it had occurred. There were usually a couple of hours between when he got home from work and when she did.

When Charlie woke up, he couldn't speak or write. He had a long recovery ahead of him, with speech therapy and learning how to function again. He had aphasia, which was a loss of ability to understand or express speech caused by brain damage. He also lost his peripheral vision in his left eye.

Overall, Charlie was very lucky. He eventually was able to walk without help and he could understand what people said to him, but he never fully regained his speech. He learned to say "yes" and "no", so we just learned to pose things to him in the form of yes or no questions. He also could say, "Huh?" or "What?" if he needed something repeated. While we were happy we still had him with us, the storyteller side of him—that part of him we all loved—was lost with the stroke.

Despite that, Charlie kept his sense of humor and loved to mess with people. We would tell people he couldn't talk, but he can say yes or no, so just ask him yes or no questions. It never failed—even with doctors—people would always respond by speaking slowly and loudly. We would say, he's not deaf, and right on cue Charlie would put his hand to his ear and say, "Huh?" just to mess with them. He would wait to see the bewildered look on the person's face and then he would laugh.

We were all grateful he made it, but it was a really rough time for my mom. She was doing a lot for our wedding while also being Charlie's main caretaker. The feeling of walking on eggshells around my mom intensified during the wedding planning. We shared a lot of good moments, but whenever I had a different opinion about something, she'd get very defensive, and I would just shut down.

THE WEIGHT OF SILENCE

Wedding planning can be stressful, even in the best of circumstances. Looking back, I'm not proud of how I acted during that time—especially with my mom, but also with my friends on a few occasions. I chose Laura and Leisa to both be my Maids of Honor. Laura was living in Oregon at the time, while Leisa lived nearby, so I thought it would help to not put all the planning on one person.

The tension with my mom, however, ran much deeper. I still had so many unresolved feelings about my mom and everything she put me through with her addiction and the divorce drama. On top of that, I was still grieving the loss of my dad. It was heartbreaking knowing he wouldn't be there to walk me down the aisle, share the father/daughter dance, or have the chance to know my husband.

For the most part, I enjoyed so much about the wedding with my mom. We had some great moments together, but there were times where I felt all my childhood wounds bubble up to the surface. As for Laura and Leisa, I must have driven them crazy with my controlling behavior and need for perfectionism.

Not only were Laura and Leisa my Maids of Honor, but the wedding party was a true family affair, with their kids being part of it as well. I chose not to have my sister in my wedding, but my niece Kayla, now age 11, was a junior bridesmaid.

At the time, there were so many things in my life that I couldn't control. In hindsight, I probably shouldn't have planned a wedding so soon after my dad died. But I was so happy with Louie, and after all the sadness, I just wanted to celebrate something good. Control was my go-to place when I was stressed.

Leisa and Laura are the polar opposites of my energy, which is just one of the many reasons why I love and need them in my life.

MELINDA VELASQUEZ

When I'm freaking out about some insignificant tiny detail, they have a way of diffusing the situation and bringing me back to center. Unfortunately, during that time, I'm pretty sure I had the opposite effect on them. I think I just stressed them the hell out.

With my mom, I felt like she owed me something after everything she had put me through, and I was determined to have the wedding I wanted. I was being driven by my emotional pain. I had no idea what she was going through dealing with being Charlie's caretaker, while still crafting things for wedding backdrops and decorations. For the first time, I was focusing on my needs and wants, but unfortunately, it came from a place of anger and bitterness, not out of love for myself or anyone else.

My emotional pain had a way of creeping up on me and taking control of how I showed up in the world. Not to mention, the stress of losing my dad, almost losing Charlie, and planning my wedding launched me back into the deepest parts of my codependency without even realizing it. I didn't realize how stressed out I was until I went to the doctor for ear pain and he told me it was the result of me grinding my teeth.

The year leading up to our wedding was an emotional roller coaster with everything that happened. Louie and I even got into the biggest fight we ever had right before our wedding when the stress of all the wedding bills coming due piled on both of us. But we got through it, and in the days before the wedding when his family arrived in town, we were able to start to enjoy all the months of planning.

My anxiety and need for everything to go perfectly kept threatening to steal my joy. However, when I woke up the morning of my wedding, I was overwhelmed with joy. Suddenly all the things I had stressed and worried about just washed away. I jumped out of bed and shouted with absolute glee, "I'M GETTING MARRIED TODAY!" And that was the energy I carried with me for the whole day.

THE WEIGHT OF SILENCE

Our wedding day was a wonderful day filled with sweet, sentimental moments, hilariously funny ones, and so much joy. I decided to have my mom walk me down the aisle, and she found the perfect dress that matched the red accents in my wedding dress perfectly.

I was standing on the steps, being photographed, when she walked up, and I finally got to see her in her beautiful dress, ready for pictures before the ceremony. She looked radiant. In that moment, I felt the same love and pride for her as I did for her when I was that little girl, excited to see her walk through my kindergarten classroom. She was beaming with pride, and she was so happy and honored that I had chosen her to walk me down the aisle.

The space we had was a little funky and dated, but we did our best to make it beautiful. What I remember most was the love that filled up the room that day. Charlie even felt good enough to be able to attend the ceremony and part of the reception. There were some hitches that happened with timing, and we were running a little behind, but I was determined to stay present in the moment and enjoy every second of the day.

The time came for the bridal party to walk down the aisle. We all lined up in the lobby, waiting for the music to start. Louie looked so handsome in his black tuxedo, with a white vest and tie. He hadn't seen me yet, but I caught a glimpse of him without him knowing. The music began, and everyone but mom and me made their way down the aisle. I could hear all the guests delighting in the kiddos as they made their entrance.

Mom and I stood there, waiting for the wedding march to come on next, but instead, the song I had initially requested—then changed—started to play. The night before the wedding, I'd got a call from a woman saying that the owner of the DJ company we hired who I had met with and planned with was not going to make it. She assured me that she was his "Senior DJ" and that she had spoken with him about our big day, and felt confident about filling in for him.

Being the kind of person I am, I tend to plan for things going wrong too. I took it in stride, asking if she had a copy of the playlist I had sent, specifically requesting songs for the day. She confirmed she had it, and I decided to let it go and trust that everything would work out.

But now, here we were, standing in the lobby waiting for the wedding march to play, and instead, she was playing the wrong damn song. I wasn't sure what was happening, but I knew I had made it clear it was supposed to be the wedding march. My mom and I looked at each other and decided to wait it out just in case. The DJ was set up at the other end of the building, so we couldn't see what was happening.

Then, in that moment, I thought to myself: *Oh shoot, what if the delay is freaking out Louie and he thinks I left him at the altar!* So, I yelled out as loudly as I could, "I'm coming Louie!"

All the guests erupted in laughter. Just then Kate—who sneaked down the side of the room—came running around the corner in her little kitten heals and said in her urgent, yet calm general manager problem-solving voice, "Hi...um, what's going on?"

I was still calm and simply turned to her and said, "They need to play the wedding march."

Kate quickly replied, "Okay! Got it!" She ran back up to the DJ and seconds later, the wedding march started playing. Mom and I came into the view of all with big smiles on our face acting like nothing had gone wrong at all. The guests applauded, and we got on with the ceremony.

It had already been an interesting day, and it was about to get even more eventful. The reverend we hired to perform the ceremony was both hilarious and very entertaining. Since I didn't grow up in church, and though Louie was raised Catholic, we decided against a church wedding, and opting instead for a non-denominational ceremony.

At one point, the reverend got to a part where he talked about my dad not being with us anymore, and I suddenly felt a wave of grief hit me hard. The tears came, and I was overwhelmed with emotion, barely able to keep it together. Just as I thought I might lose control completely, the reverend said something that caught me off guard: "His body may not be here with us today, but as you told me, I'm sure he will find a way to make his presence known."

That day I wore my hair half up, half down, with the top section styled into a bun where the comb that held my veil was securely pinned. Just as the reverend finished saying "he will make himself known," my veil unexpectedly lifted up from my hair and dropped to the ground. It didn't just fall out. According to everyone watching, it visibly lifted up as if something—someone—was guiding it, and then it dropped to the floor.

There was a collective gasp, and I couldn't help but smile through my tears, feeling in that moment like my dad had indeed found his way to make his presence known. My dad had always been the one to cheer me up when I was upset, using his mischievous sense of humor to lighten the mood. Suddenly, I was brought out of my grief, let out a laugh, turned to the guests with a big smile, pointed to the veil, and said, "And there it is!"

Once again, the guests erupted in laughter. We finished the ceremony and they announced us husband and wife. We both breathed a sigh of joy and relief as we headed back down the aisle to enjoy a quick private moment before moving onto the rest of the day. As soon as we were out of sight, we looked at each other, smiled, and said, "We did it!" We kissed again, told each other we loved each other, and walked arm in arm to rejoin our guests.

Since my dad wasn't there for the father-daughter dance, I had decided in advance to split that dance with the two men who had been there for me and were always there for me when I needed a little extra help—Jack and Kevin. We danced to the song I would have chosen for my dad, "Sailing" by Christopher Cross. My dad loved to sail. It was the song that always reminded me of him and the one magical day I got to spend with him and my mom on a friend's sailboat as a kid.

The rest of the day went by so fast, but we tried to make the best out of every second. Even the hitches and the glitches that would later become funny stories. They were part of the charm of the day, adding to the memories we'd cherish for the rest of our lives. We left the next day for our honeymoon in Maui, and spent the rest of the night and all the days after joyfully recounting every moment of our special day. It felt like a dream come true, and we were thrilled to start the rest of our life together.

Once we returned home from our beautiful honeymoon in Maui, we settled back in to daily life as a newly married couple. We were both working full-time and had a great group of friends we enjoyed spending time with on weekends. We enjoyed our cute little house in the country and hosted barbecues and badminton matches on our expansive lawn in our backyard.

Though I was still navigating the grief of losing my dad, I was also in a very happy place. I had married the love of my life, and Louie and I were building something beautiful together. But despite the joy in my personal life, I began to feel the pull of something that had been on my mind for a while—my career. I had earned my degree, but hadn't yet found the professional path I was looking for. I knew it was time to re-engage and shift some focus back to my own goals and ambitions.

CHAPTER 31

For years after earning my bachelor's degree, I struggled to find work that felt like the right fit. I realized my choice to major in history and pursue a teaching credential stemmed from fear. My mom was supportive of my passions but often let me quit when things got tough, while my dad emphasized follow-through and a clear career path. Although both perspectives came from a place of love, as a codependent, people-pleasing perfectionist shaped by my family's struggles with addiction, I found it difficult to forge my own path.

When I decided not to pursue my teaching credential, I transitioned my years of customer service experience in retail and hospitality into a more professional role. Working with people came naturally to me, and I excelled at it. I needed a break from school and time to discover what I truly wanted. After grieving the loss of my dad, adjusting to life as a newly married woman, and learning to silence the noise of other people's opinions, I began to find my way back to myself.

MELINDA VELASQUEZ

Nearly seven years after earning my bachelor's degree, I returned to school and completed a master's degree in Organization Development (OD). OD is based in psychology, social sciences, and human resource management, and for me, it was like the perfect marriage of psychology and business. Graduate school was a truly transformative experience; I finally found a field that resonated deeply with my own values and beliefs, and I formed deep, lasting connections with the people in my cohort. Yet, as grad school came to an end, I still struggled to figure out where I belonged.

Afterward, I was drawn to volunteer work, especially with youth organizations. What started as a way to network soon became something I genuinely enjoyed. I became active in my community, using my skills to help young people advocate for themselves and foster positive change. I partnered with a woman who had an incredible vision, and together, we designed and delivered the Youth Empowerment and Leadership Conference for grades six through eight, all with almost no budget. The conference was so successful for a number of years that we passed it on to a local teen center to carry on our work. I also collaborated with a group of therapists to help reshape how schools addressed adolescent female bullying.

Through my volunteer efforts, I organized and facilitated several community events. But one night, while driving to a community forum I had organized at the local library, I was suddenly overwhelmed with anxiety. I started experiencing this anxiety whenever I had to show up in a professional capacity. The focus of that anxiety was centered on my looks.

I wanted to be taken seriously and seen as a professional—a woman people wanted to work with—but my feelings of "not being enough" kept surfacing. It started with small things, like obsessing over what I wore, how I styled my hair, and trying not to look too young or inexperienced. I wasn't even getting paid for the work I was doing, yet I was fixated on being seen as *good enough* by others.

On the way to the forum, as I sat at a stoplight, I was suddenly overwhelmed with emotion and began to cry uncontrollably. I had to pull into a parking lot because I was too upset to keep driving. At first, I didn't understand what was happening, but then I realized where this was all coming from.

All the fear of not being accepted by others in my field and the frustration of not having any luck finding paid work triggered something deep inside me—something I thought I had long since buried. Suddenly, I felt like I was right back in eighth grade, drowning in fear and anxiety, wondering what my bullies would yell at me for today. Would it be my clothes, my hair, or would it just be me?

The realization hit me hard, and in that moment, I knew I needed help. I stopped crying enough to call one of the therapists I was working with in the girl-bullying group. She answered, and as soon as I tried to speak, I started crying again. Eventually, I calmed down enough to explain what had happened.

She knew my story, and as a therapist, she completely understood what I was going through in that moment. I asked if she could refer me to someone, and she told me she would make a few calls and get back to me. Despite everything I had been through with my family and the bullying, I had never seen a therapist. My whole life, I had always just pushed through my pain, burying all that trauma in an attempt to keep moving forward.

I began therapy with a woman my colleague referred me to, and it was helpful at first. But after a few months, I felt like I was just spinning my wheels. It was my first time in therapy, and I eventually realized that she just wasn't the right fit for me. I never felt like we really ever dealt with anything, it was more like talking around it. I was completely open and willing to dive deep and move toward healing, but her methodology just wasn't effective for me.

She touched on a few helpful things regarding addiction and my family, but overall, therapy with her just wasn't working for me. I decided to stop going, and planned to revisit therapy at another time when I found someone who was a better fit. Just identifying the problem and making the connection to my bullying experience helped me reduce my anxiety quite a bit. I carried on with life, trying to keep moving forward.

Around that time, I realized how passionate I was about working with youth. I had spent so much time volunteering and advocating for youth that it made sense to pursue a paid job in that field. I talked to Louie and told him that I didn't care about having a big fancy Master's Degree—I was willing to start at the bottom in order to get my foot in the door.

As always, he supported me in my quest to find my purpose. In late 2010, just over a year after grad school, I secured a job as a Family Support Counselor at an organization that provided Wraparound Services for youth and families. Wraparound was basically what it sounded like, we would wrap support services around families that were struggling, specifically if there were youth in the home at risk of being removed.

It was a non-profit organization that operated on referrals. They received cases from Child Welfare, Probation, or the School System when a child's behavior was putting them at risk of being removed from the home, school, or violating their probation. My role was to work with both the children and their caregivers. I taught them positive coping skills, connected them with sustainable resources, and helped them build natural support systems with family, close friends, and community members.

THE WEIGHT OF SILENCE

Since it was a mental health organization, we started with a week of intense training that felt a little like mental health boot camp; it was even called "Basic Training". The training week included a mix of activities and required trainings to prepare us for what we might encounter in our work. We earned a certification in a program focused on de-escalation and crisis intervention techniques, including restraints and specific moves like the bite-release for situations where a child might bite. We also learned how to get out of the grip of a child who got a hold of our hair, especially a ponytail. We became certified in CPR and AED and learned safety protocols, including how to manage exposure to bloodborne pathogens in our work.

The kids I was going to be working with had been labeled SED—Severely Emotionally Disturbed. I hated that term. What I quickly realized was that these kids had suffered a life-altering trauma, and as a result, they exhibited behaviors that could sometimes be dangerous to themselves or others. They simply didn't have the coping skills to manage the barrage of emotions resulting from trauma. Part of this training seemed to be geared towards scaring the crap out of us for what we might encounter in the field.

I took it all in, and figured I would rather know the worst-case scenarios than be caught off guard and ill-prepared. They also wove in some self-awareness and self-reflection in between all the scary talk. It was an emotionally intense week of training, filled with a great deal of personal reflection as well. Since I had done so much of that in grad school, I felt pretty confident that I knew what to expect in that regard. I was learning so much and met so many great people. I found it all very interesting, and I was doing pretty well until we got to the Mandated Reporter training.

Mandated Reporters are legally required to report any suspected abuse or neglect involving children, elders, or dependent adults. Although

MELINDA VELASQUEZ

I hadn't taken this specific training before, I was somewhat aware of what it would entail and what would be required of me. What I didn't expect was the profound impact it would have on me, personally.

I listened as they went through all the ways that a child could be neglected or abused. When they reached the last of the six types—emotional neglect—it hit home. I felt like I had been sucker-punched in the gut as the trainer highlighted the examples. There it was: "Parents may struggle to meet children's emotional needs due to a variety of reasons, such as depression or drug and alcohol abuse."

During this training, we heard horrible stories about children left for days without food, forced to eat out of the garbage. That was definitely not my life. There were also categories of mild, moderate, and severe neglect. But the more I listened, something in me clicked. I thought to myself, *I think I was neglected as a child.*

It was a shock to my system. Having someone name it so clearly, and seeing it up on the PowerPoint presentation right in front of me, brought forth a harsh reality I had never considered before. I started to mentally check out of what was happening in the room. It felt like I was thrust backwards through a long, dark tunnel. The trainer's voice faded into the background, and I could feel my face get hot as I tried to process what I had just learned.

I knew I grew up in a family struggling with addiction, and I was aware that I had issues stemming from that, but sitting in that room, hearing the trainer talk about the different types and instances of neglect, suddenly made everything I experienced feel more real and valid. I could feel my face heating up and turning red the way it did before I was about to cry, or when I was stressed. Then, I started to feel nauseous.

I started to imagine that everyone was staring at me, knowing exactly what I was feeling. So, I got up and stepped outside for some air. On the first day of class, they warned us that some of the things we learned may be triggering, but I did *not* see this coming at all. They encouraged us to take care of ourselves and even leave the room if we needed a break. In that moment, I definitely needed a break.

The group went to break after that and a woman I connected with that week came and found me sitting on the stairs outside. She said, "Hey, are you okay? You didn't look so good in there."

The fresh air helped me clear my head a bit and gave me a moment to process what had just happened. I said, "Yeah, I'm okay. Some of that stuff just hit way too close to home, and I wasn't expecting it."

She gave me a look of understanding and simply said, "Yeah, I get it." I didn't have to go into detail about what was going on for me personally, I knew she really did get it.

So many of the people in that training, and the ones who chose this type of work, had been abused or neglected themselves, or knew someone who had. They were people like me—and many had endured much worse. Part of the reason I think it hit me so hard was because I had normalized it so much that, when faced with my reality I was taken by surprise.

I had just experienced a major shock—one I probably should have sought help to process, but I didn't. Back then, I believed that simply being aware of something was enough for me to deal with it on my own and move on. I prided myself on being "the capable one," and I wasn't about to let this realization slow me down. I just kept pushing forward.

Once I finished the week of training, I was ready to go back to my home site and start the work. The organization had many locations and different types of facilities, but I would be working out in the community. When I got to my site, I clicked right away with my co-workers. Just like in grad school, I knew I had found my people.

MELINDA VELASQUEZ

I learned to get better at setting boundaries in grad school, but in mental health work, it was a requirement. Unclear boundaries could blur the lines too easily between clients, their family, and staff, which could lead to issues—especially when it came to trust and safety.

Setting boundaries also helped me protect myself from the toxic encounters with my mom and my sister. But since we still weren't dealing with the elephant in the room—addiction—those boundaries only ended up building bigger walls between my family and me. In the end, it only widened the divide between us, and the only thing that kept drawing me back was my niece, Kayla. By the time I started working in mental health, Kayla was already 17, nearly an adult.

When Kayla became old enough to drive and I helped her secure her first job, I wanted to believe she was doing well—that she had somehow escaped the impacts of family addiction. She exhibited many of the positive attributes I had—responsibility, kindness, and an upbeat attitude. Yet, beneath her outward appearance, I couldn't shake the feeling that there was pain lingering just below the surface, something she might be working hard to mask—perhaps from herself and everyone else. I wasn't sure if I sensed it or if I simply feared it, but I worried that, like me, she was carrying it in silence, playing the same role of the capable, peacekeeper.

The more I learned about different types of trauma and family systems, the more conflicted I became about whether I should have done more—or could have done more—to protect Kayla.

I knew she wasn't aware of the meth use, but she was somewhat aware of the alcohol issues involving her mom and grandma. I had worked so hard to shield her from the pain of family addiction that I was afraid to admit how much it might still be affecting her. I desperately wanted her to know the truth, hoping it could somehow protect her. But I also worried that telling her would be like dropping a bomb on our entire family—and that it could shatter my relationship with her in the process.

Things with my family were still very complicated, but between Louie and me, everything was going great. We had finally purchased our own home, which landed us back in my hometown—just around the corner from the home where my family had moved before the divorce. It also meant I was now living much closer to my mom.

After Charlie's mom passed, they received an inheritance, which allowed them to buy a home as well. Mom had retired from her job at the county after 26 years and was enjoying retirement. I did my best to keep setting boundaries with her. On the days that she was in one of her moods, Louie was amazing at stepping in and dealing with her so I didn't have to. They had formed a connection, and I was so grateful to him for that.

In early 2012, a friend and former colleague reached out to recruit me for a position at a non-profit foster family agency in the town where I lived with my dad. They were trying to expand to my county, so I would mostly work from home until enough homes were certified to warrant opening an office there.

At first, I traveled to the main office to work with someone who was doing the job locally and to acclimate myself with the organization. After that, I would go to the main office once or twice a week for meetings. The best part? They planned to expand my role by revamping and developing their agency-wide training program. I felt like someone had just offered me my dream job.

I worked there for a while when they recruited another friend and colleague—whom I'll refer to as Kate #2, not by rank, but because she was the second important friend named Kate to enter my life—to join us. Kate #2 was one of those people I just clicked with right away. She was smart, funny, and we bonded over the best hot chocolate in the county, as well as our love for Del Taco, breakdancing and old school rap and hip-hop.

Since we both lived in the same area, we often commuted together, making the hour-long drive. We called it "quality friend time," and friend time was always my favorite time. She knew all about my family and the struggles I faced with my complicated relationship with my mom.

Her energy reminded of Leisa because she had a calming effect on me, and our connection was immediate. She was nothing but love and light—with an occasional side of bossy—but it always came from a place of love. From the moment we first met, she quickly became one of my favorite people, and I was so grateful to get the chance to work with her again.

CHAPTER 32

It was Wednesday, January 23, 2013—a day like most others. On this particular day, I had to meet Kate #2 at the home of a potential foster family I had recruited, trained, and worked with all the way through the home study process. Unfortunately, we had to tell them that we would not be able to certify them.

I had been dreading having to deliver this devastating news ever since I found out. This was a family I had worked with for months, I had been in their home multiple times, and they had shared some very private, intimate details about their lives with me. Regardless of the valid reasons for not certifying them, I knew that they were genuinely loving and caring people.

As I drove to their home, I realized I hadn't heard back from my sister about what was going on with Mom. She had been feeling really tired and passed out recently. This was actually the second time she'd passed out in a span of a few months. She shrugged it off the first time by saying that she had a few drinks and hadn't eaten, but that explanation never really sat right with me.

Just before Thanksgiving, Mom went to the doctor, and they diagnosed her with a sinus infection and asthma. They prescribed some antibiotics and two inhalers because she was struggling a little with her breathing. She also had this weird high pitched, raspy voice —like someone just starting to lose their voice.

She had quit smoking about a year earlier, so I thought maybe she was dealing with some residual smoker's cough, which made sense given her voice. The sinus infection also explained why she was feeling so tired. I had dealt with many sinus infections and knew how completely drained they can make you feel.

We all made sure she rested through the holidays by pitching in more than we normally did. In fact, for the first time since I started working at 16 years old, I was able to take time off during the week of Thanksgiving. My sister and I went over to Mom's house the day before Thanksgiving to help her prep for the big dinner she hosted every year.

It was kind of a random gathering of friends and family that year, totaling around 28 people. My mom always made her home a welcoming place for the people she cared about, and she hated the thought of anyone spending the holidays alone.

That day before Thanksgiving, for me, ended up being the best day the three of us—my mom, my sister, and I— had spent together in a very long time. There was a feeling of warmth and happiness I felt that day as I peeled potatoes and sampled my mom's sweet potatoes.

We got along so well that day, and I knew, even as it was happening, that I would remember it fondly for a long time. Thanksgiving

Day itself was filled with the usual chaos and complications of family and the holidays, but that day, with just the three of us, was special. I was truly grateful for that day.

Louie and I hosted Christmas Day at our house that year, but it was just family and "Framily"—Mom, Charlie, Shelly, Kayla, and Mom and Charlie's close friends, Vera and Wade. Mom and Vera were so close they called each other sisters. We had spent many holidays together, but something about this one felt special.

We all got along, there was no negative energy and it just felt so nice. I sat back while we all opened presents and happily observed everyone in the room. I consciously captured a snapshot of that good feeling in my mind.

I had found a DVD of a Christmas movie that Shelly and I both loved growing up, "One Magic Christmas". It was one of our absolute favorite Christmas holiday movies, but it hadn't been played on television in years. Every year I searched for it, and finally, that year, I found it to buy. When Shelly opened it, she cried. I knew how much it would mean to her, and that made it even more special.

Before I knew it, January had arrived. I noticed that my mom's voice still sounded weird, so I asked her if she had been back to the doctor for a follow-up since she still seemed to be struggling. She just shrugged it off and told me she hadn't. When I pushed a little bit more, she got defensive and snapped, "Okay, I got it," In an annoyed tone.

I still wasn't sure if what was going on with her was something to worry about or if it was just a lingering effect from quitting smoking—or something else. There were always things that happened with her that could've been meth-related, but I would never know for sure because that topic was off limits.

When she got dentures, I rationalized that it was something people at her age might need. Mom had a lot of issues with her teeth her whole life, but I also knew that meth can cause your teeth to rot, commonly referred to as "Meth Mouth".

I would never know for sure if meth was the reason behind my mom's dental issues. My sister once told me that Mom didn't snort meth—she ingested it, possibly by putting it in a drink or something. Whether that was what caused issues with her teeth, I may never know.

Meth addicts can become hyper-focused on things for a period of time, and depending on what they fixate on, it can be destructive. I've seen cases where someone tries to fix a simple thing on a small appliance, and before you know it, they have taken the whole thing apart. It is like trying to fix one loose thread on a sweater, but ending up completely unraveling the whole garment.

For my mom, her version of this hyper-focus was picking at things. It often started with something like an ingrown hair. She would spend hours with tweezers trying to dig that hair out, and what began as a small irritation would turn into a sore. Then, the sore would scab, and she would pick at that too.

Something like this happened on her legs—maybe it was a cut from working in her garden—but she picked at the scabs so much that they became infected. It got so bad that she needed skin grafts to repair the damage. When I asked what happened, she just said it was a cut or something that got infected.

I'll never know for sure if it was meth-related, but the more I thought about it, the more I believed it was. It always made me sad to see how self-conscious she became about it. Her long, shapely legs had always been something she was proud of, but that pride turned into shame, and she went from showing off her legs to always trying to keep them hidden.

Because she had always hidden her addiction from me, I never really knew what was going on with her. I was so torn—she was my mom, and I loved her so much, but sometimes, she made it really hard to love her.

One moment, she could be sweet and vulnerable, making me want to lean in and spend time with her. Other times, she rebuffed me and kept me at arm's length. I tried many times to take a risk and put myself out there to trust our relationship, but any hint that I might be hurt by her again made me want to shut down. It got the point where I was afraid to try at all. It was emotionally exhausting.

When I asked her if she had gone back to the doctor after not getting better and she snapped at me, we fell right back into that toxic pattern. She went straight into avoidance, and that familiar tone triggered my instinct to shut down, to protect myself from being hurt by her again.

In grad school, I made a conscious decision about my relationship with my mom: I would do my best to focus on the good stuff. I worked hard to keep boundaries with her and my sister because, without them, they could completely drain my energy and leave me feeling the negative emotions I no longer wanted to carry.

I stopped trying to guess if and when they were using meth. I knew there was nothing I could do about it, so I had to try to let it go. Talking about addiction in our family, and everything related to it, had become an emotional minefield I was no longer willing to step into.

After the failed intervention when I was in high school, I was terrified of what would happen if I ever brought it up with my mom again. Even though Shelly used to do drugs right in front of me, as we got older, she started hiding it from me and completely denied using drugs anymore.

In my heart, I knew that they were both still meth addicts, but any time I brought it up, I somehow ended up feeling like I was the one doing something wrong. They were really good at turning things around, and suddenly, I was the awful, horrible person falsely accusing them of this unspeakable thing.

It felt similar to the intimate relationships I had been in where I just *knew* someone was being unfaithful, but I had no concrete proof. It would take so much courage for me to confront them, only for them to deny it—then get angry with me for accusing them in the first place. I was afraid to trust what I knew to be true, and it was a pattern that caused me a lot of pain in my relationships over the years.

Since my mom's addiction had been the unspoken elephant in the room for so long, some of her behaviors did not immediately raise alarms for me. I was used to her "crashing" when she was "coming down" from the drugs—staying in bed for days, binge eating, and generally being really unpleasant to be around.

I had built walls to protect me from being vulnerable with her, the result of years spent walking on eggshells. Navigating her constant emotional shifts was confusing and exhausting. The hardest part, though, was my internal battle. When I love someone, I love deeply, and not being able to trust the love coming from my own mother was ripping my heart and soul to shreds.

The wounds my mom caused ran deeper than I even realized at that time. Yet, she was my mom. Seeing her vulnerable, ill, hurt, sad, or filled with shame could shatter my walls in seconds. That is when my codependency would kick into overdrive, and I would launch right in to caretaking mode.

Something in my gut told me what was going on with her this time was different, but that hurt little girl inside me was not ready to lean into it or respond appropriately. Instead, I remember feeling almost annoyed that

THE WEIGHT OF SILENCE

I had to check in on her in the midst of a day I was already dreading. It felt like making sure my mom was okay was an inconvenience.

I carried a lot of shame about that for a long time. Now, I understand that feeling was just another defense mechanism—a way to compartmentalize and cope with what was really happening. It was the only way I knew how to protect myself.

Regardless of what I was feeling, I knew I needed to check in with my sister to find out what was going on with mom. Just a few weeks earlier, on New Year's Eve, my mom asked my sister to move in with her to help her take care of the house and Charlie. Mom had taken on a lot after his heart attack and stroke, and it was becoming too much for her to deal with alone.

Charlie had also been diagnosed with a rare form of cancer called Multiple Myeloma. They had been managing it, but it was causing issues with his kidneys. My mom went from being his life partner to being his caregiver and, at times, his voice. It was overwhelming for anyone to manage.

Shelly was only working one day a week as a bartender, so she had the time. She was also dealing with a tumultuous relationship with the boyfriend she had been dating and living with for the last 14 years or more. She spent a lot of time at Mom's anyway, so it seemed like a good idea.

Mom and Charlie had been together for nearly 15 years before they finally got married. Charlie had been married before but lost contact with his ex after they separated, and could never find her to finalize the divorce. Eventually, they went through a legal process that allowed him to get the divorce completed.

Mom and Charlie got married not long after I finished grad school in 2009. They had a small, intimate ceremony in their backyard, surrounded by my mom's beautiful flowers and plants, which were in all full bloom. In front of a backdrop of her favorite morning glory flowers they finally tied the knot. We held the reception a little later at a local lodge, where mom's sister-friend Vera worked. It was such a beautiful day, and I'll never forget how happy mom looked.

The inheritance from Charlie's mom had provided Mom and Charlie a bit of financial breathing room, something they hadn't experienced in a long time. They were able to buy a house and a newer used car—things my mom hadn't been able to do for years. However, I was concerned. Mom had never been good with money, and I worried that she would go through it too quickly. She was enjoying the freedom of not having to worry about every penny, and relished the ability to be generous, something she hadn't been able to do in a long time.

One person my mom was always generous with, even when she couldn't afford it, was my sister. For years, She had enabled Shelly by giving her money, food, or letting her borrow her car. While my sister did help around the house or in the yard from time to time, it often seemed that it was mostly my mom giving, and my sister receiving. Over time my sister had come to expect it, almost as if it were normal.

My sister continued to talk openly with me about my mom's addiction, even though she no longer admitted to her own. It was as if she had forgotten that she used to do it right in front of me and had taught me nearly everything I knew about the signs of meth use. I also had given her money to help her out more times than I could count, until I realized that my efforts—driven by love and hope that she would get help—were only enabling her to continue.

This had been the pattern for the last 25 years of my life. Anytime I had to do anything that required me to interact with my mom or my sister, all of that stuff was swirling around in my head. A pit of anxiety would form in my stomach thinking about how things would go, how they would react, and what they might say to guilt me, shame me, hurt me, frustrate me, or anger me. That day was no different.

I could feel all of that familiar anxiety building in my stomach as I drove to meet Kate #2 at the house of the couple we had to deliver the bad news to. Taking a deep breath, I put in my earpiece and called my sister on her cell phone.

As soon as I heard her say hello, my worried thoughts took over, and I blurted out, "Shelly, how is Mom doing? Did you take her to the doctor? You didn't call me back yesterday!"

Shelly replied with a slight urgency in her voice, "I was just going to call you. I'm going to take her to the emergency room. She made a doctor appointment, but when I got here, she seemed completely exhausted and barely able to do anything. I told her, that's it, I'm taking you to the E.R."

I listened, feeling a mix of worry and a strange numbness that kept me from feeling anything too intensely. I took in the information, letting her words wash over me for a moment. Then I checked back in and told her, "Okay, I have to go to this meeting, but I will call you when it is done to see what you found out at the E.R."

As I ended the call, I pulled up to the house of the family, knowing I had to hold it together. I didn't want to make Kate #2 deliver this news by herself. When she drove up, I felt a slight sense of relief seeing my good friend arrive.

I dug deep to find that capable and responsible part of me—the one raised with the belief that you don't call in sick unless you are contagious, have a high fever, or truly can't function. I could particularly hear my dad in my head, reminding me how ridiculous it would be to let people down at work if what was going on with Mom wasn't really serious.

MELINDA VELASQUEZ

Taking my mom to the emergency room definitely counted as a family emergency that would absolutely not be questioned if I needed to be released from work for the day. But I think my brain was helping my heart not go to the place where missing work would even be necessary.

We finished the meeting, but the whole thing was a blur. I just remember it being awful. They were shocked and pretty angry. I can't say I blame them. They had been through so much to get to that point, and just like that, it was over.

The meeting took just under an hour, but when I got back in my car, I wasn't ready to make that follow-up call to my sister. Kate #2 knew my family saga all too well. I told her I didn't want to call just yet, so she sat with me in my car in a nearby grocery store parking lot, where we met up to debrief after the awful meeting.

We really did need a debrief from what had just happened with the family whose dreams of fostering we had just crushed. Once we finished, we sat in the car for what felt like a long time, though it had only been about 30 minutes. I just kept saying, "I don't want to call. I don't want to go."

Kate #2 is such a good friend, and I knew she understood without judgment, which is exactly what I needed in that moment. I think it was a combination of just giving really bad news to someone, and not being ready—or willing—to hear any more bad news. On top of that, there was all the other family drama that would come along with it. I needed that brief moment of time, safe in the bubble of my little green car, with my good friend beside me. I didn't realize how much I needed that time to fortify myself for the battle ahead.

I also had this lingering feeling that I wanted to let my sister handle the responsibility of being caregiver for as long as I could. Even though she was five years older than me, my role as "the capable one" had started in my early teen years.

My codependence often pushed me to step in and handle the hard stuff—the grown-up stuff—even though I was the *younger* sister. But once I started distancing myself from my mom's moods and issues I didn't want to deal with, I got used to letting my sister take on the burden.

My mom was like me in that she was a very empathic person. That is part of what made it so hard to be hurt by her. At her core, beyond the addiction, she wanted to be a good mother. I knew that if it came down to it, she would have done anything for Shelly, Kayla, or me.

Dealing with the highs and the lows, the drama, the money issues, the health problems—it all became too much for me. I got really good at being busy in order to avoid it all. I put my head down, stayed occupied, and kept my mouth shut about the issues within my family.

The more my history swirled around in my head, the more anxious I became about making the call to my sister. But I realized I couldn't avoid it any longer. Kate #2 stayed with me as I made the call, and I was grateful for her calming presence.

I took a deep breath and made the call. "Shelly, what is going on? What happened at the E.R.?"

Shelly replied in her somewhat normal rushed tone, the one she used when managing multiple things at once: "She is still at the E.R., and they are running some tests. They are going to do a chest x-ray since she is having trouble breathing. I'm going to take Charlie home so he can eat dinner and rest."

She didn't sound super concerned, so I wasn't really sure how to respond. I asked, "So, should I go to the hospital…?" My voice was tentative, genuinely expecting her to say no.

"Yes!" she replied, more emphatically than I expected. "I'm not going back there tonight, so you should go there, and I'll stay at Mom's house and take care of Charlie."

Both my sister and I have a deep dislike of hospitals—the smells, the energy, pretty much everything. I replied, "Okay, let me check in with Louie, and then I'll head over there. I'll call you soon when I see what's going on once I get there."

Kate #2 and I said goodbye and once again, I put my earpiece in and called Louie. He was just getting off work about 45 minutes from home. I said, "Hey, Shelly took my mom to the E.R. because she was exhausted and having trouble breathing. Remember not long ago when they called the ambulance at the bar while she was shooting pool because she passed out? Shelly thought she might pass out again, so she thought she should take her to the E.R. She had to take Charlie home, so I'm going to go see Mom at the hospital."

Louie immediately asked, "Do you want me to go with you?"

I thought to myself, *oh yeah, I guess that would be a good idea*. I just wasn't that worried, for some reason. "I'm thinking that maybe it is Pneumonia or something since they are going to do a chest x-ray. She has been sick since around Thanksgiving, and she still has that weird high-pitched voice thing. Maybe that's why she hadn't gotten better after the holidays."

CHAPTER

33

Louie and I arrived at the hospital just as they finished my mom's chest x-ray. They told us they needed to admit her and wanted to do a CAT Scan to get a clearer look at her left lung. They said we'd have to wait for the results and that, for now, there wasn't much for us to do.

I gave my mom a hug and a kiss and could immediately see how exhausted she was. She could barely keep her eyes open and said she just wanted to rest. We told her we would go grab something to eat, check in with Shelly, and come back to hear the test results.

I called my sister to update her, letting her know we were just waiting and would let her know what we found out soon. After we grabbed a bite to eat, Louie and I sat in the waiting room, giving Mom some time to rest. Eventually, we decided to check if the results were back.

We walked into the room and saw the doctor holding my mom's hand. She was visibly upset. A wave of worry and confusion hit me. I asked, "What's going on? Is everything O.K.?"

MELINDA VELASQUEZ

The doctor turned to me, speaking in a calm yet eerie tone, "I was just talking with your mom about what we found. There is a four-inch diameter mass in your mom's left lung that is attached to major arteries, including being wrapped around her aorta. The mass is also paralyzing the nerve that signals the left side of her diaphragm to breathe, which is why she has been so short of breath and so exhausted. She hasn't been able to get enough air into her lungs."

As he spoke, I felt my heartbeat quicken. It had been 10 years since my dad passed away from cancer, after just eight months. In an instant, I was back there—watching cancer devour him until there was nothing left.

I screamed inside my head, *Fuck! Cancer? Again? Both of my parents?* Dad had died from liver cancer, one of the most aggressive types. But if this was lung cancer, I remembered hearing stories of successful surgeries. Clawing my way back to the present, I blurted out, "So, are you saying it's cancer?"

The doctor replied with a careful tone, "Well, no, we won't know that unless we do a biopsy and we can test the tissue to find out."

Clinging to a thread of hope, I hurriedly responded, "O.K., so we need to do the biopsy then, right? Is that what happens next?" I was desperate to take control of the situation and move forward—anything to help my mom feel better.

To my surprise, the doctor replied, "No, not exactly. The position of the mass is in a very dangerous place, and I'm concerned that if we went in for the biopsy something could go wrong and your mother would die on the table."

"What?" I gasped, my voice catching "So… what does that mean?" The gravity of the situation still hadn't hit me, so the doctor led Louie and me to the nurse's station. He pulled up the scans of my mom's lung, and suddenly it all started to sink in.

"So, what can we do for her if you are not even sure it is cancer? I asked, my voice shaking. "Can you still treat her?"

The doctor seemed to choose his words carefully, then dropped an enormous bomb that left us reeling, "We could try to treat her," he said slowly, "but she may just be happier to go home and live out the rest of her days there with her family."

"Days???!!! What do you mean days?" My voice cracked as I fought to hold back the avalanche of tears threatening to spill.

The doctor took a deep breath. "She's got maybe five days at the most."

It felt like a gut punch that neither of us saw coming. Suddenly, I couldn't fight back the tears anymore, and I lost it.

But then I did something I'd regret forever: I went right back into my role as the capable one. I refused to let my mom see me cry. I slipped into caretaking mode, shoving my own feelings aside to focus on hers.

Louie walked in and held her hand, sharing how sad he felt, while my mom admitted she was scared. I felt this overwhelming need to mask my feelings from her in order to protect *her* in some way. I hid off to the side, out of her line of sight, until I could pull myself together. I never let her see the devastation I felt at hearing she was dying.

Once I pulled myself together, I went back into her room, standing next to Louie as I held her hand. The doctor came back in the room, I looked at him and asked, "So what happens now?"

He said, "We are going to admit her to the hospital for the night so we can monitor her. An oncologist will take a look at her scans in the morning and be able to answer any questions you have."

I looked at my mom, who seemed utterly exhausted, "I'm really tired, she said. I just want to try to get some sleep."

MELINDA VELASQUEZ

We both gave her a hug and kiss and told her we loved her, and promised to be back first thing in the morning. As soon as we stepped outside the hospital, I felt a wave of disorientation. Once we were in the car, the tears started to flow again, and Louie and I sat in silence, struggling to make sense of what we had just heard. I knew we had to pull ourselves together; we still had to go back to Mom and Charlie's house and break the news to the rest of the family.

For the second time that day, I had to deliver horrible news. As we arrived at the house, we could tell by the cars present that my niece Kayla, now age 20, and her boyfriend at the time were there along with Vera and Wade and Shelly's boyfriend. I called Shelly on our way to let her know we would be there soon and we would explain everything the doctor said when we got there.

Mom and Charlie had a large room off the kitchen, with a pool table in the center, and couches and chairs lining the walls. This was the room we usually gathered during holidays or family get-togethers. Everyone was in that room waiting for us to arrive.

They were chatting casually, just like always, completely unaware of what was about to come, but I felt the energy shift the moment we walked in. They look concerned, but they had no idea what we were about to tell them. Shelly had left before the results came in, so she didn't have a clue how bad it really was.

I felt my stomach tighten up again as I took a deep breath and gave them the same information the doctor had given us. I watched their faces change from worry to shock as I explained the situation. Then I took another deep breath and delivered the hardest blow of all—that the E.R. doctor said she might only have about five days to live.

The room erupted with intensity, as if we'd unleashed an emotional storm. I looked around, absorbing the devastation. Charlie dropped his head, staring at the floor. Vera sat at the end of the couch, crying, while Wade perched on the armrest, trying to comfort her. Kayla's face turned red, her lip quivering as she tried to contain her sobs, wiping away tears with the sleeves of her sweatshirt. Her boyfriend leaned in close, offering what little comfort he could.

Shelly, who had been standing near the kitchen, took a hesitant yet deliberate step toward me. Her eyes locked onto both Louie and me, brimming with tears. In a voice filled with distress, she cried out, "What?"

Then Shelly's boyfriend yelled out in frustration and shock, "What the fuck? Why the hell would he say something like that?"

Louie spoke up and said, "We saw the scans you guys, it's pretty bad."

I added, "They have checked her in to the hospital for the night, but they said we could come back in the morning so we can talk to the Oncologist to get more information."

As the news started to sink in, my sister's emotions were on the verge of erupting. She walked straight over to the bar and downed a shot of tequila. Vera cleared her throat, trying to pull herself together to speak, and said, "Okay, so maybe the E.R. doctor doesn't really know what he's looking at. Let's wait until we talk to the Oncologist before jumping to the worst-case scenario."

Louie and I tried to share their optimism, but I just had this nagging feeling. I said, "We will go there in the morning, and talk to the Oncologist, and get a second opinion. I just want to prepare you that I don't think that doctor would say something so devastating if he wasn't certain. But I agree, I want to hear what the Oncologist has to say too."

MELINDA VELASQUEZ

Louie and I headed home after what felt like the longest day of my life. I was completely exhausted, but every time I drifted off, I would wake up again, unable to stay asleep. In the morning, I took a quick shower to wake myself up and to have a good cry. The shower has always been a place where I can cry in private, allowing the water to cleanse and refresh my energy. That morning, I needed that time to let my emotions out.

We arrived at the hospital as soon as visiting hours began at 9 a.m. and gathered in Mom's hospital room with the Oncologist. He brought up her scans and explained a lot of things I can't quite remember, but he basically confirmed what the E.R. doctor had told us the night before, but not as specific.

As soon as the doctor finished speaking, the room grew heavy with the weight of the news. It was clear the rest of the family now felt what Louie and I had felt the night before. My mom turned to us and said, "Can I get something for my anxiety?" The nurse came in and gave her an Ativan. Then Mom looked at me and said, "I want to go home."

The doctor said he would give us a few minutes alone and stepped out into the hallway. At that moment, I caught a glimpse of Shelly's face; she was clearly panicking. She blurted out, "This is too much! I need a cigarette."

She bolted out the door, and I ran after her, with Louie close behind. I caught up, grabbed her arm, and said in an urgent tone, "No! We need to talk to the doctor right now and figure out exactly what is happening and what we need to do."

She stopped, and a nurse went to get the doctor, leading us to a small meeting room with just a small couch and two chairs. The doctor returned, and now that mom wasn't in the room, I pushed him for a clearer answer, "We need you to tell us exactly what is happening and what we need to do next. Is our mom going to die?"

He said simply, "Yes, I don't think she will be able to go much longer with her breathing being compromised the way it is. I recommend getting her set up with Hospice today. They can get her set up with a bed and oxygen and meds that will keep her comfortable. I can send over a social worker to help you get that set up."

Shelly was crying, pacing around the room, repeating "Oh my God" over and over. I knew she wouldn't be able to handle any of this. Social workers were my people—I worked with them every day in Child Welfare. I knew they would connect us with resources and help manage all the paperwork we needed to deal with so we could get Mom home, where she wanted to be.

I shifted right into planner mode. Charlie had stayed right by Mom's side the whole time, along with my niece, her boyfriend, Vera, and Wade. Louie sat with me while I talked to the social worker, selected a Hospice provider, and filled out paperwork. Shelly took Charlie home to start preparing the house for Mom's arrival, while Kayla, her boyfriend, Vera, and Wade stayed behind with Mom.

Within two hours, we had a hospital bed set up in the living room of Mom's house, as close to her garden as we could manage. They brought oxygen and showed us how to set it up and use it. They also delivered a commode and a big package of adult diapers called Chucks. I was glad we were prepared, but it was all happening so fast—it was really overwhelming. I had serious stuff to manage though, so I really didn't have the time to fully process what all of this really meant.

When Mom came home, she refused to get in the hospital bed and insisted on being in her own bed. I felt a small sense of relief having her back home, but none of us really knew what to expect. By the time we got Mom settled, we were all exhausted.

MELINDA VELASQUEZ

We were sitting in the pool room when Kayla's boyfriend came back from the bathroom with a confused look on his face. "I just threw up," he said. "It was so weird—it felt like my head was going to explode, and then my whole sub sandwich just came out."

He said he hadn't felt good after eating the sandwich, but we figured it might be food poisoning or something. He still didn't feel great, so he and Kayla decided to leave. Shelly offered to stay the night with Mom and Charlie, while Louie and I planned to come back in the morning.

Louie and I were finally able to fall asleep, but around 2 a.m., my cell phone rang—it was my mom's home number. I shot up in bed and answered. It was Shelly and she was frantic, "Charlie just threw up all over the bathroom, and Mom keeps trying to get up out of the bed! I'm afraid she's going to fall, and I can't deal with both. You gotta come back over here!"

I sat there, stunned, trying to process what she was saying, then quickly replied, "Okay. We will be there as soon as we can."

Louie sat up and asked, "What's going on?" I filled him in, and we got dressed as fast as we could. Luckily, we only lived about five minutes away from Mom's house.

When we arrived, Shelly was stressed out. She said, "I just got the guest bathroom clean. It was so crazy it was like projectile vomit all over the place!"

I said, "If he is sick, we need to get Mom out of their bedroom and onto the hospital bed. The last thing we need is for her to get whatever he has. Let's get her moved and quarantine him in their bedroom so we all don't get sick."

We got Mom moved into the hospital bed and got Charlie set up in their bedroom. Louie went back to our house to pick up the air mattress, and we set it up in the pool room so we could stay the night. Shelly and Vera were scheduled to bartend for a wedding the next night, and since Shelly needed the money, she decided to go while Louie and I stayed with Mom and Charlie.

Shelly asked if she could stay at home after she was done working and return in the morning. Since she was working so late and her house was close to her job we figured it was a good idea. Mom was restless all night, so Louie and I barely got any sleep. By the time morning arrived, we were eager for Shelly's return, desperate for a break from the chaos and stress of the past few days. We just wanted to go home, take showers, and get a little respite.

Since Mom got home, she remained on Ativan, which kept her calm and helped with her breathing. She was very unstable on her feet, so whenever she moved around, we had to make sure she didn't fall. She also slept a lot during the day; because when you are nearing end of life, sleep cycles tend to shift.

Shelly had only been home a few minutes when she ran to the bathroom and got sick. For a moment, I thought she drank while she worked and was just hungover. Then Wade called to tell us that Vera had gotten really sick and had to stop the car on her way home from work the night before to throw up. I turned to Louie and said, "What the fuck is happening?"

We soon learned that the woman who had shared the hospital room with Mom had a HIGHLY contagious airborne virus called the Norovirus. Almost everyone who had spent the most time in Mom's hospital room was now sick, having been exposed to the virus for the longest.

Shelly had been exposed last since she'd cleaned up after Charlie when he got sick in the bathroom.

MELINDA VELASQUEZ

Kayla's boyfriend was sick, but Kayla and Wade were still fine. We checked in with everyone, and they all described the same symptoms. So, we decided to quarantine Shelly in the guest room and sanitized the entire house. It was now Saturday, and this virus was knocking out the entire family one-by-one.

Word had started to spread about Mom, and she had friends who wanted to come say their goodbyes to her. But we were worried about exposing anyone else—or worse, exposing Mom to something new. The fact that she had been on oxygen in the hospital and since she had been home probably saved her from getting it. The situation was already stressful; the last thing I needed was to handle an unstable patient dealing with vomiting or, even worse, diarrhea!

Louie went home for a bit to take care of a few things at our house, while trusted friends began helping in any way they could. Kate #1 was recovering from surgery at the time, and she was heartbroken that she wasn't able to be there. Until everything that happened with my mom, I had planned to help her out when she got home from surgery.

Leisa couldn't stay that day, but she went to the store and bought a bunch of bleach wipes for sanitizing. I asked her to bring me a double shot of wheat grass. I was doing everything I could to stay healthy and needed the nutrient boost.

Laura drove down from almost four hours away, and brought a bunch of my favorite foods and her spirit to cheer me up. My sister's friend, whom I was close with since high school, also came over. She brought us some masks and gloves from the medical office where she worked and, most importantly, helped me with the task I had been dreading—changing my mom's diaper.

Jenny came over too. It felt so good to have my people there supporting me. She also worked in the medical field and was not squeamish like I was. Before she left, she told me, "I don't have to be anywhere early in the morning. If you need me to come back, you call me no matter what time of night and I will be here."

That night, with everyone else sick, it was just me, Louie, and Kayla on shift, and it turned out to be the worst night yet. Mom was really restless, constantly trying to get out of bed. Louie and Kayla fell asleep, but I couldn't. I knew I had to stay awake and listen for her.

At one point, she got up, and she was freakishly strong. I yelled for Kayla and Louie to come help me. I realized I needed to change her diaper, but I didn't want Kayla or Louie to have to see that. So I asked them hold her and lift her nightgown while they looked away. While she stood there, I got down on the floor and changed her diaper as quickly as I could.

It was exhausting and crazy. We finally managed to get her back in bed, but I was terrified that it would happen again. Louie and Kayla were able to fall back asleep, but I just lay there crying. By 2 a.m., I picked up my phone and called Jenny.

She was obviously asleep when I called her, and I was still crying and said, "I need you. Can you please come here?"

She didn't even hesitate and replied, "I'm on my way."

Jenny sat with me on the couch next to my mom's hospital bed for hours. I just needed my friend. I knew if anything like that happened again, she would be calm and she could handle it. The thought of putting Louie and Kayla through something like that again was too much for me. They never complained, but I didn't want Kayla's memories of her grandma to be clouded by those moments. I needed reinforcements.

MELINDA VELASQUEZ

The rest of the night, Mom was calm, and Jenny stayed with me until I assured her I was okay. There are no words to express how grateful I was to her for her being there. That morning I called Hospice for some help with keeping Mom asleep at night. They sent someone to bring a prescription and gave her a sponge bath, too.

By Sunday, we found out that Wade had gotten sick too, and after Kayla left, she called to tell me she was now sick as well. Then Louie went home again to check on a few things, and he called and told me he was sick too. After I got off the phone with Louie, I sat down in the pool room by myself and said a prayer.

I am not religious, but I am spiritual, and I believe in the Universe and that there is a higher power out there somewhere. That day, I called on every angel I had and said, "I get why I am probably the only one in this family with enough positive coping skills to deal with all that is coming at me, and I can handle a lot, but please, please do not let me get this damn Norovirus. That would throw me over the edge."

Watching my mom die was already hard enough, but this virus made everything I was dealing with so much more brutal. Each time someone got sick, everything in the house had to be sanitized because it was airborne and highly contagious. We were also warned that it could even be transferred on food, so we had to throw away food that people who had gotten sick had touched.

We had been told that if you hadn't vomited or had diarrhea in 24 hours, you were no longer contagious. Vera hadn't been able to come see my mom since the hospital, but she said she was feeling better and hadn't been sick in 24 hours. She said she would come and stay Sunday night so I could get some sleep.

By the time she arrived, I was the only one who hadn't gotten sick.

I had also been awake for about 38 hours straight and hadn't showered since Thursday morning before we went to the hospital. I was desperately in need of a break. Sleep would come first and then a shower.

The meds they gave Mom helped her stay calm, but we had to set an alarm to give them to her every couple of hours. So I managed to get a little sleep in between alarms. Vera said, "This is crazy, you need sleep. This is too much to manage by the people who love her. Let's look into hiring an in-home aide that can come work the night shift."

We found a nurse who was set to come to stay with her that Monday night, and I was so relieved. After dinner, I took a shower—my first real moment to unwind in days. I planned to relax and watch something on TV, desperately needing some sort of mindless distraction.

I barely stepped out of the shower when Shelly, now feeling better, called out, "Hey come here. Something is happening with Mom. She just started breathing weird."

We all gathered around her, and I remembered that not long before my dad passed away, he had acted the same way. We could tell she was struggling, and we all wished for her suffering to end. We knew she had been the one who kept us together for holidays and family gatherings, so I said, "Mom, don't worry, we will all stay together when you're gone."

And just like that, she let go.

She was 65 years old. It was almost five days to the hour from when the E.R. doctor had given us that devastating prediction that she had maybe five days to live. Those five days were the most difficult days of my life. I was so exhausted and sleep-deprived from the emotional roller coaster that when she finally passed, I felt numb at first.

Charlie sat beside her, holding her hand and crying. Vera broke down, resting her head on Mom's chest as she held her hand and cried.

My sister left the room and started to cry. I felt my face grow hot, and a few tears slipped out, but I was still holding it all together while everyone around me was falling apart.

I called Louie, who was also feeling better by then, and said, "Mom just passed. I need you here with me."

After hanging up, I called Hospice to let them know she had passed, and Vera called the nurse to cancel her visit. We had made all the arrangements in advance with Hospice and the funeral home near where Mom wanted to be buried. That is one of the great things about Hospice—they get everything set in advance, so the loved ones don't have to deal with that in the midst of their grief.

I made one more call to Leisa. Earlier, I had told her we planned to have the nurse come, and she told me to call her if I needed her. She picked up right away, and I said, "Mom just passed."

She replied, "I'm so sorry, Min. what can I do?"

She mentioned that she didn't want to see Mom sick because she didn't want to remember her that way, and I understood that. I said, "Can you come over? You can just come in the pool room with me; you don't have to see her."

She didn't hesitate and said, "I'll be right there."

Louie arrived before Leisa, and we all waited for the mortuary to show up to take her away. When they finally got there, I told Leisa, "I can't watch them take her out of here."

"You don't have to," she said, lying down on the air mattress next to me, her back turned away from the room where they were loading up Mom onto the gurney, shielding both of us from seeing them wheel her out.

THE WEIGHT OF SILENCE

Once I knew that everything was handled and there was nothing left for me to do, I started to cry and couldn't stop. Leisa whispered to me in her comforting, motherly tone, "It's okay Minna. Just let it all out." After that, I released everything I had been holding in, crying and wailing like a little child while she held me in her arms.

CHAPTER

34

After they took Mom away, it was pretty late, and all I wanted was to go home. I hadn't been able to go home since we got that first call from Shelly about Charlie throwing up. Those five days felt like one long, traumatic blur. During the day, things were manageable, but the nights seemed endless; that was when Mom was the most unsettled, and I felt helpless and alone.

My home is my sanctuary, and I just needed to be there to have space to process everything that had happened. Shelly was feeling better, so she was able to stay with Charlie that night. But now that Mom had passed, I knew we would need to figure out a more permanent arrangement for Charlie's care. We planned to meet up at Mom's the next morning to decide what needed to happen next.

While Mom was sick, I tried to take a step back and let Shelly take on some responsibility, but it never seemed to work out, and I was always forced to step in and handle things. Before she got sick, Mom was not only Charlie's caregiver, but also held power of attorney. Once Mom was back home, everything—Mom's and Charlie's affairs—was signed over to me, giving me access to bank accounts and the authority to make important decisions.

I knew my mom had asked Shelly to move in before all this happened, and I genuinely wanted to give her the chance to step up. But Vera, Wade, and other family and friends that were there were adamant that it should be me. Logically, I knew they were right, but I was so tired of it *always* having to be me.

We all met up at Mom's the next day, and right away I felt a weird energy coming from my sister. She was doing what she always did—making everything about her. She kept saying things like, "I lost my mom and my best friend. What am I going to do?" She was grieving, and she had the right to, but almost immediately I felt as if she was sucking all the energy out of the room.

She also did what she had been doing since we first found out about Mom— walking over to the antique bar cabinet in the pool room and taking shots of tequila. She'd became an addict around age 17, and whenever she was overwhelmed, that 17-year-old version of her would resurface. Now, at 42, she still had zero positive coping skills, and her unresolved issues were spilling over onto all of us.

After everything I'd been through, mostly on my own over the last few days, I was in no mood to handle her pity party. I blurted out, "Shelly, I am five years younger than you. You are my *older* sister, and I have just been through hell taking care of Mom and everyone else. I am sitting here, facing the fact that I have lost both of my parents before I even turned 40. Could you, for one second, as my big sister, have some empathy for what I'm going through and offer *me* some comfort?"

MELINDA VELASQUEZ

She just sat there, silent, with a look of shock on her face. She was not used to seeing me fall apart or calling her out. Like mom, she was good at taking care of people in certain situations. I remembered the time I had my wisdom teeth removed and developed dry socket—she rushed over when I called her because I was in so much pain, and Louie was at work. She showed up for me that day and a few other times, too. But overall, I had felt for years that she didn't do anything for anyone unless she got something out of it.

I even felt that way about her relationship with Mom. They seemed close, but I knew Mom gave her money, food, and let her use her car. She would spend time with mom and then turn around and complain to me about Mom's drug use, even though she was also an addict.

She could be very helpful and nurturing, but it almost always came at a cost. I no longer trusted her or looked up to her the way I had as a kid, when I just wanted to hang out with my big sister. I still loved her deeply, but, like with my mom, I had built a wall to protect myself from the emotional damage she had caused over the years.

We were all standing in the room where Mom had passed, and after my outburst, I broke down in tears and headed into the kitchen. Louie followed, trying to comfort me. The tension in the house was undeniable. Shelly became even more upset, and Kayla did too. Just as it seemed like everything was spiraling in a bad direction, we heard a cat meowing loudly outside the kitchen window.

It pulled our attention away from the argument, and I looked out to see a small cat standing on the fence, meowing. It was more of an older kitten, with white paws, a white belly, and grey on its back. None of us had ever seen it before, and it didn't belong to any of the neighbors. Wherever it had come from, it broke the tension in that moment and stopped us from arguing.

Over the next few days, whenever things got tense or heated within the family, the cat would show up, meowing so loudly that we couldn't ignore it. I remembered the promise we had made to Mom just before she passed, and it didn't feel like a coincidence that this random cat kept showing up out of nowhere. We all felt that this little cat was a spiritual messenger, carrying Mom's energy, so we named it Grandma Kitty.

Just a few days after Mom passed, Charlie wasn't feeling well. We called the doctor, and after a series of questions, they found out that he was having trouble breathing, so they told us to take him to the emergency room. After his heart attack and stroke, Charlie had a defibrillator put in and was on blood thinners. He hadn't been doing well before Mom passed, but he held it together like he always did for us.

He was dehydrated, and his vitals were not good. They admitted him, and it really wasn't looking good. I went to see him and said, "Charlie, I know you're tired and you've been through a lot, but I'm not ready to lose you too." He looked at me, smiled, and patted my hand with whatever strength he could muster.

Thankfully, Charlie pulled through, but it was a rough few days. Once we got him home, he was still weak but feeling much better. We hadn't even begun to think about planning Mom's memorial service yet. She had wanted to be buried in the cemetery in the town where she had lived with her grandmother, where many of our relatives on Mom's side were also buried.

We decided to hold Mom's Celebration of Life in early March. After Charlie's hospitalization and everything else, we needed some time to breathe. That's when we realized Mom didn't have a will. She did have some life insurance, which helped cover her casket, headstone, and other burial costs. She had named Shelly, Kayla, and me as beneficiaries.

MELINDA VELASQUEZ

Since Charlie was still not divorced when they bought their home, only Mom's name was on the deed to the house. Because they hadn't been legally married for very long and there was no will, this meant Mom's estate—including the house—went into probate.

This was another big shock, because Mom had told us she was going to put everything in a trust, the way Charlie's mom had done, but she never got around to it. At first, I had no idea what probate meant, but I was about to become an expert—because, once again, I was put in charge of figuring it all out.

The house and the car were basically Mom's only assets, but since Charlie's name was also on the car's pink slip, that left just the home. Shelly, Charlie, and I were easily identified as beneficiaries, but there was a long, drawn-out court process, and we had to hire an estate lawyer to guide us through the whole thing.

While all of that was being figured out, we had to figure out care for Charlie. He was functional, but couldn't drive or really speak or write. Mom had been his voice and advocate, taking him to every appointment. Vera and Wade were the closest people to Mom and Charlie, and were like family to us, and I was grateful to have their support as we navigated everything.

Vera was especially good at stepping in when Shelly became too much for me to handle; she could be firm with her in a way that I couldn't. I had my suspicions, but at that time I didn't know for sure that Vera and Wade were addicts too. Vera had always been the bridge between Shelly and Mom. Mom was open with Vera about her drug use, and in some ways, Shelly was as well. Vera had her own issues, but for me, especially during that time, she was a helpful ally.

We agreed that Shelly would stay in the house, take care of Charlie, handle his doctor appointments, manage his meds, and look after the house. Since Mom had already asked her to move in and help before she passed, it seemed like the most logical arrangement. I would be in charge of the money and the bills.

We got Shelly set up with a bank account at the same bank that Mom and Charlie used—one that I also used—so I could easily transfer money from their account to hers when she needed it. Charlie's prescriptions were already set up through an online pharmacy, so all Shelly had to do was login in to his account whenever he needed prescription refills.

I could tell that Shelly wasn't happy about having to do all of that, and even less so about having to ask me for money. Everyone, except Kayla, knew that Shelly was a drug addict, but even Kayla knew her mom couldn't be trusted with money.

At that time, Shelly made her living as a bartender, but she struggled to work enough shifts to pay her bills or contribute to rent consistently. I did some research and found out that Shelly might qualify for providing In-Home Support Services (IHSS). I told her if she qualified as a caregiver, she could get some steady money of her own coming in as way to help supplement her expenses.

My uncle was able to come out from out of state, and he stayed in a hotel. He was devastated that he hadn't been able to make it out before Mom passed away, but I had been keeping him updated by phone during her final days. I was happy he could make it for the service, especially knowing how close he and Mom had been. He was the youngest of four siblings in their family and was now the only one left.

MELINDA VELASQUEZ

I was nervous at first about spending time with my uncle since I hadn't seen in him years. While I was glad he found something that helped him in his recovery, his strong religious beliefs sometimes felt a bit overwhelming. I'm comfortable with spirituality, but have never been drawn to organized religion. At times, he could be a bit pushy about his opinions and beliefs and it made me uncomfortable.

I went to pick him up from his hotel, and within minutes I realized how happy I was to see him. Being with him made me feel closer to my mom and gave me a sense of comfort and someone for *me* to lean on instead of holding everything on my own. He was helpful without being pushy, and being with him during that time was more healing to me than I ever could have imagined.

I saw the uncle I loved as a kid—his sense of humor was still there, along with a heart full of memories of my mom and my dad that brought me a sense of peace I desperately needed. He shared stories about his life and about growing up with my mom under the shadow of their alcoholic and extremely abusive father that I never knew about.

Having worked in child welfare for years, I understood the impact childhood trauma and abuse can have on kids. I had seen kids who got help, resources, and consistent therapy, yet they still struggled to function in their life. My mom never received that kind of help. She managed to escape her father's relentless abuse by moving to California as a teenager, but the pain and trauma she witnessed—and endured herself—haunted her throughout her life.

Hearing what my mom and uncle went through as the children of a physically and emotionally abusive alcoholic father helped open up my heart to both of them in a new way. The years I spent learning about trauma-informed care allowed me to see my mom's experiences through a different lens. Seeing the pain it still caused my uncle after all those years, helped me begin to heal some of the wounds my mom had inadvertently passed down to me. It was a huge step in my healing to realize just how much of how my mom reacted and responded *to* me was not *about* me at all.

In some ways, it was freeing, but in others, it made my grief so much more intense. I carried a lot of shame because my relationship with my mom had become so complicated that at times, I thought I would feel relieved if she wasn't here anymore. But now that she was gone, it felt like there was an actual physical void in my heart—a piece of me was missing.

During the day, I worked, took care of things, and showed up like I always did—"the capable one." Yet every night, I would go home and cry myself to sleep. I shared my feelings with Kate #2, expressing that I needed to hold something close to my chest to fill that void I felt. Kate #2 told her mom—whom I had never met before—what I shared with her, and she knitted me a small blanket in my favorite colors that I could hold to comfort me.

We still had a bottle of mom's perfume, and I sprayed it on the blanket so I could smell her as I held it. Like I did with my dad, I took one of her shirts that didn't just smell like her perfume but truly smelled like *her*. I held it close to my heart whenever I felt that void. I preserved that shirt in a Ziploc bag to keep the scent and started holding the blanket instead.

Just like I felt her presence with Grandma Kitty, I could feel her with me when I was really struggling. One particularly rough day, while I was in my bedroom, I felt a gust of air that smelled like her sweep past me. There were no windows or doors open, and the blanket with her perfume was nowhere near me.

MELINDA VELASQUEZ

I knew it was her gliding through the room, just as I remembered her doing when I was a little girl in my kindergarten classroom, leaving a trail of her perfume in her wake. She was there to comfort me in that same way she did when I was a child. It felt like her way of letting me know she was there for me again, even if she was not in her physical body anymore. It brought me a much-needed sense of peace.

Once the initial tensions calmed down, Grandma Kitty suddenly disappeared, and we never saw her again. However, knowing that my mom would always be with me was a comforting thought that lingered. When the time came for the celebration of life, I looked forward to a day of celebrating her, sharing stories, laughs, and tears with everyone who loved her. So many people showed up for Mom and us that day; it was truly beautiful.

As the day came to an end, I was happy to retreat back to our home with Louie and a few close friends to reflect on everything that had happened. It was the first moment in over a month that I could exhale without stressing about planning something or worrying about someone who was sick or dying. I felt so thankful for that little window of peace amidst the chaos.

CHAPTER 35

Before Mom's Celebration of Life, Louie and I loaned Shelly some money to help her get by until a few small life insurance checks arrived. She needed a new phone and a few other things. I hadn't given her any money in a long time, knowing it only enabled her, but this time we made an exception because it felt like the right thing to do. Everything was fine until she started asking for more.

It wasn't just that she wanted more money—it was the way she approached us, as though we owed it to her. I had been down this road with her before. It felt like, with Mom gone, she assumed the responsibility of taking care of her now fell to Louie and me. Since she had a place to live, a car to drive, food to eat, and all she had to do was help take care of Charlie, we saw no reason to give her more money, so we said no.

We were also frustrated because she wasn't holding up her end of taking care of Charlie. We found out she had been taking their car to the bar at night and constantly calling me to handle things that were supposed to be her responsibility. On top of that, I hadn't realized how little Charlie trusted Shelly, which became the biggest issue of all.

When things started going sideways with Shelly and Charlie, I was confused about what was going on until Vera clued me in about everything. She told me that when Shelly lived with Mom and Charlie, she stole from them a lot—usually small amounts of money or little items, but over time, it all added up.

I asked Charlie about it, and he confirmed that he didn't trust her. We confronted Shelly about it, but she denied everything. He showed me evidence he'd found in the garage of drug use involving one of Shelly's friends who'd been over to the house.

Charlie managed to express that he didn't trust her at all and believed she was going through things in the garage and the house, taking whatever she wanted without his permission. Mom and Charlie were collectors, and they had a three-car garage full of things they had accumulated over the years. I constantly had to play referee between them. It was clear he didn't trust her, and she had no respect for his boundaries.

Louie and I were both working full-time jobs and managing our own household, while also handling everything for Charlie's house. I was constantly getting calls from Shelly complaining about Charlie, and whenever I went over, Charlie was furious about something Shelly had done.

Although Charlie still couldn't talk, he was very expressive and found ways to communicate his emotions. I'd gotten really good at asking him yes-or-no questions to help him convey what he was feeling or needed. I hoped Shelly would step up and take on the responsibilities of helping care for Charlie, but once again, it became clear that, it would all fall on me.

It was the middle of the week; I was working from home and I got a frantic call from Shelly on Charlie's home phone. I barely had a chance to say hello before she interrupted me, her tone aggressively demanding, "You need to get over here now!"

My heart jumped into my throat, fearing something had happened to Charlie again. I felt my stomach tighten up as I asked, "What's going on? Is Charlie okay?"

She refused to give me any details and just said, "You just need to get over here right now," before hanging up. I sat there for a second, in shock, trying to prepare myself for whatever I might be walking into. I felt like I hadn't had a moment of peace since we first found out about Mom's diagnosis, and ever since, it had been one traumatic event after another. My nerves were shot.

I got in the car and drove as quickly as I could over to the house. As I approached the last curve in the road, I held my breath, fully expecting to see an ambulance or other emergency vehicles in front of the house. Rounding the corner, I saw none. In that moment, I couldn't decide if that was good or bad.

I pulled up in the driveway and walked into the house, relieved to see that Charlie was fine and everything looked normal. But now, I was pissed that Shelly had put me through all of that again. I asked, "What the hell is going on?"

Shelly replied, "He just went off on me because I didn't get his medication ordered in time." Charlie motioned me over, showing me the bottle, and communicated that he had asked her to reorder it, but she hadn't, and now he was going to have a lapse in his medication.

It was so easy to stay on top of his prescriptions because the online system alerts you when it's time to place a refill order. I was beyond frustrated. Making sure that Charlie had his medications was her main job, and she couldn't even manage that. I wanted to turn to Shelly and say, *You had ONE job!* Instead, I remained calm and turned to Shelly to hear her side of things.

She said, "I just didn't realize he was running low, and when I finally went to order it, there was a delay because it needed doctor approval. But he just got angry with me. That's it, Minna, I'm done. I'm done!"

I stood there for a moment, processing everything they'd said and everything that had happened up to this point. Taking a deep breath, I calmly said, "Okay. It's clear this arrangement isn't working, and that you two just can't live together. I'll take over, so go ahead, grab your things, and head home. I'll handle things here."

Without hesitation, she gathered her things and left the house in a huff. I don't think she realized that, although she'd said she was done, it was actually *me* who was done. I was done dealing with her moods and her selfish behavior, done with her using me and everyone else to get what she wanted. I was done pretending she didn't have a problem when she clearly did.

I had spent the last 25 years of my life walking on eggshells around my mom and my sister. I stopped calling them out on their hurtful behavior and poor choices because that always led to the inevitable discussion about their addiction, which never ended well for me. I kept their secret because I feared losing my family and, most importantly, losing Kayla. But now Mom was gone, Dad was gone, and Kayla was 20 years old—old enough to take care of herself.

Kayla became the one constant that probably held us together as a family from the moment she was born. She was the reason I showed up for holidays and put on a happy face with the family—it was all to make sure I remained a stable presence in her life.

Kayla also had a very close relationship with my mom. I watched as Mom became the nurturing figure with Kayla that she had been with me as a child, and it gave me hope. Over the years, Mom, Charlie, and I each played a part in helping to raise Kayla. She lived with Mom and Charlie for a while, and I always kept a close eye on her, especially when she was little.

It is not surprising that I chose a career in Child Welfare—always working to help kids and families in ways I couldn't help my own. As the years passed, I realized deep down that my mom and sister would probably never move toward recovery. I often wished I could have done more for Kayla, but the fear of exposing our family's secret kept me quiet when she was younger, just as it did when I was younger.

By the time Kayla graduated from high school, I felt a huge sense of relief. We had managed to get her this far, relatively unscathed. I'd spent so much time worrying about her, and it wasn't until that moment that I realized just how much it had weighed on me.

Louie and I made a conscious decision not to have kids. He had his own reasons, but for me, I simply didn't have the energy to give to a child. I had spent my entire life taking care of others, always focused on someone else's needs, and I was exhausted. I had a lot of healing to do and knew I needed to focus on myself for a while.

Kayla was now an adult, and I believed I had done all I could do to protect her—or so I thought. I could see the familiar tensions growing between Kayla and Shelly, echoing the dynamic between Shelly and my mom. Some days, they could be as close as ever, only to be yelling and screaming at each other ten minutes later.

Kayla had always been stubborn; I saw that trait in her as early as age two. She would battle with her mom and she would never back down. Both born under the sign of Taurus, and it often felt like watching two bulls butting heads. Kayla was usually the one who wouldn't give in until she won.

I believe I had become to Kayla, what my dad had been to me. While there was good in that, there were also unintended, unhealthy consequences. As she grew older, I noticed her putting on a brave front with me, even when she was scared or uncertain. No matter how much I told her I loved her and was always there for her, I saw myself in her—the way she tried to people please me, just as I had done with others.

My codependence kicked into overdrive with Kayla. I hoped that having me in her life would provide some kind of balance. I wanted her to have someone who wouldn't react to her the way my mom and sister did to me for most of my life. I tried to be a safe port in the storm for her, and I think I succeeded. However, by continuing to keep our family's secret from her, I unknowingly perpetuating the same cycle that had harmed my own self-esteem and self-worth.

After Shelly moved out of Charlie's house, I took over all of his care. It was really hard, stressful, and sometimes really overwhelming, but it was still better than dealing with the constant drama of Shelly living there. After a week or two, Shelly reached out to tell me she was ready to come back. What she didn't know was that Charlie was also done. He told me she was no longer welcome at the house and he didn't want to see her again.

I had to be the one to break the news to her, which wasn't fun, but Charlie was adamant. He had watched for years as she drifted in and out, using him and my mom. She helped my mom around the house, but it always came at a cost. Whether it was a place to crash after a fight with her boyfriend, money, food, or the use of their nice new car when she needed it, there was always a price for her help.

Charlie had not realized how much of his mother's estate my mom had spent by the time she passed, and he wasn't happy about it. Mom had managed their finances, and he was aware Mom often gave Shelly money. While Mom was alive, there was nothing he could do about it, but now things were different. I kept everything transparent with him, always letting him know exactly how much money he had and how much was going toward bills, groceries, and other household expenses.

Shelly was not happy about no longer having access to what she still called "Mom's house." I reminded her that it was now *Charlie's* house and that you can't disrespect people and expect them to welcome you back. Keeping Shelly at arm's length was also helpful for me, as it allowed me to re-establish some much-needed boundaries with her.

Since everything that happened with Mom, I felt overwhelmed by Shelly's constant demands, always about what *she* wanted or needed, rarely considering anyone else. Charlie may have been the one to push her away, but I was left dealing with the fallout. I could manage my sister, but when Kayla stepped in acting as a peacekeeper on her mom's behalf, something shifted for me.

Seeing Kayla take on the role I used to play in our dysfunctional family set off alarm bells. She tried to get *me* to understand her mom's point of view, attempting to help *her mom* clean up the mess she had made. I knew that Kayla didn't have the whole story, or the entire truth. She didn't understand that what was happening with her mom was not just the result of one bad choice—it was the consequence of a lifetime of shit we have all endured because of her addiction.

I knew Kayla was aware her mom had issues with alcohol, and that her mom and Gram could be really moody and not fun to be around sometimes. But I was pretty sure she didn't know the full depth of it all—or anything about the meth.

MELINDA VELASQUEZ

I was now faced with the most difficult decision of my life, and it weighed heavily on my heart. I could either keep the family secret from Kayla or tell her the truth. If I kept quiet, I risked allowing this disease to keep destroying our family and putting Kayla at more risk by leaving her in the dark. But If I chose to pull back the curtain to finally reveal what was truly going on, there was no way to know if it would help Kayla—or make things worse.

I knew that the longer we kept the truth from her, the more she was at risk of the cycle continuing. I was also painfully aware that her dad had struggled with alcohol and meth when she was young, putting her at double the risk. I didn't want to be the one to blow up my family by telling Kayla the truth, yet I couldn't keep letting this secret rip me apart—and potentially do the same to her.

Before deciding, I spoke to Vera and a close friend of my sister's whom I'd also stayed connected with. Since Shelly had stopped admitting to me that she was still doing meth, I needed to be absolutely sure before I lit the fuse on this bomb. They both confirmed, in detail, what I had feared, giving me the clarity to trust that I wasn't imagining things: Shelly was still using.

I also started seeing a therapist after my mom passed away who specialized in family systems and addiction. I was so stressed out with everything I had been dealing with, and I needed help coping with it all. She helped me to realize how much I had normalized the very abnormal behavior that was happening within my family over the years.

She gave me a new lens to view my family through, offering a fresh, unbiased, and professional perspective. The previous therapist I'd seen had definitely talked about my family's addiction, but this woman laid it out for me in no uncertain terms: what I experienced with my family was a trauma, and I was severely codependent.

THE WEIGHT OF SILENCE

At first, it was shocking to hear—I had minimized its impact after dealing with it for so long—but soon, I felt validated. I began to recognize the real effects that growing up in a family of addicts had on my life and how I present myself in the world. I had done a lot of self-development in grad school and beyond, but working with her made me realize that all of that had only scratched the surface. If I didn't confront my pain and peel back the layers caused by my family's addiction, I would never be free of it.

I shared with her what was currently happening with my sister and my concerns for Kayla. She helped me reach the incredibly difficult decision to tell Kayla the truth—not just about her mom, but about my mom as well. My intent was not to ruin the image she held of her mom or her grandmother; it was to finally end this painful family secret.

My therapist also pointed out that keeping Kayla in the dark put her at greater risk of continuing the cycle. She needed to know and understand the severity of her family's history to avoid unconsciously following the same path. This was something I had already worried about, but it helped to have it reiterated from an unbiased professional who specialized in addiction.

I knew Kayla would have a lot of questions, and I also knew I didn't have all the answers. Vera and Shelly's friend offered to come over and be there with me when I told Kayla the truth, as they were the ones who had confirmed for me what was really going on with Shelly and my mom. I was grateful to have their support.

Shelly's friend had done drugs with her in the past but had been clean for a long time. Vera also used meth, but she was honest with me about it and knew everything about my mom. Hearing some of the things about my mom was painful, but it also brought a sense of relief, having someone confirm what I'd always known in my heart to be true.

MELINDA VELASQUEZ

One afternoon, we all gathered around my dining room table, bracing ourselves for what we were about to do. We knew that telling Kayla the truth would likely send Shelly into a rage, but we all agreed it was the right thing to do. When Kayla arrived, she sat down with a smile, happy to see everyone. Meanwhile, a sense of dread was building inside me, knowing that what we were about to reveal would change everything.

She took a seat at the head of the table, and I began, "So, I wanted to talk to you today because I know you've been trying to talk to me about what's been happening with your mom and trying to make things better."

She replied, "Well yeah, I can see both sides of what's been going on, and I wanted to talk to you to try to help you see her side of things."

I nodded and said, "I know, and I want you to know that I do see both sides of things, and in a normal situation, things might have been able to be settled. But this situation is far from normal, and there is a lot that has happened that you don't know about. I realized that it's not fair to you to continue to keep you in the dark about something this big."

The smile on her face started to fade and she looked at me with nervous anticipation and asked, "Okay...what is going on?"

I took a deep breath. "You know how you and I have talked about your mom having issues with alcohol?"

She said, "Well yeah, I have known for a while that the way she drinks, especially sometimes is not healthy. She gets mean sometimes, and we get in fights. I just can't be around her."

I continued, "Yes, and how, since you were a teenager, you have had a job, and she would often ask *you* for money? And she has trouble keeping a job and paying her bills…"

Kayla looked confused. "Yeah, but what does that have to do with what is happening now?"

I leaned in closer and said gently, "Honey, your mom is an addict…but alcohol is not the only addiction she has. She is also addicted to meth, which is short for methamphetamine."

Kayla leaned back in the chair, processing this, and then asked, "So what does that do to her? Why does she take it, and how does she take it?"

I took a moment to explain it all to her, why people use it, and the types of behaviors it brought out in people. I told her, "It's affected her ability to function, to take care of herself, and sometimes to take care of you. It's also caused a lot of strain on her relationships, including with me and with Charlie."

I paused and checked in with her to see how she was doing with all of this information. I saw a few tears roll off her cheeks and she reached up to wipe them away with her shirt as she said trying to fight back her tears, "This actually explains a lot."

I took a deep breath, feeling a tiny bit of relief at her response. I remembered being in her position, hearing Shelly tell me about my own mom's meth addiction. It was hard to hear the truth, but it also shed light on so many things that never really made sense before.

I looked at her and said, "I'm so sorry to be the one to tell you all of this. I wanted to tell you so many times when you were struggling with your mom, and I knew what was going on. But I was scared if I told you that I would lose you. I know your mom is going to hate me for telling you, but I just couldn't keep this secret anymore. I finally realized it was doing more harm than good to not tell you the truth."

She said, "I'm glad you told me. I'm just thinking about so many things that have happened and how she reacted. Knowing this makes all of it make more sense."

MELINDA VELASQUEZ

I made it through telling her about her mom, but now I had to tell her about her Gram, my mom. "There is something else I need to tell you, too," I said. "I can understand everything you're feeling right now because… your mom isn't the only meth addict in the family, Gram—my mom was addicted to meth too."

She began to cry again and asked in a shaky voice, "Did that have anything to do with why she died?"

I glanced over at Vera and Shelly's friend, took a deep breath, and said, "We have no way of knowing for sure, but it probably didn't help. She smoked for a really long time and it is entirely possible that the mass they found was cancer in her lungs."

Vera chimed in and said, "She was so terrified of her doctors figuring out that she was using drugs that she was afraid to take blood tests. I told her to get a chest x-ray after she quit smoking, but she never went. I kept telling her that they had to do a very specific test to find drugs in her system, but she would still avoid any of that if she could."

Hearing that was new to me, too. I remembered how defensive she'd been when I'd asked her why she hadn't gone back to the doctor when she wasn't getting better. We all sat together, with Kayla and I asking Vera and Shelly's friend questions. I still worried about how Kayla was really doing with the information, but also for the first time, it felt like a weight I'd carried my entire life had finally been lifted.

For years, my mom and sister gaslighted me into believing that I was wrong about them. Even though I knew I was right, I felt like if I didn't see them use drugs with my own eyes, how could I really be sure? I didn't realize the toll that took on me until I finally heard the irrefutable truth from people who had no reason to lie to me.

THE WEIGHT OF SILENCE

There was also a part of me that wanted to believe I was wrong, because I didn't want to accept the reality about the people I loved. I was probably one of the few people on earth who truly understood what Kayla was feeling in that moment. I knew it was a lot to take; but, as hard as it was to tell her, it also felt like I had broken free from a prison that held my soul captive for over 25 years.

I didn't just dump this on her and then send her out into the world. I told her about my therapist and invited her to come to a session with me. I also went with her to a Codependents Anonymous (CODA) meeting. I had been to CODA meetings before, and realized it was not the right thing for me, but I wanted to support her and let her find what worked best for her.

She had a lot of questions answered during our session with the therapist, and we discussed the possibility of doing an intervention for her mom. In my own sessions, my therapist had recommended a book I had been reading called *The Lost Years: Surviving a Mother and Daughter's Worst Nightmare* by Kristina Wandzilak and Constance Curry.

The book was written by a mother and her daughter, sharing their story of the daughter's addiction and the mother's codependence. Each chapter traded off telling the same story from each of their perspectives. That book changed my life.

Kristine Wandzilak, the daughter, became a professional interventionist who was outspoken about how sometimes an intervention isn't the best approach—especially the kind where the addict is ambushed. From my own experience with mom, I understood how wrong things can go and how hurtful it can be for the loved ones involved. I also knew that for rehab to be effective, the person has to admit they have a problem and genuinely want to get help.

MELINDA VELASQUEZ

I talked to my sister before about going to rehab, back when she was still open with me about her drug use, but she was extremely resistant. After living in denial for so long, I wasn't sure if her reaction now would be any different. I wanted to hold onto some hope for Kayla's sake that she might be willing, but deep down, I knew better.

Kayla wanted to be the one to tell Shelly that she knew, so I let her decide how she wanted to handle it. We talked about trying to do some kind of intervention, but decided to see how she reacted to Kayla knowing first. I expected that she might hate me and not want to talk to me ever again, but I couldn't have anticipated the firestorm that was about to hit.

CHAPTER

36

Kayla let me know when she planned to tell her mom that she knew about her meth addiction, and I braced myself for the fallout. As soon as Kayla left, Shelly called me. I decided to let it go to voicemail, hoping it would give me a sense of what I was dealing with before I engaged with her. She left me a message unleashing every mean and nasty thing she could think of to say to me.

She told me what an awful person I was and how I was trying to turn Kayla against her. She told me she hated me and that I was no longer her sister. It was all pretty horrible, but it was her final words that hit the hardest, she said, "I should come over to your house and kill myself on your front porch. How would that make you feel?"

Louie was sitting beside me as I listened to the message, and I just sat there in a stunned silence, her words echoing in my head. Louie, however was pissed. Normally, he stayed neutral in the family drama, which was grounding for me, as he often acted as a buffer when things got tough. But after everything he had seen me go through with my mom and how my sister acted throughout, and how much stress she added to our lives, he'd had enough.

Louie has always been *fiercely* protective of me, and hearing her threatening to kill herself on our doorstep, all because I told the truth, was a bridge too far. He looked at me and said, "That's it, babe, I'm done. Your sister is no longer welcome at our home, and if she shows up, I'm calling the police."

I felt a mix of emotions. Part of me was genuinely worried that she might hurt herself, but I was also scared for what she might do to us or our home. I hoped it was just her lashing out, but that first week after her call, I was constantly on edge, not knowing what to expect.

I talked to Kayla, and she told me that Shelly admitted that she used to do meth in the past but claimed she didn't anymore. I knew that wasn't the truth, but I had done all I could. Kayla would have to decide how she was going to deal with the information. I knew when I told Kayla the truth that it could create a rift between Shelly and me, but it was a risk I was willing to take. This secret had been eating me alive, and I just couldn't keep living with it hidden.

I understood that Kayla needed to make her own choices, and I completely respected her desire to keep her mom in her life. I had made a similar decision about my own mom just a few years before she passed away. The angry messages from Shelly had finally subsided, but I knew I needed to communicate something important to her. I wanted her to know that, despite everything, I loved her deeply—but that I was no longer willing to pretend like she wasn't an addict.

THE WEIGHT OF SILENCE

Finding the right words was hard. I needed to be clear yet loving, to take a firm stand while still expressing how much I cared and wanted the best for her. During this time, I was still reading *The Lost Years*, and in one section, written by the daughter, I found the perfect words. The words were from the mother to her daughter when she showed up at their home once again after many near death experiences and failed attempts at rehab, which put her family through hell worrying about her, "I am overjoyed that you are alive, but I can no longer live with addiction in my life. You, Kristina, are not welcome in my home or in my life until you complete treatment and are living a life of recovery."

Those words captured exactly what I needed to say.

I knew I didn't want to see her in person, but I needed to make my feelings clear and convey that my intention was not to hurt her. I knew there was a good chance my words wouldn't land with her the way I hoped, but I did my best to convey love in my message. I decided to send her an email, ending it with, "I love you, but I can no longer live with addiction in my life. You, Shelly, are not welcome in my home or in my life until you complete treatment and are living a life of recovery." When I hit send, I finally felt a sense of release.

I still wished the best for her, but I was no longer going to be in her life or allow her in mine if she continued to live in denial. It was not an easy decision for me, but it is not one I regret. She was all that I had left of my immediate family— my only sibling, and the only person who shared memories of the family we once had.

At the same time, I had to admit that, as much as I loved her, she was also a person who brought far more stress and chaos into my life than peace or comfort. Letting go of the big sister I had once looked up to—the sister I had always wanted to spend time with me—was one of the most difficult decisions I have ever made in my life. But it was also one of the best decisions I have ever made for my own well-being.

I still had to have some contact with her since mom and Charlie's house was going through probate, but I tried to do as much as I could through the lawyer. After Mom had been gone for about six months, managing everything—taking care of Charlie, shopping for his house and ours, planning meals, commuting an hour away twice a week and basically running two households—became extremely taxing on me. I never complained to Charlie, but I think he knew it was too much.

He let me know that he wanted to find an assisted living facility and sell their house. Living alone in a three-bedroom house with a big yard, he understood that the upkeep on the house would eventually be too much, especially on a fixed income. We went out together, found a great place about 20 minutes from where I lived, and by the summer of the year Mom passed, we got him settled into his new home.

I spent a lot of time with him, and he told me more than once that he was ready to go but didn't know why he was still here. He knew he had many health issues, and he'd made peace with dying just days after Mom passed, when he was in the hospital. But that was when I told him I wasn't ready for him to go yet—that I still needed and wanted him here.

Once we got him settled in his new home, it was time to clean out the house and get it ready to sell. A few good friends helped me sort through everything and set up for an estate sale, but it was a long process because my mom had kept EVERYTHING. It got to the point where I dreaded opening each new drawer, worried I would find it crammed with paperwork that I'd have to sift through in case anything important was buried there.

THE WEIGHT OF SILENCE

The whole experience was exhausting and completely all-consuming—sometimes it felt like digging a hole in the sand. But as I sorted through dozens upon dozens of documents, I was also able to find some peace.

My journey toward forgiving my mom had started with conversations I'd had with my uncle about the trauma he and my mom experienced living with their father. It continued as I planned her memorial, created a slideshow, and wrote a poem about her to display that day. Suddenly, my heart was full again, overflowing with emotion I had held back for so many years, but it was bittersweet.

I finally felt safe opening my heart to her again, but it was only possible because she was no longer here.

Mother's Day had always been a struggle for me when it came to picking out a card for her. All the cards spoke of amazing, wonderful mothers, but it was never that simple for me. I felt so much pain and anger towards her for not being the mother she had been when I was little, and giving her a card like that felt like a lie. But as I sorted through her things and saw all of the things she'd saved of mine, I could see that the mother I loved was always there, even if I didn't always feel her presence.

She had saved report cards, class pictures, drawings I'd made as a kid, tons of copies of the first article I wrote that was published in the school newspaper, and even the poem I'd written that also got published. There were keepsakes from my whole life, showing just how proud she was of me and how much she loved me.

I found the death certificate for my mom's best friend, who had died by suicide at just 30 years old. I was 37 when Mom passed, and suddenly, I understood the profound impact it must have had on her to lose her closest friend so tragically at that age. I remembered being young when it happened, and how close this woman was to our family. I was the flower girl in her wedding, and we spent a lot of time with her and her husband. I also remember the funeral, and how my mom showed incredible patience and strength during a time that must have been deeply painful for her.

I also came across a bunch of documents detailing what she had to deal with when Charlie came home from the hospital after his heart attack and stroke. I flashed back to the silly things I got annoyed with her about during that time, and I never once considered the amount of stress she was under taking care of Charlie. Everything that happened since she died not only allowed me to forgive her, but it also allowed me to love her again—and that was the greatest gift I could have received.

When we held the estate sale, Shelly showed up, even though she knew Charlie didn't want her there. As soon as I saw her, I felt like I had seen a ghost. I stood there, frozen, feeling a wave of sadness and anxiety wash over me. I looked at Louie and said, "I can't deal with this today." I didn't know if she was going to cause a scene or not.

Louie went to talk to her, and she said she wasn't there to cause any problems—she just wanted to walk around and look. I was fine with it and understood her desire to be there, so I told Louie to tell her that if there was something she really wanted that wasn't a big item, she could have it. I also mentioned that after the sale, we would reach out to her and she could take whatever she wanted that we hadn't sold.

I wanted to honor Charlie, since most of the money was going to him and it was technically his stuff now, but I also wanted her to be able to have things of my mom's that mattered to her. A lot of the things I knew she wanted didn't sell, and I was happy she was able to come and get them. That would be the last time I saw her in person for a long time.

The house sold quickly. And by April of the year after Mom died, the probate case was finally settled. The money from the sale of the house was split evenly between Charlie, Shelly, and me. Not long after that, Charlie's health began to steadily decline, and he decided he wanted to enter Hospice care. One day, as I sat with him in his new home, we had a conversation, and I reminded him, "I know you kept saying you were ready to go but you didn't know why you were still here."

He said, "Yes."

I continued, "I think you were waiting for all of this stuff with mom's estate to be settled to make sure I didn't have to deal with all of this alone."

He just smiled and nodded his head in agreement, saying, "Yeah."

I began to speak, I could feel tears welling up. "I'm so grateful for your love and support through all of this. Thank you for everything and for loving my mom and all of us."

I leaned over and gave him a hug. He placed his hand over his heart and, using his version of sign language, told me, "Love you and thank you for everything."

His 67th birthday was that May, and I threw him a surprise birthday in a small private dining room where he lived. Louie, Kayla, her boyfriend, Wade, and Vera all came, and he genuinely seemed to enjoy it.

When he first moved to the new place, it lifted his spirits and gave him a sense of community again. It was really good for him, and it took a lot of pressure off of me. By the time his birthday came, we could all see that he was not feeling well anymore.

He had stage-five kidney disease, and once he decided to go on hospice, they advised him to have his defibrillator turned off. It was a shock to both of us when they brought it up. When the nurse asked him if he was ready to go, she explained that the defibrillator would prevent that from happening. He had signed a DNR order, so in theory, it made sense, but it still felt strange to me. I left the decision up to him, and he chose to turn it off.

I went to visit him in the beginning of July and called Wade and Louie after I left because he wasn't looking good to me; he seemed really tired. Wade went over again to check on him, and he felt the same way.

Early on the morning of July 4th, my phone rang. I had a special ring programmed for Charlie's calls, so I jumped up the way I always did when he called. He only called if something was wrong because he couldn't really talk, so whenever I heard that ring, I knew it wasn't good news. I answered the phone, saying hastily, "Charlie, are you okay?"

An unfamiliar man's voice replied back, "Hello, is this Melinda Velasquez?"

A sudden sense of dread came over me, and I held my breath as I responded, "Yes, this is Melinda. This is my stepdad's phone number. Who is this?"

He said, "I'm an EMT, and I'm here with your stepdad. I'm sorry to tell you that he has passed away."

Even though I had known it was likely coming, I still felt a huge sense of shock and began to cry. All I could manage to say was, "Oh no." Louie asked me what was going on, and I replied, "Charlie passed away."

I was confused as to why there were EMTs on the scene since we were told by hospice to call them first if something happened. I said, "He's on hospice. There is a note by the phone specifically saying not to call 9-1-1, but to call hospice if anything happened. Did *he* call 9-1-1?"

The EMT responded, "It appears he might have had a heart attack based on what we've seen. When it happened, he pushed his emergency alert button. The young man who responded to the alert panicked and called 9-1-1. We can see the number for hospice, if you would like, we can call them and let them know what happened."

I was still and shock, taking it all in, and it was early in the morning. I said, "Yes, please do, and I will follow-up with them, too. Thank you for calling me and letting me know."

The man with the kind voice replied, "No problem, ma'am. I'm very sorry for your loss."

Almost exactly a year and a half after Mom passed away, Charlie joined her. Thankfully, after Mom's passing, we had learned the importance of planning ahead. We had Charlie sit down with a lawyer to draw up a will. He named Kayla and me as beneficiaries. The house had been sold, so after settling all of his expenses, the remaining money from the house and whatever was left in his bank account was split between us.

It felt fitting that Charlie passed on the 4th of July—typical of him to go out with a bang on a day filled with fireworks and celebrations. We celebrated his life and cleared out his belongings, and for the first time in almost two years, I was no longer a caregiver for someone else.

In June of that year, Louie and I decided to leave our jobs and use some of the money from Mom's life insurance to support us while we started a mobile auto repair business. My job was increasingly requiring me to travel to the main office, which was an hour away from home. With everything I had gone through while taking care of Charlie, I knew I needed a change.

I hadn't really had the chance to grieve the loss of my mom. It felt like I had been running a two-year marathon, and I was desperately in need of a break. For the first time in my life, I didn't feel responsible for taking care of anyone else. Louie and I decided to take a much needed vacation before diving into setting up our new business. We took about two weeks off and took a road trip up to Oregon.

In the midst of managing Mom's estate and caring for Charlie, we took a leap and adopted a rescue dog. She was the exact breed I said I would never get—a chihuahua/terrier mix—but she found us, and we both fell in love with her. She quickly became our cherished fur baby, and she joined us on the road trip through Oregon, where we explored the beautiful landscape and enjoyed a much-needed break from the whirlwind of the past two years.

Back home, we tackled the house projects we had been putting off, then turned our attention to starting a new business. I knew I was capable, but I quickly realized I had taken on too much too fast. Louie and I are hard workers, so we made it work, but I was struggling.

Louie, the mechanic and face of the business, allowed me to stay behind the scenes handling the books, creating policies and procedures, designing the website, managing marketing, and taking care of all the paperwork. My days were filled with emails while Louie took on phone calls and face-to-face interactions. I managed community outreach and marketing but spent much of my time at home, often in sweats, feeling disconnected from the vibrant, outgoing person I once was.

I gained about 30 pounds of what I called "grief weight," mainly because I simply didn't have the energy to shop or prepare regular meals. Takeout became our staple. I just felt so raw—exposed and vulnerable, like an open wound. I hadn't truly processed losing my mom, the unraveling of my family, or Charlie's passing. Once I got past the initial hurdle of starting our business, I realized I could no longer just push through the pain; I had to sit with it if I wanted to heal.

Louie was the only one who witnessed my daily struggle, though even he didn't know the depth of it—how often I cried in the shower or woke up weeping from dreams of my mom. We were both exhausted, and he buried himself in work while I withdrew from the world.

Running the business from the background worked for about a year, but eventually, I felt ready to re-engage. The business was steady, but I knew it was time to put myself out there again. I asked the Universe for part-time work that would make good use of my skills, and shortly after, a colleague from the Foster Kinship Care Education program at the local junior college offered me a position helping with trainings, conferences, and events.

It was exactly what I needed to pull me out of my grief cave and back into work I felt passionate about.

Having experienced so much loss in such a short time, I've learned that grief is an ongoing journey. My parents are gone, and the family I cherished as a child no longer exists. Kayla is still in my life, though our interactions have lessened as she grows older. My relationship with my sister has become less volatile, but she's no longer part of my life. It was a hard decision but one I don't regret. Even if my sister were to stop using and drinking, that alone wouldn't be enough. I love and miss her, but I've chosen peace for myself. If she were to come back into my life, I'd want to see more than temporary sobriety—I'd want her to find true healing.

I've come to understand that recovery from addiction and codependency requires addressing the deep roots of suffering. One must look within, confront the pain, and face the darkness to begin healing. Just like grief, true healing is an ongoing process.

MELINDA VELASQUEZ

I've done significant work to heal from trauma and to break the cycle of codependency that shaped my life. I know the work is continuous, but I'm ready to take life as it comes, learning to ride the waves and staying open to what lies ahead.

As Maya Angelou beautifully said, *"We delight in the beauty of the butterfly, but rarely admit the changes it has gone through to achieve that beauty."*

Like the butterfly, I've embraced my transformation—recognizing that growth often comes through struggle. And though the journey is far from over, I'm ready to continue unfolding, one moment at a time.

The journey isn't over—my story continues to unfold, and I invite you to join me in the next chapter, where we'll explore strength, healing, and the tools to help us all grow.

ACKNOWLEDGEMENTS

To Jillian Navarro, *my friend, first editor, and mentor: You were the first person I trusted with the initial draft of my manuscript, offering guidance at a time when I felt completely overwhelmed. If you hadn't reached out when you did, I don't know how long it would have taken me to take the next step in the process. Although our in-person interactions were few, I knew from the moment we met that we had a connection. When you told me you felt the same, I realized our meeting was no accident.*

"Thank you" doesn't seem sufficient for all you did for me, for this book, and for the cherished conversations we had along the way. I'm proud of the work we did together, and the end result wouldn't be what it is without your input. Thank you for strengthening my writing while honoring my voice.

Rest in peace, my friend, and thank you again.

To my cover artist, Laura Duffy: *Thank you for bringing your knowledge and expertise to this project and for capturing my vision beautifully!*

To my formatter, Aubrey Labitigan of Jai Design, *I'm so grateful you were able to sweep in and format my book in the eleventh hour. You not only delivered faster and better than the people I had been struggling with for months, but you also relieved an enormous amount of stress at a criti cal point in my self-publishing process.*

To my beta readers, Jacob and Jody: *I'm so grateful to you both. Thank you for your invaluable insights and for lending fresh eyes to the pieces I could no longer see!*

To my unofficial photographer, soul sister and daily sounding board, Andora: *I'm so grateful for your friendship, your keen eye, and your willingness to step in and help in any way without hesitation. Thank you for always being there for me, and lifting me up when things got to be too much. I'm truly thankful we found each other at this point in our lives!*

To my dear friends and family*—those mentioned in the book and those not—who have supported me throughout my life and during the long, iterative process of writing this book: I feel incredibly blessed to have so many amazing people in my life—those girlfriends I grew up with who feel more like sisters, as well as those "soul sisters" from my "soul pod" whom I met later in life. From the moment we met, I felt a magical, instant connection, and I can't imagine my life without all of you. Thank you for your love and support. I love you deeply!*

And finally, to my love, my Louie: *From the moment we met, you have been a blessing. You are my greatest protector, and you've helped heal parts of me that I wasn't sure I could ever mend, simply by being who you are. I'm so glad that, throughout all these years, we've learned to grow together instead of apart. Thank you for always having my back and for working so hard to ensure we have what we need. You were the first person I felt safe asking for help, and time and again, you've proven that you will always be there for me. You've made it possible for me to pursue my goals and dreams, and although I know there have been times when it was difficult—for both of us—to trust the process, your support has meant the world to me. I love you so much and am grateful every day that you came into my life.*

REFERENCES AND RESOURCES

"What Codependency Looks Like in a Relationship," Dr. Nicole LePera, The Holistic Psychologist

While I was unable to track down the exact article where I found this information, I want to ensure Dr. LePera receives credit for her invaluable work. Please find her social media contact below to connect with her and explore more of her insights: Instagram: @the.holistic.psychologist

Queen Bees and Wannabes: Helping Your Daughter Survive Cliques, Gossip, Boyfriends, and Other Realities of Adolescence by Rosalind Wiseman

Just a few of the books I have found provided helpful insights:

The Lost Years by Kristina Wandzilak & Constance Curry

The Body Keeps the Score by Bessel Van Der Kolk, M.D.

The Gifts of Imperfection by Brene Brown

Codependent No More by Melody Beattie

Are You the One for Me? Knowing Who's Right and Avoiding Who's Wrong by Barbara De Angelis Ph.D.

Adult Children of Emotionally Immature Parents: How to Heal from Distant, Rejecting, or Self-Involved Parents by Lindsay C. Gibson, PsyD

Made in the USA
Monee, IL
02 April 2025